The Promise of Narrative Theology

The
Promise of
Narrative Theology

GEORGE W. STROUP

SCM PRESS LTD

Copyright © John Knox Press 1981

*Unless otherwise indicated scripture quotations are from the
Revised Standard Version of the Bible, copyright 1946,
1952 and © 1971, 1973 by the Division of Christian Education, National Council of the Churches of Christ in
America, and used by permission.*

334 01315 1

First British edition published 1984
by SCM Press Ltd
26–30 Tottenham Road, London N1 4BZ

Typeset in the United States of America
and printed in Great Britain by
Richard Clay (The Chaucer Press) Ltd
Bungay, Suffolk

For Dorothy Lucille Meyer
1922–1977

Preface

During the last ten years a new approach to theological reflection has emerged under the rubric of "narrative theology." As is the case with most new proposals in theology it remains to be seen whether narrative theology is only another fad in theological discussion or whether it is a substantive contribution to the task of making Christian faith intelligible in the modern world. One seminary president has already written the obituary for narrative theology, dismissing it as "a one-string violin" which will soon go the way of the "genitive theologies" of the past few decades. That prediction may turn out to be accurate, but such a judgment is at best premature. For some time it has seemed to me that the use of narrative in theology provides rich possibilities for understanding and interpreting the content of Christian faith. Furthermore, narrative theology appears to open new channels of conversation between the systematic theologian, the biblical scholar, the social scientist, and, most importantly, the layperson who long ago gave up on the theologian as a resource for understanding the Christian faith.

This book is an experiment in systematic theology. It is an attempt to see if a particular interpretation of Christian narrative speaks to the situation of Christians in affluent, Western cultures, a situation in which Christian identity is increasingly problematic. And it is an attempt to determine if the use of narrative in theology casts any new light on what Christians mean by "revelation," the doctrine some Christian theologians have appealed to as the basis for what Christians know and confess about God. As an experiment some of the proposals in this book are both tentative and incomplete. A number of important questions are left unanswered, perhaps the most important of which is the "criteriological question"—what criteria are at work in my description of the content of Christian narrative (why, for example, the emphasis on the Gospel of Mark). In my mind the criteriological question could be answered only by extending the themes developed in this manuscript in the direction of christology. Although closely related to the themes in this essay the criteriological question demands its own ground and will have to await another day. The issues I have taken up, especially those of revelation and Christian identity, are what I understand to be prolegomena to the development of christology and the doctrine of God.

I first discovered my major themes in the process of writing a Ph.D. dissertation in theology at Vanderbilt University in 1973. Professors Peter C. Hodgson and Edward Farley provided both criticism and encouragement as I first tried to understand the shape and function of Christian narrative.

In the years since, I have had the opportunity to rethink and reconceive my original proposal. I am deeply indebted to The Association of Theological Schools in the United States and Canada for a grant which enabled me to write this manuscript during the 1978–79 academic year.

I also am grateful for the advice and criticism of many friends and colleagues. I am especially indebted to Diogenes Allen, Wallace Alston, David Bartlett, J. Christiaan Beker, Freda Gardner, James Heaney, Seward Hiltner, Vic Hunter, John F. Jansen, W. Eugene March, and Daniel Migliore. Although each of them would have serious reservations about some aspect of this essay, their criticisms have assisted me in clarifying and refining my argument.

A conversation partner who has been of great help to me

throughout this project is Professor Thomas W. Mann of Converse College. Professor Mann's students and colleagues will recognize that much of what I have to say about Deuteronomy and its function in Christian hermeneutics is borrowed from many conversations with him. The errors in my interpretation of Deuteronomy are not his but those of an ill-equipped systematic theologian.

Richard Ray, Donald Hardy, and Joan Crawford of John Knox Press have been responsible for turning a rough manuscript into something resembling a book. Their patience, encouragement, and advice enabled me to survive the final stages of this project. I would also like to thank Lewis C. Allen, Gregory D. McDonnell, and Patricia K. Willey of Austin Presbyterian Theological Seminary for proofreading, checking footnotes, and preparing the index.

Some of the theological terms that appear in this essay which are of central importance are grace, faithfulness, and promise. What these terms mean in relation to God is always in part a mystery, not in the sense that they are irrational or unintelligible but in the sense that they finally transcend all human explanations. In my life Donna Fox Stroup and Lucille Elizabeth Stroup are daily, visible reminders of the wonder and mystery of God's grace.

George W. Stroup
Austin, Texas

Contents

That every individual life between birth and death can eventually be told as a story with beginning and end is the prepolitical and prehistorical condition of history, the great story without beginning and end. But the reason why each human life tells its story and why history ultimately becomes the storybook of mankind, with many actors and speakers and yet without any tangible authors, is that both are the outcome of action.

Hannah Arendt, The Human Condition

Look into my heart, O Lord, for it was your will that I should remember these things and confess them to you. I pray now that my soul may cling to you, for it was you who released it from the deadly snare in which it was so firmly caught. It was in a state of misery and you probed its wound to the quick, pricking it on to leave all else and turn to you to be healed, to turn to you who are above all things and without whom nothing could exist.

Augustine, Confessions

Nearly all the wisdom we possess, that is to say, true and sound wisdom, consists of two parts: the knowledge of God and of ourselves. But while joined by many bonds, which one precedes and brings forth the other is not easy to discern.

John Calvin, Institutes of the Christian Religion

This means that it is not the children of the flesh who are the children of God, but the children of the promise are reckoned as descendants.

Romans 9:8

PART I

Toward a Narrative Theology

Chapter I

The Crisis
in Christian Identity

In different historical periods and in various geographical and cultural settings readers of the Bible have recognized that a turning point in the Gospel narratives is the question Jesus addresses to his disciples at Caesarea Philippi: "But who do you say that I am?" (Matt. 16:15; Mark 8:29; and Luke 9:20). The question marks a turning point in Jesus' relation to the disciples and in the larger narrative itself because it points to a central feature of Christian faith—namely that a person's understanding of Jesus' identity is inseparable from his or her understanding of the nature of discipleship. What a person believes about Jesus cannot be separated from how he or she lives in the world. Faith in the God who reveals himself in Jesus Christ has serious but unavoidable consequences for daily life, from the most mundane issues to questions of life and death.

At the center of Christian faith is the question of identity, a question that is two-sided. On the one hand it is a question about Jesus of Nazareth and the God whom Christians confess to be disclosed in Jesus' life, death, and resurrection. Christian theology is the attempt to think through and understand what faith confesses about the God revealed in Jesus Christ. But that is only one side of the identity question in Christian faith and only one part of the task of theology. Equally important are the consequences of what it means to confess that Jesus Christ is "the only begotten Son of God." Traditionally Christians have claimed that anyone who makes that confession is led to reconsider what kind of person one is and how one lives in the world. In more cases than not that confession seems to require a person to "turn around," reinterpret personal identity, and live differently in the world. What a person believes about Jesus Christ cannot be separated from how one lives in the world without tearing apart the fabric of Christian faith. But while the two go hand in hand they also are never perfectly conjoined. The agony of Christian existence in both its personal and its corporate forms is that what one believes and confesses is rarely demonstrated consistently and without distortion in daily life. Sin remains as much a reality for Christians as for non-Christians. Yet the two-sided question of Christian identity—who one understands Jesus of Nazareth to be and what it means to confess him as Lord—stands at the very center of Christian faith.

Because the identity question is so central to Christian faith it is an issue which every Christian and every church has had to face in some form. To be sure, during some periods in the church's history the question of identity has been unusually urgent. Whenever Christians have been in a non-Christian culture the question of identity has been paramount. But in every situation Christians have had to ask what Christian faith means in their culture at that point in history. In other words, Christians always have had to deal with the question of discipleship.

Although it is a perennial theological topic, it may be that the question of Christian identity has taken on a new form in the Western world. In the past few decades the explosion in communications and the news media has reduced the size of the world dramatically to the dimensions of a television screen. People who live in Western cultures are increasingly aware of the world's cultural and religious pluralism. They recognize that Christian faith is only one of many religious traditions in the world by which people celebrate the sacred and experience the reality of grace. It is no longer possible for Christians to dismiss or ignore the religious traditions of other cultures.

While cultural pluralism and the diversity it represents are now an unavoidable reality, yet another force is at work in Western society which emphasizes not the diversity of human life but the common features of human existence. Secularism, particularly its manifestations in modern science and technology, has created one culture out of many, a culture in which ethnic and social differences are leveled by human dependence on computer technology and a shared perception of reality which is shaped primarily by the high priests of modern science.

For many Christians the issue is not secularism, which is simply a fact of life, but whether Christian faith and identity can be maintained in a culture whose political and social values increasingly have little or nothing to do with the Christian tradition.

In the remainder of this chapter we will look at some additional features of the problem of Christian identity and its distinctive symptoms in the Christian church. In the chapters that follow we will examine how the crisis in Christian identity is reflected in different aspects of Christian life, not the least of which is the sphere of Christian theology and therein the confusion that now surrounds what Christians mean by "revelation." Many Christians simply no longer understand what revelation means. Because of their awareness of the integrity and legitimacy of other religious traditions it has become difficult for Christians to make universal and imperialistic truth claims about Christian faith, claims that often were based on a doctrine of revelation.

From the opposite quarter, in the midst of the numbing commonality that characterizes secular culture, Christians often ask what, if anything, is distinctive about Christian faith and participation in the Christian community, a distinctiveness that once was described partially by means of a doctrine of revelation. The crisis in Christian identity, therefore, has had serious consequences for the structure and content of Christian theology, consequences that are most clearly visible in the problematic status of the doctrine of revelation in contemporary theology.

Two foci make up the structure of this essay: the first is the existential problem of Christian identity and the second is the confusion in Christian theology about the meaning of revelation. The premise of this book is that these two issues are so closely bound that the one cannot be resolved without addressing the other. In order to address both themes and their relation to one another we will make use of the emerging discussion of "narrative" or "story" theology. In Chapter III we will survey some recent contributions to this diverse yet growing body of literature. One of the strengths of narrative theology has been that it provides a foundation for theology by uniting experience and reflection in a way that other recent forms of systematic theology apparently have been unable to do. Narrative theology is not simply a matter of storytelling. Narrative theology does recognize, however, that Christian faith is rooted in particular historical events which are recounted in the narratives of Christian Scripture and tradition, that these historical narratives are the basis for Christian affirmations about the nature of God and the reality of grace, and that these historical narratives and the faith they spawn are redemptive when they are appropriated at the level of personal identity and existence. Hence Christian narrative is a primary datum for theological reflection and the appropriate context in which to re-examine the nature of Christian identity and what Christians mean by "revelation."

Knowledge of God and Knowledge of Self

Christians have long claimed that faith in Jesus Christ entails the reinterpretation of one's personal identity and the alteration of one's daily existence. That claim is based in Scripture and nowhere appears more prominently than in the dichotomy Paul draws between life under the law and life in Jesus Christ.

> But thanks be to God, that you who were once slaves of sin have become obedient from the heart to the standard of teaching to which you were committed, and, having been set free from sin, have become slaves of righteousness.
>
> (Rom. 6:17–18)

This righteousness that characterizes Christian life is manifested in a peculiar kind of freedom. It is not a freedom that knows no restraints—the freedom to be or do anything—but a special kind of freedom, the freedom for which "Christ has set us free" (Gal. 5:1). One of the distinctions theologians often use to describe Christian freedom is to insist that it is not freedom *from* everything, but freedom *for* a particular way of life. It is the freedom to love God and to love other people.

Christian freedom has many implications, but it is only fully and properly understood when it is seen to be rooted in the freedom of God. God's freedom is the freedom to be for the world, a freedom which Christians believe they see in the life, death, and resurrection of Jesus of Nazareth. God's freedom is his freedom to love, and God's love describes the nature of God's freedom. The freedom and love that characterize Christian righteousness are rooted in God's freedom and love. The freedom of the Christian life is derived from the freedom with which God loves the world. And in loving God the Christian receives the promise that finally, in God's good time, one's own self shall be understood.

For now I see in a mirror dimly, but then face to face. Now I know in part; then I shall understand fully, even as I have been fully understood.

(1 Cor. 13:12)

In the context of the freedom and love that describe Christian existence a person grows in the knowledge of God and of self. In loving God and becoming free to love other people, becoming "slaves of righteousness," Christians come to a fuller knowledge of God and of themselves. The knowledge of one's self that emerges in the Christian life of freedom and love, the knowledge of who one truly and really is, is inseparable from knowledge of God. And there is no better example of the search for self-knowledge by means of knowledge of God than a treatise that is fifteen hundred years old, Augustine's *Confessions*. It would not be unfair to describe the whole of this treatise, written in the form of a prayer, as the reconstruction of a person's self-identity in light of Christian faith and knowledge of God.[1]

To those familiar with the Christian tradition perhaps an even more compelling example of the relation between knowledge of self and knowledge of God can be found at the beginning of John Calvin's *Institutes of the Christian Religion*, where all "true and sound wisdom" is described as "the knowledge of God and ourselves." A person has true self-understanding only in so far as he or she knows the God who is Creator and Redeemer of everything that is. And one knows God as Creator and Redeemer only in so far as one knows one's personal identity to be dependent on God's grace. Hence, knowledge of God in Christian faith is correlative with knowledge of self.[2] The two are dialectically related. All true self-knowledge requires knowledge of God, but knowledge of God is sterile and "academic" unless it discloses true knowledge of the self. The relation between the two is extremely complex, but in Christian faith they are inextricably joined, although difficult to untangle.

But, while joined by many bonds, which one precedes and brings forth the other is not easy to discern. In the first place, no one can look upon himself without immediately turning his thoughts to the contemplation of God, in whom he "lives and moves" [Acts 17:28].[3]

The God in whom one lives and moves is the decisive reality for the true and proper articulation of personal identity and the interpretation of the meaning and structure of one's world. At least that has been the persistent claim of the Christian community since its beginning.

There have been some periods in the Christian tradition when true Christian identity was perhaps more discernible than in others, which is simply to say that Christian faith ebbs and flows and that some communities have been more faithful to the gospel than others. But faithfulness to the gospel is at least partially determined by the nature of the relation between knowledge of God and knowledge of self. Christian identity, of course, is never determined wholly by an undefiled, pristine knowledge of God. All human knowledge is shaped by cultural and historical location. The question that endures and which must be answered by every Christian individual and community is the degree to which its self-understanding has been shaped by its knowledge of the God who is Creator and Redeemer and the degree to which it uses "God" only as religious dress for its own moral, political, and cultural values. Questions about Christian identity are at their root questions about Christian faith. An investigation of the Christian identity of any individual or community is an inquiry into its understanding, interpretation, and appropriation of Christian faith. Hence it is a "hermeneutical" question. And by "hermeneutical" I mean not simply that narrow task of determining the rules for the proper interpretation of a text, but also the broader process of understanding which takes place in the encounter between persons, texts, and communities. In this larger sense of "hermeneutics" attention is given to the problems created by historical and cultural diversity in any attempt at understanding.

To some degree, of course, Christian self-understanding always reflects both Christian faith and the values of a particular culture. The problem arises when Christian identity ceases to be shaped by knowledge of God. It then becomes problematic and confused. Christian identity which is not formed by what faith confesses about God quickly degenerates into civil religion and cultural nostalgia, and knowledge of God which does not have visible consequences in personal and communal existence soon becomes irrelevant. In either case, the disruption of the relation between knowledge of God and self results in a distorted understanding of Christian faith and the dissolution of true Christian identity. There is ample evidence in modern culture that Christian faith and identity have become obscure and uncertain and that this hermeneutical problem has become the ecclesiastical and theological crisis of our day.

2. The Shape of the Problem

The crisis that now confronts the Christian community is more insidious, more elusive than many of those crises the church has faced in the past—persecution by the state, the struggle with non-Christian religions, the search for an ecumenical consensus within Christianity. The present crisis manifests itself in a vague sense of uneasiness that troubles many Christians regardless of their denominational affiliation or tradition. Upon closer examination this uneasiness seems to be rooted in a pervasive uncertainty about the identity of the Christian community.

This crisis that now besets the Christian church, both in the United States and in most other affluent parts of the world, is no less serious than the more overt, dramatic crises that the church has faced in the past. Nor is this crisis in Christian identity anything new. There is indeed a sense in which it is perennial and must be dealt with by every Christian generation. In the modern world, however, in the world shaped by intellectual and social forces let loose since the Enlightenment, the identity question has become increasingly complex. It simply is no longer apparent to many people what role Christian faith and participation in the life of the church should play in the self-understanding of Christians.

Individuals seriously committed to Christian faith and participation in the life of the church have responded to the present crisis in various ways. Some have engaged in forms of ecclesiastical nostalgia in which everything contemporary is decried and the past is lifted up and glorified at the expense of modern sensibilities and responsible participation in society. The church plays the ostrich, hides its head in the past, and prays that the modern world with all its perplexing problems will go away. Christians of this sort valiantly battle modernity by means of the faith of their parents and joust against the windmills of the contemporary world. Other Christians not only glorify the past but they cling desperately to the Bible as the inerrant Word of God and dismiss the problems of life in the twentieth century as the result of unbelief. It may not be readily apparent how the difficult issues of life in modern culture are resolved simply by quoting from the Bible or the church's confessions, but these traditional resources have been used by many conservative Christians as at least one way of making sense out of their lives and their world.

These popular solutions to the identity crisis in the Christian community—glorifying the past and clinging to an inerrant Bible—pose difficult problems for those Christians who have learned that quoting from Scripture cannot bridge the chasm in understanding that separates the first from the twentieth century. The pastor must make some kind of sense out of the odd legends and stories in Scripture and minister to a congregation that honestly wants to know what Christian faith has to say about divorce, abortion, welfare, the environment, and a host of other personal and social issues. At the same time, the theologically trained pastor knows that this fundamental task demands much more than simply reciting apparently appropriate verses from the Bible. Conservative churches are growing in the United States because they offer a distinct, easily discernible Christian identity in the midst of the increasing flux and homogeneity of American middle-class culture. While the ostrich-like posture of conservative churches is distasteful to many Christians, it has become abundantly clear in recent years that conservative Christianity has been remarkably successful, if one measures "success" in terms of increased budgets and the number of new members (by no means the only or even the relevant criteria for assessing whether the gospel has been proclaimed). No doubt one reason for that success has been that conservative churches offer an easily identifiable alternative to the confusion and uncertainty that is rampant in mainstream, liberal Protestant churches.

But it is not surprising that after careful scrutiny the conservative alternative to the crisis in Christian identity strikes many people as superficial and inadequate. For all its homage to the authority of Scripture, conservative Christianity continues to mix and confuse the regional, parochial interests of the American middle class with the promises, claims, and demands of Christian faith. Although the inadequacies in the conservative program are glaring, it will no longer do for liberal Christianity to look down its nose at conservative churches and dismiss them out of hand as unworthy of serious attention. The challenge now facing those Christian communities who do not look upon the last two hundred years of theological and biblical scholarship, from Schleiermacher to Bultmann, as either a heresy or a tragic mistake is to offer a compelling description of what it means to live and to understand one's self in the contemporary world by means of Christian faith.

The present crisis in Christian identity also suggests that "religious pluralism" may not be the paramount theological issue of our time, at least not as that issue has been formulated recently in some academic circles. The most urgent theological issue is not whether there is some common ground between Christian faith and other religious traditions, theistic or secular, nor the question of whether Christianity is superior to other religious traditions. The crucial theological issue of our day is not whether the Christian community can find acceptance and understanding in other religious communities. On the contrary the question is whether the church can rediscover the sense in which it stands in and lives out of a tradition, reinterpret that tradition so that it is intelligible in the contemporary world, and offer a clear description of Christian faith which makes it relevant to the urgent questions and issues of modern society. In sum, the present crisis in the church is a deep-seated confusion about Christian identity, and that crisis cannot be resolved by sociological analysis or psychological treatment because it is at root theological and must be treated as such.

3. Symptoms of the Crisis

The crisis in Christian identity manifests itself in a number of symptoms which are prevalent in the Christian community, symptoms which suggest that all is not well with the church. Four of these symptoms are especially important: the curious status of the Bible in the church's life, the church's loss of its theological tradition, the absence of theological reflection at all levels of the church's life, and the inability of many Christians to make sense out of their personal identity by means of Christian faith. These "symptoms" illustrate a problem in the common life of the Christian community, a problem that is also evident in the personal lives of many of us who live in and are committed to the church. The fact that these symptoms are prevalent does not mean the demise of the church is imminent. The symptoms do suggest that there is a problem in the church's general health which deserves serious attention.

The first of these symptoms is the silence of Scripture in the life of the church. One could argue that questions about the authority of Scripture and the nature of hermeneutics have been the dominant issues in Christian theology during the past two hundred years.[4] Certainly questions about the proper interpretation of Scripture and the role of the Bible in Christian life are nothing new. What is new, however, is a phenomenon which James Smart has described aptly as "the strange silence of the Bible in the church."[5] Protestant churches which stand in traditions that come out of the sixteenth-century Reformation understand the Bible to be of crucial significance for understanding and living Christian faith. Those churches nurtured by Heinrich Bullinger's Second Helvetic Confession of 1566 and The Westminster Confession of Faith of 1647 still repeat the words, "For God himself spoke to the fathers, prophets, apostles, and still speaks to us through the Holy Scriptures."[6] But it is unusual to discover a Protestant congregation whose faith is informed by a Reformed understanding of Scripture's witness to God's Word and a proper interpretation of the relation between the Bible, the Word of God, the Spirit, and the world. Such a Reformed understanding of the relation between Scripture and the world has nothing to do with teaching children to memorize the Bible in order that they learn a proper morality, a practice that remains widespread in conservative churches. In both conservative and liberal churches homage is still paid to the authority of the Word of God and Scripture's witness to God's revelation, but beneath the public pronouncements subtle shifts have occurred in the church's life which have had seismic consequences.

As is clear in confessions such as the Second Helvetic and Westminster, at one time an essential feature of the identity of the Protestant church was the authority Scripture exercised in the life of the community. Although most Protestant churches still claim that Scripture is the basis for their understanding of Christian faith and continue to repeat the theologically appropriate statements about its importance, in fact the Bible no longer exercises anything like the authority it once did in many Christian communities. And in those communities where the Bible continues to exercise its traditional role there is little or no serious engagement with the problems of the twentieth century. A remarkable number of Bibles continues to be published and sold each year and there are few Christian homes (not to mention motels and hotels) in which a Bible cannot be found. But despite its increasing growth rate, the Bible no longer exercises the same authority or plays the same role it once did, even in those conservative churches where appearances suggest otherwise.

Most Christians own a copy of the Bible but few know what to do with it. More often than not the Bible is found buried on the top shelf of the bookcase in the den or covered with dust on the bottom shelf of the coffee table. If it is read at all, it is used as a desperate treatment for insomnia when drugstore medicines fail.[7] How strange that those Christian communities who traditionally have sought to understand faith and life by listening for God's Word in the witness of Scripture should now suffer the silence of the Bible and a growing unfamiliarity with its content and use. It is little wonder that the apparent demise of Scripture in the life of the Protestant community has resulted in widespread confusion and has prompted serious questions about the church's self-understanding and identity.

The confusion about the role of Scripture is apparent in the growing lack of knowledge in the church of the content of Scripture. In recent years Christian education at all levels has focused on important questions about the meaning of faith and its implications for life in modern culture. It is not unusual to discover an adult church class considering themes in recent fiction or the moral consequences of euthanasia. These are important topics and deserve to be studied in the church, but they also should not constitute the entire program of Christian education. There is now a widespread unfamiliarity in the church with what were at one time old and familiar names and stories in Scripture. "Biblical illiteracy" has become a serious problem at all levels of the church's life.

If this were the extent of the problem then the church could address biblical illiteracy by means of some kind of massive education program. New members could be required to demonstrate some knowledge of the content of Scripture and greater attention could be devoted to Scripture in adult education. Unfortunately, biblical illiteracy is only a surface manifestation of a problem that lies much deeper in the church's life and is more difficult to unearth. The problem is not just that many people no longer know what is in the Bible; it is also a mystery to many people what the Bible has to do with life in the twentieth century. Even many of those individuals in the church who know something of the content of Scripture do not understand how to apply it to their personal and social existence. What is sometimes referred to as "the hermeneutical gap" between the first and twentieth centuries has become more like an unbridgeable chasm.[8] What Karl Barth once referred to as "the strange new world of the Bible" seems so strange and so alien to the modern Christian that only a schizophrenic could inhabit both worlds simultaneously.[9] Among other Christians that strange new world has become so familiar, so domesticated, that it seems to be simply a mirror reflection of contemporary culture and its values and worldview. In 1941, Rudolf Bultmann gave classic expression to this hermeneutical dilemma in his essay on "New Testament and Mythology." "It is impossible," he wrote, "to use electric light and the wireless and to avail ourselves of modern medical and surgical discoveries, and at the same time to believe in the New Testament world of spirits and miracles."[10] Although many important objections have been raised to Bultmann's program for the demythologization of the New Testament, his essay does reflect the hermeneutical confusion over the function and meaning of Scripture that pervades the Christian community today.

Ironically the silence of Scripture and the church's uncertainty about the role of Scripture is in part the result of advances in biblical scholarship and theology during the last two hundred years. Although many branches of Protestantism have resisted the use of scholarly tools in the study of Scripture, most pastors and teachers from the major traditions have been trained in what has come to be known as "the historical-critical method," which actually is several methods for analyzing and interpreting a biblical text. For many of these people the discovery of the historical-critical tools was a liberating experience. It freed them to read the text without the blinders of literalism and it opened new, richer vistas within the text that were hitherto unknown. One would have thought that the training of pastors in these skills eventually would have altered the way in which the Bible is used and understood in the church. But to the disappointment and the dismay of many scholars, critical methodology seems to have had little or no effect on the life of the church.

Having been exposed to a critical reading of Scripture in their seminary education, it is difficult for pastors to return to a pre-critical reading of the text. But once the pastor enters his or her first parish the tools of historical-criticism remain a closely guarded secret. Very little that the pastor learned about how to read and interpret Scripture is passed on to the laity. Pastors have been content to let those in the church who have not had a theological education continue to read the Bible as though it were a history lesson or a science text. Obviously this situation has had serious consequences for the life of the church. The pastor reads and understands the text in one way and the parishioner reads and hears something else. For various reasons pastors apparently either cannot or will not lay their exegesis on the table for the congregation, and at some level of consciousness the congregation senses that its understanding of Scripture is quite different from that of its pastor.

For those who teach in many Protestant seminaries the silence of Scripture and the ineffectiveness of the critical method are cause for considerable worry. Only recently a reappraisal of the historical-critical method has begun in earnest in several quarters. Not many Christians who have benefitted from the insights of the historical-critical method would agree with the conclusion that "Historical biblical criticism is bankrupt."[11] But many people, including a few in the professional guild of biblical scholars, are beginning to re-examine the limits and usefulness of the historical-critical method as the sole approach to the interpretation of Scripture. The issue is not whether the critical tools of modern biblical scholarship are bankrupt, but whether they can be expected to disclose the full meaning of the text in all its richness and depth. Although one dimension of the text may be illumined by a knowledge of the historical context in which it was written (hence the importance of the history of religions, form criticism, and redaction criticism), it may also be that what the text *means* must be understood not entirely in terms of its historical development but rather in terms of what it says. What a text says may be only partially illumined by knowledge of the author's intentions and the historical and social context in which the text was written. If that is the case, the decisive question then becomes that of the proper relation between those critical methods which explore the history of the text and the claims made on the reader by the text itself.[12]

Whether the silence of the Bible in the church is due to the unwillingness or the failure of biblical scholars and theologically trained pastors to pass along the discoveries of the historical-critical method is difficult to assess. What is clear is that those churches which traditionally have pointed to Scripture for their understanding of Christian faith and have appealed to categories

such as "Word of God" and "revelation" to explain the importance they attribute to Scripture no longer do so, or if they continue to make such appeals they are no longer certain what they
mean. As a result many Protestant churches no longer know what
they mean by "authority," what role Scripture should play in the
life of the church, and, finally, when all is said and done, what
the Bible has to do with life in the modern world.[13]

The second symptom of the emerging crisis in Christian identity is the loss of theological tradition. The sense of living out of
a theological tradition no longer seems to inform the life of many
Christian communities. An understanding of the meaning and
importance of a historical tradition that begins with the confession "My father was a wandering Aramean" and extends through
the formation of the Christian community and its development
since the first century is not a common characteristic of many
churches. Unfortunately, many Christians confuse tradition with
the mindless repetition of past rites and the preservation of
anachronistic rules and institutions. They fail to see that a "living
tradition" is not a museum. In a sense this is not a new development, for a significant part of the Protestant church in the United
States has never known what to make of "history" and has considered it useless and irrelevant. Many Christian sects and denominations assume some kind of direct continuity between Jesus,
Paul, and their congregation in the twentieth century, a curious
application of the virgin birth to ecclesiology. In the period between the first and the twentieth centuries they believe the
church was either dormant or hidden.

Those Protestant churches which look to the Reformation and
to Luther and Calvin for a theological understanding of their origin and development appeal not only to Scripture but also to
particular creeds and confessions written in different and often
distant historical periods by individuals and communities who
shared neither the same culture nor vision of the world but who
did share a similar understanding of the meaning and shape of

Christian faith. For some time Protestant theologians have recognized that *sola scriptura* does not mean that the reader has access
to the pristine meaning of Scripture.[14] Every reader comes to the
text with a particular cultural background, worldview, and interpretive frame by means of which the text is read and understood. Hence there can be no encounter between an "unpreju-
diced" reader and a pristine text. Every encounter with a text is
colored by the reader's presuppositions, and one function of the
church's creeds and confessions has been to provide the reader
with some categories and principles for the proper interpretation
of Scripture and the meaning of Christian faith. The church's
confessions provide the formal categories for the interpretation of
Scripture (such as Trinity, justification by faith, etc.), but they
do not resolve the question of what the text and these principles
mean in any given historical situation. As it engages in the difficult process of reinterpreting Christian faith in different periods, situations, and cultures, the church has found that it needs
not only the Bible but also those creeds and confessions which
illumine and explain the meaning of faith. "Tradition," therefore,
refers to more than simply a collection of creeds and confessions,
more than simply a museum of theological artifacts; it refers to
the whole history of the church's interpretation of Scripture and
therein the living history of its understanding of faith.[15]

Scripture no longer seems to exercise authority in the daily
life of the church. Neither does "tradition" and it is often misunderstood. To appeal to tradition in the process of resolving a
theological argument or a practical matter in the daily life of the
church is to run the risk of being labeled a musty antiquarian
hopelessly out of touch with the contemporary world. It is a curious development that in those Protestant churches whose understanding of Christian faith has been shaped by Augustine,
Luther, and Calvin one seldom hears the tradition discussed as a
resource for contemporary issues, except in those unfortunate
cases in which the tradition is used as an excuse to avoid the

modern world. At one time in the history of the church it would
have been difficult to find educated Christians who had not read
Augustine's *Confessions*, but it is not unusual today to find seminary students who assume the book is a television soap opera.
The consequences of this loss of tradition in the church's life are
enormous. Far too many Christians have no idea what Augustine,
Luther, and Calvin have to do with their congregation and its
understanding of Christian faith. If the issue is pressed one soon
discovers that many people in the church are uncertain what, if
anything, is distinctive about their church, be it Presbyterian,
Baptist, or any other denomination.

Whether one is Presbyterian or Baptist is not the most important question that should be asked of an individual or a
church. The problem, however, is that people are not amor-
phously Christian, or at least they should not be. Admittedly
there is a form of civil faith that masquerades under the title
"Christian" in many American suburban communities, but this
amorphous Christianity is unaware of whence it came and is often
unable to separate its values and principles from those of middle-
class, white America. Furthermore, this amorphous Christianity
neither understands nor values the development of the church's
faith, nor is it rooted in any particular tradition within Christen-
dom. It may use the same language and symbols as other
Christian communities but it does not understand the historicity
of that language and its basis in redemptive experience in the
same way as do other Christians. Consequently the piety and
religious passion of amorphous Christians is of a very different
sort from the piety of those churches self-consciously rooted in a
particular theological tradition.[16]

The reasons why tradition is not a powerful voice in the life
are manifold and complex, but regardless of the difficulty of the
problem, for the church to give up its tradition and in so doing
cut itself off from its historical roots would be to court disaster.
There are many aspects of Christian doctrine, language, and

ritual that have been and still must be reformed. Contemporary interpretations of Christian faith are distorted by sexism and racism. There is much in its tradition for which the church needs to repent, but even if the Christian tradition does need to be reworked and reinterpreted the church cannot live without it. A Christian community unaware of its theological tradition may suffer a form of religious and spiritual amnesia.[17] The tradition provides the hermeneutical categories by which the community reconstructs and reinterprets its identity. While the symbols "God the Father" and "resurrection" may function differently now and mean something else than they did in the first or sixteenth centuries, they are carried into the present by a tradition, and the doctrines and creeds which have been used in the past to elucidate these symbols give each Christian community its identity and continuity with the churches of past generations. A church which no longer understands or is unaware of its theological tradition is a church without a memory, and memory is indispensable for what Christian faith affirms about God.

A third symptom of the identity crisis in the church is closely related to the first two symptoms, and, although perhaps not as apparent, equally serious. Scripture and the Christian tradition are not the only traditional resources which seem to have fallen on bad times in the church. It is also rare to hear the discipline of theology, in any form, appealed to or employed in the church's life. As is the case with Scripture and tradition, most churches still pay lip service to the importance of theology, but it is unusual when theological reflection plays an actual role in a church's decision-making process. Regardless of whether the issue is the ordination of homosexuals or the restructuring of the denomination's bureaucracy, pragmatic concerns about finances and public image play a far more important role than theological reflection.

Unfortunately it is not only those in the pew who shun theology. Nowhere is the demise of theology more apparent than among the church's clergy. In both the national offices of major denominations and in small, rural churches one seldom encounters anything even resembling theological reflection. In order to keep budget-raising up-to-date the church's denominational administrators quickly adopt whatever language and newest breed of systems analysis is in vogue in the business community. The expertise and in that sense the vocational identity of church administrators consists of the management and business skills with which they assess the needs of the church and structure its programs and life. In similar fashion parish ministers eagerly embrace transactional analysis or whatever is the most recent psychological fad as one way of demonstrating that they too, like the doctors and lawyers in their congregations, possess professional skills. Whether it is transactional analysis or the newest technique in business management it must offer immediate results, provide the pastor with an expertise which few others in the congregation can claim to possess, and, most importantly, be something that can be mastered quickly, at least within a three-day retreat or a two-week study leave. The tragedy, of course, is that the pastors and church leaders who eagerly embrace these techniques do not understand their vocational identity to be what they were trained to do—to bring Christian faith with its Scripture and theological tradition to bear on the ambiguities and complexities of the contemporary world.

By no means is it entirely the fault of parish ministers that theology is almost an extinct discipline in the local church and in denominational headquarters. Protestant seminaries which undertook the theological education of these pastors must shoulder a major share of the responsibility for the problem. Students in many seminaries were taught the tools of historical-critical research and the basic doctrines of the Christian tradition, but they were not taught how to apply these tools and doctrines to personal issues such as divorce and abortion or social issues such as the size of the defense budget or a proposal to pave the church parking lot instead of increasing benevolence giving. Apparently seminaries assumed that their responsibility was simply to provide basic tools and information, and it was the student's task to learn how to use them. Since understanding is in part a matter of knowing how to do something, and not simply a matter of knowing the proper answer to a question, it is not surprising that many pastors either gave up any attempt at theological reflection once they entered the parish or found that because they did not know how to use the discipline they were unable to teach their congregations how to think theologically for themselves. As a result the most important advances in theological scholarship during the last two hundred years—the emergence of historical-critical tools such as form and redaction criticism—have had little or no impact on the life of the church. In the local church basic questions about the use of Scripture and the significance of Christian faith for personal and social issues are discussed today in much the same terms as they were several generations ago.

The church can no more afford to give up theological reflection than it can Scripture or the Christian tradition. Properly understood theology is not an esoteric mystery studied only by seminary professors who are unwilling or unable to earn an honest living; nor is it just the Saturday morning hobby of the parish minister. Theological reflection is of primary importance to every Christian who wants to understand what it is he or she believes and what are the implications of Christian faith for all aspects of life. It is the discipline of theological reflection which serves as the bridge between the church's established resources, such as Scripture and tradition, and the challenges posed to Christian faith by the modern world. If it does not know how to think theologically (as opposed to other modes of reflection), the church will become a prisoner of the past, repeat what it has memorized in Scripture and tradition, and play hide-and-seek with the modern world, or it will discard its Scripture and its creeds as anachronisms and wander through modernity in search of an uncertain identity. In either case the church will not be responsible to the faith it confesses. It is the ability to think theologically which enables the church to engage the world by means of the resources of the past.

Finally, a fourth symptom of the crisis in Christian identity is the inability of individuals within the Christian community to make sense out of their personal identity by means of Christian faith. Obviously this fourth symptom is closely related to the first three. When Christians no longer know what to do with the theological resources for the interpretation of Christian faith, such as Scripture and the creeds, they may continue to give them lip service and they may continue to participate in the life of the Christian community, but their identities—who they are, what kind of people they understand themselves to be—are shaped by other communities and other narratives. No one lives entirely within the Christian community. Most people live in various communities (nation, race, family, vocation) and personal identity is constructed out of these different communities and the narratives peculiar to them. Although a person may live in different communities and participate in various narratives, Christians claim that anyone who professes faith in Jesus Christ must assess these other communities and their narratives from the perspective of Christian faith and its truth claims. Regardless of a person's race, nationality, and vocation, the personal identity of Christians must finally be interpreted in light of and by means of Christian faith. The crisis in the church is that the personal identity of many Christians is no longer shaped by Christian faith and the narratives that articulate that faith but by other communities and other narratives, narratives which have no necessary relation to the Christian community.

To put the problem in its clearest form, when individuals who participate actively in the church identify themselves to other people, neither the language of Christian faith nor the fact of participation in the Christian community seem to play prominent roles in those identity narratives. Where one comes from, the composition of one's present family, a person's vocation, political, and economic preferences—these are usually some of the bare facts that make up the formal narrative, and when a person broods over this narrative and struggles to understand it and come to terms with the realities glossed over or ignored in the formal narrative—rejection by parents, divorce, runaway children, etc.—there is often little or no evidence that Christian faith or the realities supposedly encountered by participation in the Christian community play any significant role in this identity narrative or its interpretation. For many of those individuals most active in the church, Christian faith does not appear to play an obvious role in the way in which they construct and articulate their personal identity in either a simple or a sophisticated form. The crisis in Christian identity is that it is not apparent to observers outside or inside the church what role Christian faith plays in the narratives Christians recite in order to explain who they are and what kind of people they think they are. These identity narratives appear to be no different from those recited by individuals who have little or no commitment to Christian faith. Two people, who are executive vice presidents of World Oil Company, belong to Evergreen Country Club, and are staunch Republicans, refer to basically the same facts and use the same categories and symbols for interpreting their identity, despite the fact that one of them is a committed participant in the Christian community.

The other symptoms we have discussed—the silence of Scripture, the loss of tradition, the absence of theological reflection—are only further indications of the crisis in Christian identity in its most virulent form, the crisis in personal identity that seems to be widespread among those individuals who have lived in and supposedly have been nurtured by the Christian community. It is beside the point to ask whether Scripture is silent in the Christian community because the personal identity of Christians has become confused and uncertain, or whether there is a crisis in

Chapter II
Revelation
Under Siege

What we have described as a crisis in the daily life of the Christian community has had important theological consequences during the latter half of the twentieth century. While Christians have been troubled in their daily existence about the meaning of Christian identity in the modern world, Christian theologians have watched doctrines which at one time formed the centerpiece of the church's theology crumble under the strain of unrelenting criticism. This doctrinal collapse has been most evident in what Christian theologians refer to as the doctrine of revelation. During the first half of the twentieth century, Protestant theology, especially that movement loosely labeled "neo-orthodoxy," made revelation the systematic principle for the elucidation of the other doctrines of Christian faith. Books such as the first two volumes of Karl Barth's *Church Dogmatics*, Emil Brunner's *Revelation and Reason*, and H. Richard Niebuhr's *The Meaning of Revelation* are evidence of the preoccupation with revelation by theologians during the 1930s and 1940s. Revelation became the foundation on which twentieth-century theologians rebuilt the theological edifice that was in shambles after the collapse of nineteenth-century liberalism in 1914. Although neither neo-orthodoxy nor the doctrine of revelation were greeted with universal acceptance for many years following the First World War, the major contributions in theological scholarship during that period came from figures who shared a common commitment to a specific interpretation of revelation. Therefore, when the doctrine of revelation and the theological positions erected on it came under increasingly heavy fire during the 1950s and 1960s it was not surprising that the discipline of theology and its related fields were thrown into disarray and confusion.

It is not an accident that the attack on revelation occurred when it did. What we described in the first chapter as the crisis in Christian identity became increasingly apparent during the same period in which neo-orthodox interpretations of revelation came under heavy attack. While there may be no direct or immediate causal relation between the two, it is understandable why Christian identity might become questionable if that doctrine at the center of Christian faith proves unable to bear the weight laid upon it. So too if Christian identity in contemporary society becomes confused and uncertain one might expect questions to be raised about the coherence and the intelligibility of that doctrine which functions as the epistemological foundation of Christian faith. The attack on neo-orthodox interpretations of revelation reflects at the level of the church's intellectual life the crisis in identity which Christians were experiencing at the more primordial level of lived experience. In this chapter we will examine briefly what revelation means, Karl Barth's interpretation of revelation, the attack launched against Barth's interpretation, and an alternative interpretation of revelation.

1. What Revelation Means

Much confusion now surrounds the doctrine of revelation. The air is filled with attacks and counterattacks, and there is clearly no consensus among contemporary theologians as to what revelation means. A casual reading of contemporary theology quickly discloses that there are a variety of proposals for how to construe the meaning of revelation and differing opinions as to its role and significance in the explication of Christian faith. Nor is the confusion and debate over revelation strictly a discussion among professional theologians. Both inside and outside the church many people still understand revelation to be a matter of accepting propositions which cannot be demonstrated by reason but which must be accepted by faith. To others revelation suggests miraculous moments of ecstasy and illumination, dusty roads and blinding lights, or football stadiums and "moments of decision." It is probably not an exaggeration to conclude that the doctrine of revelation, despite its importance in recent theological discussion, has been widely understood by people in the church to be a mysterious, if not exotic, doctrine that is beyond mortal powers of comprehension. If that is true, it is unfortunate because the rough parameters of what theologians mean by revelation are neither mysterious nor difficult to understand.

As is the case with the doctrine of the Trinity, there is no doctrine of revelation as such in Scripture. Most theologians would probably claim that what they mean by revelation is based in part on Scripture's description of how people come to know God, but few theologians outside the circle of rigid conservatives would claim that Scripture itself teaches a doctrine of revelation. Contemporary theological discussions of revelation are often quite different from earlier more traditional discussions. Initially, revelation was understood to refer to truths which were not accessible to reason. Revelation referred to those propositions and doctrines about God, such as the Trinity, which were known to be true because of God's gracious illumination of the intellect. In the period following the Reformation, revelation was not understood primarily in terms of its relation to reason, but in terms of the inspiration of Scripture. Revelation was still understood to refer to truths about God, but now these truths were understood to be revealed in an inspired (and in some parts of Protestantism an "infallible") Bible. In the last two hundred years, following the Enlightenment, with the development of historical criticism and an emerging awareness of the historical relativity of all human statements and truth-claims, the contemporary discussion of revelation has shifted yet again from its Medieval and Reformation forms.[1] In the broadest sense of the term, revelation, as it appears in most contemporary theological discussions, refers to the unveiling or disclosure of a reality that is not accessible to human discovery and which is of decisive significance for human destiny and well-being.[2] Three aspects of this general description of revelation are worth noting.

In the first place, revelation means an unveiling or, to use a more contemporary term, a "disclosure." It refers to an event in which a veil is dropped or removed, an event in which that which is masked or hidden from view is disclosed and made known. In this sense revelation does not refer to an event in which new realities are created or come into being, but only to events in which existing realities previously beyond the reach of human knowledge become accessible and knowable. In revelation the veil that masks or hides a reality is dropped and what previously had been unknown or known only as hidden becomes an unveiled reality. Also, what is known in revelation cannot be abstracted from the time and circumstances, the "event," in which it is encountered and known. The unveiling described as revelation refers both to the circumstances in which revelation takes place and to what it is that is known in the disclosive event. Consequently what one knows in revelation is not an idea or a proposition that is universally true without reference to the time and circumstances in which the event of disclosure takes place. What is unveiled or disclosed in revelation cannot be separated from the event in which it makes itself known. *What* one knows in revelation cannot be separated from a description of *how* revelation takes place. Knowledge of the event of revelation is inseparable from knowledge of that which is revealed.

Secondly, the event in which revelation takes place is not one that can be initiated by human will. A person who experiences revelation is not so much the subject as the object in this event. That is, revelation or disclosure is not something a person effects or creates. From the individual's perspective revelation is an event in which he or she is wholly passive, simply the recipient of what takes place. It is not the knower who does the disclosing, unless one wants to say that the real knower is the one who is unveiled. The person who experiences revelation is really only the passive object in this event and the disclosure is initiated by that which is disclosed.

It follows as a corollary of the second point that what is known in revelation, both in principle and in fact, is inaccessible to human inquiry and investigation. In other words, what one knows in a revelatory event is not something that could have been discovered given enough time and ingenuity. Revelation is not just another piece of knowledge like that which comes from research and exploration or extended reflection. What is disclosed in the revelatory event is not new information, not more data in addition to that already accumulated and classified by human science, nor new ideas and insights. The very use of the words "unveiledness" and "disclosure" suggests that what makes itself known in the revelatory moment is the stuff of mystery. Revelation yields not the solution to a problem but the unveiling of a mystery.

Thirdly, in strictly theistic language this interpretation of revelation suggests that God is disclosed or revealed to human beings only because God does the disclosing.[3] The unveiling is what God does and in no sense is it a human act. For Christians this means that every doctrine of revelation is also a statement about the grace of God. In the sense in which we will be using the term, revelation takes place only by means of the activity of an other and therefore is a gracious event. Because revelation is an event that takes place only by means of God's grace it is a redemptive event for all those who participate in and respond to it. Hence what one knows in revelation cannot be known dispassionately or disinterestedly, for it is knowledge about human well-being and destiny, knowledge that is unto salvation.

Revelation, therefore, in one sense of the word refers to an event in which something is unveiled or disclosed, and what is known in this event cannot be separated from the givenness and particularity of the event. What is disclosed in revelation is not just one more phenomenon in the natural order but a mystery that is the very ground of that order, a mystery Christians understand to be a personal reality. And finally, revelation is a gracious event, and as such, it is not susceptible to human initiative or manipulation.

2. Barth's Discussion of Revelation

The most comprehensive and formidable statement of a doctrine of revelation as the basis for Christian theology is the work of Karl Barth. In the first two volumes of his *Church Dogmatics* (subtitled "Prolegomena to Church Dogmatics"), Barth discusses the nature of revelation and the relation between revelation and the Word of God. As Barth describes it, revelation is neither a formal category nor a description of general religious experience. Revelation refers to a specific event and a particular act; it "signifies the Word of God itself, the act of its utterance."[4] Revelation means *Deus dixit*, and it is not possible in the context of Barth's theology to separate revelation from the Word of God. It is in this sense that revelation, understood as a description of universal religious experience, has nothing to do with what Barth means by the term. Revelation always refers to that particular event in which God's Word is spoken.

In Barth's theology the Word of God appears in three forms.

The first of these is real proclamation, the Word of God preached and the Word celebrated in the sacraments.[5] Not all proclamation is real proclamation because not all preaching is the preaching of the Word of God. "Real proclamation" is that event in which "man's language about God is not only man's language, but also and primarily and decisively God's own language."[6] Not every sermon is the proclamation of the Word of God. A sermon is nothing more nor less than one person's attempt "to express in his own words in the form of an exposition of a portion of the Biblical testimony to revelation, and to make comprehensible to men of his day, the promise of God's revelation, reconciliation and calling, as they are to be expected here and now."[7] In this attempt to bring the witness of Scripture to bear on human experience and contemporary history there is no guarantee that the sermon will be the Word of God preached. Simply because this event occupies a familiar place in a church's worship service and is the occasion for language many people might refer to as "religious" does not necessarily mean that the Word of God has been preached. Human words about God may have been spoken but that in itself does not mean that the Word of God has been preached. Proclamation as "the Word of God preached" refers to an event in which the Word of God is heard in the midst of human words and not simply to any event in which there is human language about God.[8] Real proclamation, as opposed to any and all forms of proclamation, refers only to those events in which language about God becomes an occasion for God's grace, when "human language about God is not set aside, but rather exalted."[9] In describing real proclamation in this manner Barth suggests a parallel between the Word of God preached and the Incarnation; "As Christ became true man and also remains true man to all eternity, so real proclamation becomes an event on the level of all other human events."[10]

The second form of the Word of God is the Word written, the witness of Scripture. Scripture is the church's recollection of or attestation to those events in the past which the church refers to as the locus for God's revelation, events in which God has spoken and acted as Creator and Redeemer. Scripture is not itself the Word of God but the human (and hence fallible) witness to God's activity in history.[11]

The "authority" of Scripture is not for Barth some property intrinsic to Scripture, nothing Scripture magically exercises in itself; rather its authority is that of a witness. It points to the decisive thing and in so doing directs attention to what ultimately matters. As far as Barth is concerned it is a mistake of the first order to confuse the witness, Scripture, with that reality to which it witnesses. "Therefore we do the Bible a poor honour, and one unwelcome to itself, when we directly identify it with this something else, with revelation itself."[12] Even though Scripture is not itself God's Word, it, like the human words of proclamation, may become God's Word. The claim that the Bible is God's Word "is a confession of faith, a statement made by the faith that hears God Himself speak in the human word of the Bible."[13] There is nothing that the church can do nor anything that any individual interpreter can do to make Scripture become the Word of God. But from time to time, through God's grace, the human witness of Scripture becomes the occasion for the Word of God. In this sense the Bible is God's Word written, but only "so far as God lets it be His Word, so far as God speaks through it."[14]

The third form of the Word of God is really the first in as much as it is the presupposition for the first two forms. What is preached in real proclamation and witnessed to in Scripture is the revealed Word of God. In the first two forms of the Word of God, "proclaimed" and "written" describe those occasions in which God's Word can be heard in the midst of human words. Such is not the case, however, with the term "revealed." The latter term is "nothing but a transcription, a second designation of the subject itself"; and as such it "signifies the Word of God itself, the act of its utterance."[15] Revelation, as the third form of the Word of God, refers to that historical event in which God's Word was immediately present and directly visible. Revelation, therefore, is synonymous with Incarnation, "the Word became flesh," "God with us," or as Barth describes it, "Revelation in fact does not differ from the Person of Jesus Christ, and again does not differ from the reconciliation that took place in Him."[16] Although Barth insists that proclamation and Scripture must not under any circumstances be identified with God's Word, that is not true of revelation. While the human words of proclamation and Scripture from time to time through God's grace may become God's Word, in the sense that God's Word may be heard in them, revelation is immediately and directly what proclamation and Scripture are only indirectly and by mediation.[17] To speak of "revelation" is not to speak of human words which become God's Word but to speak of God's Word itself, Jesus Christ.

In the context of Barth's theology it is clear that revelation refers only to this third form of the Word of God, the event of Incarnation. One must remember, however, that in the early volumes of the *Church Dogmatics* Barth emphasized the objectivity and givenness of God's redemptive acts over against what he perceived to be the prevailing subjectivity and emphasis on religious experience bequeathed the church by nineteenth-century liberalism. Barth attempted to turn the tables, to insist that the objective reality of what God has done precedes the question of its possibility, that the ontic precedes the noetic. Even with this historical note in mind it is clear that revelation actually functions in a double sense in Barth's theology. On the one hand, as we have seen, revelation refers to that event in history in which God's Word became a fleshly, tangible reality in the person and life of Jesus of Nazareth, what Christians refer to as the "Incarnation." This historical event in which God's Word became a visible reality is what Barth refers to as the third form of the Word of God or what he also describes as "the objective reality of

revelation."[18] "God reveals himself in his Word" means that
God's acts and intentions are disclosed in the life and death of
Jesus of Nazareth. Revelation is "objective," therefore, in that it
has a historical referent which can be looked at, examined, and
discussed.

In addition to this objective dimension in Barth's interpretation of revelation there is yet another dimension. For various reasons Christians have insisted that revelation is not just a historical
event, not just something that happened only once, there and
then in the distant past, but also a reality that reoccurs from time
to time in the experience of contemporary individuals and communities. The third form of the Word, the revelation of God in
Jesus of Nazareth, is the presupposition for the other forms of
the Word, occasions in which human words, words spoken in the
present, become bearers of God's Word. Through God's grace the
human words of Scripture, preaching, and the sacraments may
become occasions in which God's Word becomes a present reality.
What happened there and then in the life and person of Jesus of
Nazareth becomes a here-and-now reality. When this happens the
human words of Scripture and proclamation become authentic
witnesses to that event in which God's Word was revealed in the
humiliation and exaltation of Jesus Christ.[19] Human words do
not cease to be human just as Jesus of Nazareth does not cease to
be fully human, but human words are "exalted" and "elevated."
These human words which witness to and attest to God's Word
become God's Word in the sense that they are confirmed, preserved, and fulfilled.[20] The objective reality that was a historical
event becomes what Barth calls a "subjective reality" in the experience of individuals and communities. And it is God in his
mode of being which Christians call "Holy Spirit" who makes
possible the subjective reality of revelation, the human encounter
with God's Word in Jesus Christ.[21]

Yet another way of describing Barth's twofold use of revelation, his distinction between the objective and subjective dimen-

sions, is the distinction between content and form. The objective reality of revelation is a description of *what* (or more precisely *whom*) is revealed, the cognitive content of revelation, which Christians believe to be God's self-disclosure in Jesus of Nazareth. The subjective reality of revelation, on the other hand, is a description of the form which God's Word assumes, regardless of whether it is the unmediated (or immediate) appearance of the Word in the Incarnation or the mediated sense in which the human words of proclamation and Scripture become God's Word. The subjective reality of revelation describes *how* God's Word becomes a reality in the midst of human words. This distinction between the objective and subjective realities of revelation, between the content and the form of the Word, enabled Barth to speak of God's Word as the primary authority in Christian life and theology and to identify that Word with Jesus of Nazareth. At the same time, Barth was able to attribute a relative authority to the human words of Scripture and proclamation in so far as they fulfill their proper function as witnesses to God's primary self-disclosure in Jesus of Nazareth.

Barth's interpretation of revelation provided pastors and theologians with a formulation of the doctrine of revelation which did not have to be reworked after each new discovery in natural science and the historical investigation of Scripture. Because he refused to identify the human words of Scripture and proclamation with God's Word, Barth was able to describe revelation so that it did not diminish either the human character of faith or God's freedom. To identify the human words of Scripture and proclamation with God's Word would be to make them something more or less than human words. The fatal consequence of that mistake is to introduce a not so subtle docetism into Christian life and worship. By definition the sermon becomes God's Word, regardless of its content, and the preacher becomes a high priest delivering an infallible message received directly from God. Such an understanding of the sermon places an impossible burden on anyone who dares to preach, for it denies the pastor's essential humanity and makes him or her into a religious and moral demi-god. Similarly, to identify the human words of Scripture with God's Word would be to make the Bible into a "paper Pope," an infallible oracle of divine wisdom. Once this move has been made it is no longer possible to draw a distinction between that to which Scripture witnesses and Scripture itself. Christian faith becomes faith in the Bible rather than faith in the redemptive grace of God. The historical investigation of Scripture becomes irrelevant if not irreverent, and it becomes impossible to separate the significance of what the Bible says about Jesus Christ from what it says about the role of women and slaves in the church and the natural structure of the cosmos. Not only does such an identification deny the human character of faith, but it also attempts arbitrarily to limit God's freedom. The Word of God is now confined to those occasions and to those human words with which it has been identified. The Spirit is no longer free to move where it wills, the Word no longer free to stand over against any and every human word either in confirmation or in judgment. Barth's formulation of the nature of revelation and its relation to the Word of God provided a context for the development and celebration of Christian faith in response to the grace and freedom of God.

Not only did Barth protect both the human character of faith and God's freedom, but by giving priority to the doctrine of revelation Barth linked Christian faith and the identity of the Christian community to an interpretation of specific historical events in which Christians believe they witness the presence and the activity of that reality Jesus called "Abba." Hence revelation and the Word of God have an inescapably historical referent. Although they may be forms of the Word of God, the human artifacts of Scripture and proclamation are not the only resources for understanding the identity of the Christian community. They may be necessary for a proper interpretation of God's self-disclosure, but neither in itself is sufficient nor a final criterion for

assessing the meaning of Christian faith. They function properly
only when they witness to Jesus Christ, but it is God's Word as
it is revealed in Jesus Christ that is the sole authority for faith
and theology and the source of identity for the Christian community. This aspect of Barth's theology is hardly new. By insisting that Scripture is not itself God's Word but the witness to
those events in which the Word appeared, Barth only echoes
Luther's claim that "this much is beyond question, that all the
Scriptures point to Christ alone."[22] For Barth and Luther the
human words of Scripture and proclamation are God's Word only
in so far as they point to and witness to the revelation of God's
Word in Jesus Christ.

In many respects Barth's description of revelation is attractive
and compelling. It is not, however, without its problems, as we
shall see in the following section. A major problem in Barth's
discussion is his reluctance to describe what he calls "the subjective reality of revelation." How does the objective reality of revelation, the Incarnation of God's Word in Jesus Christ, become a
subjective reality in the experience of men and women today?
Barth denies that it is human ingenuity that enables this to happen. "On the contrary," he writes, "the fact that this takes place
is something which we must accept as quite beyond our understanding."[23] But if it is beyond our understanding and beyond
human description, then it begins to sound like an event to
which only a select number are privy. If all that we can say about
the subjective reality of revelation is that it is the work of the
Spirit, then it is understandable why serious questions might be
raised about the intelligibility of the doctrine and its appropriateness as the foundation for the elucidation of Christian faith.

3. Attacks on Revelation

It is not surprising that what we have described as the crisis
in Christian identity—with its attendant symptoms of the si-

lence of Scripture, the loss of tradition, the absence of theology, and the inability to use Christian faith for interpreting personal identity—began to become a serious problem in the middle of the twentieth century. That was also the period during which fundamental questions were raised about the neo-orthodox interpretation of revelation, especially Barth's position. The theological position commonly referred to as neo-orthodoxy came under unrelenting attack, and the doctrine of revelation, especially Barth's formulation of it, was the target of serious and sustained criticism. The debate was not merely a squabble among professional theologians. The attack on the doctrine of revelation also called into question the place of Scripture, preaching, and the sacraments in the church and other doctrines and rites which traditionally had provided the Christian community its identity. The confusion and disputes among professional theologians only reflected the more widespread crisis of identity within the Christian community.

The attacks on revelation came from several quarters. Some of the objections were directed only against the doctrine of revelation as it had been formulated in neo-orthodox circles. Since there were significant disagreements among neo-orthodox theologians as to how revelation should be construed, the objections often were against the position of a particular theologian, such as Barth. Other attacks were wider in scope and were directed at features of the doctrine of revelation found both within and without neo-orthodox circles, such as all those interpretations of revelation that appeal to history. For our purposes we can separate the attacks on revelation into four camps: (1) those who argue that some interpretations of the category Word of God suggest a bifurcation of reality and a supernatural interpretation of revelation; (2) those who question the claim that revelation refers to God's self-disclosure; (3) those who dispute the correlation of revelation with historical events; and (4) those who question the primary role given revelation by some twentieth-century theologians.

A common feature of most neo-orthodox interpretations of revelation is to link revelation with the Word of God. As we have seen, Barth describes revelation as the unmediated form of the Word of God, the Word incarnate in Jesus Christ. What Emil Brunner describes as "the unity of revelation" is to be found in the unity of the Word; "The center of the Bible and of the history of revelation is the revelation in the Incarnation of the Word, Jesus Christ."[24] The Word of God, then, is both the content of a revelatory event and a description of how revelation takes place. As Barth describes it, from time to time in the midst of certain human words, such as Scripture and proclamation, God's Word appears. When this happens human words are "taken up," "exalted," and "elevated." They do not cease to be human words, but they become human words in and through which God's Word is heard.

But for some theologians the way in which Barth links revelation to the Word and his interpretation of the Word implies a sharp dichotomy between the natural order and some other-worldly supernatural sphere. The result is that the Word of God, like a creature from some other world, occasionally intrudes into the natural order and revelation becomes some kind of supernatural event. Those theologians influenced by Dietrich Bonhoeffer have found this bifurcation of reality into a natural and a supernatural order unwarranted and religiously mistaken. A case in point is the Lutheran theologian, Gerhard Ebeling, who argues that the Word of God is not an appendage or something other than what we call the natural order of reality. It is a fundamental misunderstanding, Ebeling insists, to describe God's Word as "so to speak a separate class of word alongside the word spoken between men, which is otherwise the only thing we usually call word."[25] Ebeling fears that Barth reduces God's Word to a formal concept and in so doing separates the world from the domain of the Word with the inevitable but unfortunate result that revelation becomes a supernatural, otherworldly event.[26] Ebeling appeals to John 1:14, which he understands to be not a statement about two kinds of word, the earthly and the heavenly, but a statement about a human word which is the true and authentic word. What the Bible describes as God's Word is not some otherworldly reality which from time to time intrudes into the natural order, but simply "word as word—word that as far as its word-character is concerned is completely normal, let us not hesitate to say: natural, oral word taking place between man and man."[27]

Closely related to the concern about the supernaturalism and the bifurcation of reality in some neo-orthodox descriptions of revelation is the uncertainty among many theologians as to the meaning and intelligibility of language about "God acting." As we noted previously in our discussion of the meaning of revelation, most theologians describe revelation as a gracious event which cannot be initiated, summoned, controlled, or manipulated but can only be received in thankfulness and joy as a gift. Revelation is not a human act but God's act. For sometime, however, there has been an extended discussion among theologians as to what an "act of God" is and what such language implies.[28] If there is confusion and uncertainty about what it means to say "God acts," then revelation, since it is usually attributed to God, will also be confused and unclear.

In addition to those who fear that Barth's description of the Word of God suggests a formal concept that stands somewhere apart from the natural world and depicts revelation as a supernatural event, there is a second group of theologians who question Barth's claim that God's revelation in his Word represents God's full self-disclosure. The most familiar version of this accusation emerged in 1961 from a circle of German theologians, the best known of whom is Wolfhart Pannenberg. The so-called "Pannenberg circle" of theologians published a collection of essays under the title *Revelation as History*, and in the "Introduction" to that volume Pannenberg raised what he understood to be the decisive issue, "the present consensus that revelation is, in essence, the self-revelation of God."[29] Pannenberg attributed that consensus in recent theology to Barth's influence, but in a broader historical context he understood it to be the result of two factors: successful Enlightenment attacks on the traditional idea that revelation could be identified with the transmission of supernatural truths, and the development in German Idealism, and Hegel in particular, of the idea that revelation refers to "the self-revelation of the absolute."[30] The very notion of revelation as God's *self*-revelation enabled both Hegel and Barth to attribute uniqueness (or in Hegel's case "absoluteness") to Christianity. After examining the biblical material and summarizing the results of the other essays in the volume, Pannenberg argued that there is no basis in the biblical tradition for describing revelation as God's self-disclosure. The announcement of the divine name in Exodus 3 does not mean that one has a complete understanding of the bearer of the name. Furthermore, the term "Word of God" in the Bible has various meanings and suggests direct self-disclosure only in those texts that seem to be influenced by Gnosticism. Nor does the distinction between law and gospel refer to the self-revelation of God, for neither law nor gospel is itself revelation but an interpretation of it. On the basis of this evidence Pannenberg concluded that there is no justification for describing revelation as God's full and direct self-disclosure.

In place of this mistaken interpretation Pannenberg argues that revelation is not direct, as in a theophany, but is indirect and is produced by the acts of God in history. It is "a reflex of his activity in history."[31] In another essay in the same volume, Pannenberg lays out his constructive position by means of seven theses.[32] In place of a special series of events within history, some form of *Heilsgeschichte*, as the scope of revelation, Pannenberg argues that the true locus of revelation is all of history—universal history as it is comprehended from its end. Revelation is "indirect" in that it can be fully known only at the end of history. Christians, however, and anyone else for that matter who has eyes to see, can anticipate history's end because it has been disclosed in the fate of Jesus of Nazareth. Although Pannenberg obviously thinks it a mistake for Christian theology to embrace Hegel's notion that revelation refers to the self-disclosure of the absolute, his constructive position is indebted to Hegel's insight that universal history is the proper arena for interpreting revelation. Whether Pannenberg's alternative interpretation succeeds in avoiding the Gnosticism he believes to be implicit in Barth's position and whether Pannenberg fully appreciates the particularity and radical nature of evil are questions that must be raised about his position.[33] In any case, Pannenberg's objections to Barth's description of revelation as God's full self-disclosure are formidable and worthy of consideration in their own right, regardless of what one may think of Pannenberg's constructive position.

These first two objections to revelation have been confined to the neo-orthodox interpretation of the doctrine and to Barth's position in particular. From other quarters, however, questions have been raised about features of the doctrine of revelation that seem to be shared by most contemporary interpretations of it, even those outside the neo-orthodox circle. Perhaps the most significant of these has been James Barr's challenge to what he understands to be the unqualified acceptance by contemporary theologians of the principle that history is the only channel for revelation. The formula "revelation through history," Barr argues, has not been seriously challenged and for sometime has functioned as a "unifying factor in modern theology."[34] Barr does not deny that revelation through history is a major theme in the Bible, and he readily acknowledges that it serves "a real apologetic purpose" and has enabled theologians of all stripes (conservatives, existentialists, liberals, and even some archaeologists) to find warrants for their position in the biblical text. "It has been rather like the great tree in Nebuchadnezzar's dream, under which all the beasts of the field find shadow."[35]

As valuable as the formula "revelation through history" may be for apologetic purposes, Barr finds it seriously deficient on other grounds. In the first place, as an Old Testament scholar, Barr rejects the notion that revelation through history is the only axis that runs through Scripture or even that it is the normative theme. There are other motifs in Scripture which deserve to be listened to as attentively as those texts which appeal to historical events. The Wisdom literature constitutes a significant portion of the biblical canon and certainly cannot be forced into the mold of revelation through history. Secondly, there are some texts, such as Exodus 3, which are not really interpretations of historical events but are direct verbal communications between God and individuals. Barr denies that texts such as this one are "a commentary on, or an interpretation of, the divine acts." On the contrary, "the speeches and conversations are a precondition of the divine acts to just as great an extent as they are a consequence of them."[36] Thirdly, there are various kinds of narrative in the Old Testament and Barr wonders whether the one term "history" can be applied to them all without being stretched to such an extent that it is virtually meaningless. For example, in what sense can the one term "history" be applied to the creation, the flood, the Exodus, and the destruction of Jerusalem by Nebuchadnezzar? Barr is willing to admit that all of these may be "stories," but he doubts that they all can be said to be "history."[37]

For these reasons and others Barr concludes that it is a fundamental mistake to make "revelation through history" the normative basis for biblical theology. Those theologians and biblical scholars who embrace the category use the term "history" in such diverse senses that it would be misleading to attempt to group them in one camp. The different uses of the term "history" by contemporary theologians suggest a category that has no equivalent in the Bible. "The Bible itself has no linguistic bracket cor-

responding to 'history,' and, as we have seen, its narrative revelatory passages are not constant but variable in their relation to
what we can by any definition call 'history.'"[38]

Finally, in addition to these objections to the doctrine of revelation, some theologians have raised questions that extend beyond Barth's position to most other interpretations of revelation.
They find the category of "revelation" itself to be either unintelligible or inadequate as the primary principle for the exposition
of Christian faith. As long ago as 1941, Paul Althaus protested
against "the inflation of the concept of revelation in contemporary
theology."[39] Althaus pointed out that theology's infatuation with
revelation has been a recent development and that it is not self-
evident that revelation can or should function as the basic principle in systematic theology.

A more recent indictment of the category of revelation is
F. Gerald Downing's book, *Has Christianity a Revelation?*[40] He
argues that there are two problems in most Christian discussions
of revelation: "One is the difficulty of using the word logically
and coherently; the other is the difficulty of finding a biblical
basis for the ideas it is used to convey."[41] It is not always clear
what Downing means by a "biblical basis," but since he devoted
most of his attention to word studies in the Old and New Testaments, apparently he thinks that if nothing like the present theological concept of revelation can be found in biblical terminology
"it must be very doubtful whether God is really believed to 'reveal himself'."[42] By means of that criterion, of course, many doctrines of Christian faith, including the Trinity, could be demonstrated to have no "biblical basis." In addition to his questions
about the biblical basis for revelation Downing also doubts that
revelation can be used logically and coherently. He believes that
the term exacerbates rather than clarifies the confusion between
"natural" and "revealed" religion, that it is "incurably intellectualistic," and that it is no help in apologetics. Finally, Downing

concludes that God "cannot be said to have 'revealed' himself, unless the word 'reveal' is evacuated of most if not all meaning."[43]

In Downing's case, as in the other attacks that have been launched against the apparent influence of revelation (or some particular interpretation of it) in recent theology, one need not accept the constructive alternatives that are attached to each attack in order to agree that the critical questions that have been raised deserve careful scrutiny. It is also apparent that any attempt to answer even a few of these issues would soon lead one far afield and into most of the major doctrines in systematic theology, because, as we have seen, hard on the heels of questions about the meaning of revelation follow questions about God (what does it mean to say "God acts?"), Christology (in what sense is Jesus of Nazareth the Word of God?), and eschatology (does revelation take place in history or at the end of history?). But it is also clear that because Christian identity has something to do with the interrelation of knowledge of God and knowledge of self and because revelation describes how that knowledge of God comes to bear on personal identity, any attempt to sort through the confusion in Christian identity will entail some consideration of what is involved in the doctrine of revelation. Of particular importance for our consideration will be the hermeneutical questions that are related to the doctrine of revelation, questions about how that which has been revealed at some point in history becomes a reality in the contemporary experience of individuals and communities.

4. Internal and External History

The question of how historical events become revelatory in contemporary experience was an important one for H. Richard Niebuhr. His book, *The Meaning of Revelation*, first published in 1941, remains one of the most provocative discussions of this issue in recent theology. Although there are a number of features of Niebuhr's discussion that suggest that he belongs in the camp of "neo-orthodoxy," there are also important differences between his description of revelation and the interpretations of other neo-orthodox theologians.

The context for Niebuhr's discussion of revelation, what he calls "the point of view," is the problem posed for theology by historical relativism. By "historical relativism" he means the conviction that all forms of human knowledge are conditioned by the point of view of the observer, by his or her location in time and space. As Niebuhr describes it, "historical relativism affirms the historicity of the subject even more than that of the object; man, it points out, is not only in time but time is in man."[44] And because human beings are "in time" all knowledge, including theology, is temporally conditioned; that is, it is relative to the particular point and place in time from which one perceives and knows. The relativism of all knowledge does not lead inexorably to some form of extreme subjectivism, such as skepticism, but it does mean that theology has no choice but to begin with history and with a particular historical faith, which is to say that revelation must be examined from the perspective of a "confessional theology." Historical relativism, therefore, is not something theology should fear or attempt to deny but an indispensable category for understanding the context in which theology does its work.[45] In this context a theological account of revelation means "not only that in religion, as in other affairs, men are historically conditioned but also that to the limited point of view of historic Christian faith a reality discloses itself which invites all the trust and devotion of finite, temporal men."[46]

Christian faith cannot be separated from history. The symbols and texts of the Christian community refer to people and events in history and make claims about the meaning and goal of history. The theological problem that emerges for Niebuhr is this: how can statements which appeal to revelation be both about

God and history? It would seem that revelation deals with one or the other but not with both. Either its statements are about God and not subject to relativity or theological statements are about historical events and subject to the relativity that pervades all historical judgments. If the theologian's focus is on historical events and if the theologian accepts the inherent relativity of all statements about history, then it would seem that there is no room for a reality which transcends time and history; "what is seen in history is not a universal, absolute, independent source and goal of existence, not impartial justice nor infinite mercy, but particularity, finiteness, opinions that pass, caprice, arbitrariness, accident, brutality, wrong on the throne and right on the scaffold."[47]

Niebuhr believed that it was possible to resolve this apparent dichotomy between what "subjective faith" confesses and what an "objective" investigation of history discloses by means of a distinction between history as it is observed and history as it is lived. Revelation, he argued, refers primarily to the latter, "to *our* history, to the history of selves or to history as it is lived and apprehended from within."[48] Historical events which do not existentially engage a person are "objective" in the sense that they do not play a constitutive role in the articulation of personal identity. Other events, however, which bear heavily on a person's sense of self, identity, and world are of a different sort. While external history has to do with an impersonal account of objects, internal history is concerned with subjects and is by definition an intensely personal discipline. From the perspective of external history, value is concerned with the relative weight or importance to be attributed to an event—for example, its effect on other events. In internal history, value is a category more concerned with quality than it is with strength or influence. So too if one examines time and human association from the perspective of external history these refer to serial time recounted by the chronicler and the external forces that bind together atomic individuals into one whole. From the perspective of internal history time does not refer so much to serial moments, duration, but to remembered time, "not a number but a living, a stream of consciousness, a flow of feeling, thought and will."[49] And human association is more a community of selves than it is a set of objective forces; it means "the participation of each living self in a common memory and common hope no less than in a common world of nature."[50]

Niebuhr describes these two perspectives on history as "the two-aspect theory of history," and argues that their relation is finally a paradox rooted in the deepest convictions of Christian faith about the nature of this world and that which transcends it. Niebuhr does not think it possible to resolve this apparent dualism between external and internal history either metaphysically or historically and insists that a proper description of revelation demands that we hold these two in dialectical tension. Although revelation refers primarily to those events that have happened to a person and are constitutive of that person's identity, revelation is not wholly a subjective reality. External history should not be dismissed nor absorbed into internal history. It is precisely a community's external history as it is reported by it to others which provides a basis for self-criticism. The Christian community should closely examine its external history as it hears it recounted by others in order to determine whether it bears any similarity to its internal interpretation of that history. If it does not then the community must at least raise the question of whether it is engaged in some form of collective self-deception. To listen to that external history as it is recounted by others "may be described as an effort to see itself with the eyes of God."[51]

Revelation, therefore, refers to "that part of our inner history which illuminates the rest of it and which is itself intelligible."[52] It is that event or set of events that serves as the basis for the interpretation of all other events in a person's or a community's life-history and which gives meaning to the whole. This revelatory event is of overwhelming importance for the identity of both individuals and communities. As Niebuhr describes it the revelatory moment serves a threefold function: "Through it we understand what we remember, remember what we have forgotten and appropriate as our own past much that seemed alien to us."[53] Hence, the first function of the revelatory moment is that it enables a person or a community to understand the remembered past. What had previously been a chaotic and therefore meaningless personal history takes on an order and a pattern, and by means of the revelatory event the life-history is imbued with meaning. Secondly, the revelatory event enables a person or a community to recover those events in the past which had been either forgotten or repressed. The past cannot be destroyed nor does it cease to exist, but it can be forced from consciousness. The revelatory event both demands and enables one to bring to light those events which previously had no meaning or which had so much meaning that they were too painful to examine. What happens in this dimension of the revelatory moment bears some similarity to what takes place in psychoanalysis. Both situations may be the occasion for "total recall on the part of a patient or of bringing into the light of day what had been a source of anguish while it remained suppressed."[54] And finally the revelatory moment enables individuals and communities to appropriate other events and other histories that had previously appeared alien and unintelligible. This third function—appropriation—has a universal thrust that includes the whole sweep of creation; "Through Christ we become immigrants into the empire of God which extends over all the world and learn to remember the history of that empire, that is of men in all times and places, as our history."[55]

An important feature of Niebuhr's description of revelation is the role of the community. Although revelation is an event that takes place in a person's inner history and illumines the rest of it, as Niebuhr describes it revelation is in no way a private event.

The function of the community is indispensable for understanding how revelation takes place. The community provides the necessary context for this event because it is the community that is the bearer of the history and the narratives and symbols which, if they cease to be merely external history and become a part of a person's internal history, may become the occasion for revelation. When Christians talk about revelation they refer to specific historical events and understand those events to have overwhelming significance for the interpretation of their personal history. But this appeal to history is an appeal to events that make up a community's narrative, events that are carried in the community's collective memory. "What distinguishes such historic recall from the private histories of mystics is that it refers to communal events, remembered by a community and in a community."[56]

Individuals, like communities, remember events by means of images, images that seem to have disclosive power. Revelation is that occasion "which provides us with an image by means of which all the occasions of personal and common life become intelligible."[57] When this "event" occurs an image or set of images enables a person to understand, recollect, and appropriate his or her internal history. Clearly images play a decisive role in this process but that observation only raises the question of which images and from where do they come?[58] It is at this point that Niebuhr made an important contribution to the contemporary discussion of the meaning of revelation. He recognized the obscure but essential role that imagination plays in the process of revelation. The imagination provides the images which a person uses to bring order and meaning to the apparent chaos of personal history. But the revelatory images provided by the imagination are no substitute for reason. As Niebuhr describes them reason and revelation are complementary realities and the one cannot perform the function of the other. In a revelatory event certain images, sparked by the imagination, take on an illuminating and disclosive power, and it becomes the task of reason, what Niebuhr calls "the reasoning heart," to search through memory with the assistance of these revelatory images for a "pattern of dramatic unity" by which "the heart can understand what has happened, is happening and will happen to selves in their community."[59]

· Although the imagination provides reason with images by which it can search the past and examine the present, there is no guarantee that these are the right or appropriate images. The imagination is as susceptible to the powers of evil as is reason. What Niebuhr refers to as an "evil" or "false" imagination is one that provides reason with false images, images which "do not apply to the experience at hand" and which lead reason "to false expectations and to inept reactions."[60] Apparently, Niebuhr's only criterion for distinguishing between a true and false imagination is teleological; that is, imaginations are shown to be evil "by their consequences to selves and communities just as erroneous concepts and hypotheses in external knowledge are shown to be fallacious by their results."[61] An evil imagination is not the result of its failure to function but the result of the imagination's perverse activity. In most forms of insanity the imagination does not cease to function, but the images provided by the imagination bear little or no relation to the situation at hand or to reality.

If this were the whole of Niebuhr's description of revelation then he might justly be accused of contriving a theological category for what is nothing more than the common human experience of self-discovery. But Niebuhr believes that there is something else at work in this event other than a person's appropriation of internal history. This "something else," Niebuhr argues, is the self-revelation of God. Not only is revelation that moment in which an event and an image illumine a person's internal history, but it is also "the moment in our history through which we know ourselves to be known from beginning to end, in which we are apprehended by the knower; it means the self-disclosing of that eternal knower."[62] What is experienced in revelation is not just the meaning of one's own personal history but "knowledge of someone there in the darkness and the void of human life."[63]

Although history is the context in which Niebuhr examines the meaning of revelation, what is revealed in revelation is not primarily the meaning of history. History only serves as the medium through which God's self-revelation occurs. Like many other neo-orthodox theologians Niebuhr understands revelation to be a relational reality in which individuals come face to face with that personal reality called God who knows them for what they are. What is known in revelation is not a proposition but the identity of the ultimate agent. "We acknowledge revelation by no third-person proposition, such as that there is a God, but only in the direct confession of the heart, 'Thou art my God.'"[64] History is only the sphere in which this intensely personal, I-Thou encounter takes place.

As attractive and compelling as Niebuhr's position is, it is not without its problems. Unlike Barth, Niebuhr does not link revelation to the category "Word of God," nor does he tie revelation as tightly to historical events in the first century as did Barth. Niebuhr does place great emphasis on history as the arena in which revelation takes place, and he does insist that revelation refers to God's self-disclosure. It is not clear how Niebuhr would have responded to the attacks leveled against revelation by figures such as Pannenberg, Barr, and Downing. But perhaps the most engaging feature of Niebuhr's position is his attempt to describe what Barth referred to as "the subjective reality of revelation," that process in which events in the distant past become a reality in the contemporary experience of individuals and communities. The bulk of Niebuhr's book is devoted more to this question than it is to issues such as those raised by Pannenberg, Barr, and Downing—what it means to say "God acts" and whether revelation refers to God's self-disclosure. However, Niebuhr's position suggests themes that could be used in the formulation of a response to the critiques of revelation. Niebuhr's use of the categories "internal" and "external" history may avoid some of the problems that beset traditional forms of *Heilsgeschichte*, and he does not make revelation dependent on supernatural intervention in the natural order.

But as is the case with every provocative theological argument Niebuhr's account raises a host of problems and questions. Niebuhr does not really address the difficult hermeneutical question of how events and realities recorded in external history become disclosive, meaning-filled moments at the level of internal history. The public execution of a first-century Jew can be investigated and discussed by any secular historian, but how that objective event becomes a redemptive moment in an individual's personal history is a far more difficult question to untangle. It will not do simply to appeal to the imagination as the solution to the hermeneutical problem without offering a convincing description of how the imagination facilitates understanding and appropriation.

A related problem is Niebuhr's use of Scripture. He describes the revelatory moment as one in which the imagination presents to reason certain images or sets of images which illumine the past and imbue it with meaning. In Niebuhr's description Scripture is not revelation nor even the history of revelation; Scripture is "the history of Israel understood and unified by means of revelation."[65] The images which unify history are often found in Scripture, but Niebuhr does not explain the role of Scripture in this process in which the heart searches the past with disclosive images given by the imagination. While Barth's interpretation of revelation may suffer from too rigid a description of the relation between Scripture and revelation, Niebuhr never clearly explains how Scripture functions in the revelatory process. Memory occupies a central position in Niebuhr's analysis, but only because the relation between memory and interpretation illumines the appropriation that takes place in revelation. But the ambiguity in his description of the relation between external and internal history and in his interpretation of the role of Scripture in revelation only emphasizes the importance of the hermeneutical issues that attend any discussion of the meaning of revelation.

5. A Narrative Interpretation

Niebuhr has directed our attention to the encounter which takes place between events in "objective" or "external" history and the personal histories of individuals and communities. In the collision between these two histories or narratives something like what Barth refers to as the subjective reality of revelation occurs. It is in the context of this encounter between narratives that we have every reason to search for both the meaning of revelation and the structure of Christian identity. Also, we have reason to suspect that revelation and Christian identity are interrelated, that the former is a doctrinal formulation of the meaning and experience of the latter, and that a crisis in one leads to a crisis in the other.

Events which took place two thousand years ago enter the present and transform it by means of disclosure and redemptive power. From the perspective of Christian faith Barth is surely correct in his claim that the encounter or collision between the church's narratives and those of a person's internal history take place only by means of the gracious activity of the Spirit. That does not mean, however, that it is either impossible or unfaithful to attempt to say something else about this very human event. Ultimately it may be that it is indeed the Spirit who makes it possible for the events of external history to redemptively transform the personal histories of individuals. That would seem to be the necessary implication of the Reformation claim that "faith is the principal work of the Holy Spirit."[66] But penultimately this momentous human event is subject to inquiry and description from several perspectives, including the various disciplines of the social sciences. The theologian pursues the task of inquiry and description not in order to profane the holy but in order better to understand what it is that faith confesses about the God who reveals himself in Jesus Christ. Furthermore, if the doctrine of revelation is central to the Protestant understanding of Christian faith, then it is essential that revelation be described in as intelligible a manner as possible. The identity crisis in the Christian community may not be resolved by a reinterpretation of the doctrine of revelation, but, as we have seen, basic theological questions about Christian identity are at issue in any interpretation of revelation, and the discussion of the nature of Christian identity seems to lead eventually to questions about the meaning of revelation.

In addition to directing our attention to the distinction between external and internal history, Niebuhr made the provocative claim that revelation includes the appropriation of external events at the level of internal history and that this "appropriation" necessarily assumes the form of a story, what Niebuhr referred to as "the story of our life." In fact, Niebuhr claimed that the experience of faith, which is a human response to the event of revelation, compels the Christian to confess faith by means of a narrative. "The church's compulsion arises out of its need—since it is a living church—to say truly what it stands for and out of its inability to do so otherwise than by telling the story of its life."[67] Although he lifts up the category of narrative as a clue to the meaning of revelation (and therein to the structure of Christian identity), Niebuhr does not fully explain how understanding and appropriation take place in this process. In the following chapters we will take up these questions, but first we must examine the category of narrative and its significance for theological reflection.

Chapter III
The Emergence
of Narrative Theology

Three themes in Niebuhr's discussion of revelation are especially important and may provide clues for a reconstruction of the doctrine of revelation and an interpretation of the nature of Christian identity. The first of these was Niebuhr's claim that revelation cannot be separated from history and that revelation has its true locus in the internal or personal histories of individuals and communities. Secondly, Niebuhr made the intriguing suggestion that when Christians articulate or give expression to their appropriation of Christian faith they do so by means of a story or narrative, "the story of our life." Finally, Niebuhr argued that the context in which this narrative recital of faith is learned and appropriated is the shared life of the Christian community. These three themes—historical event, narrative account, and communal context—have been the subject of considerable discussion among those theologians concerned about the crisis in Christian identity and among those who believe an intelligible description of revelation to be a necessary ingredient in the theological resolution of the crisis.

Of particular interest has been Niebuhr's introduction of the category of "story" or what is sometimes referred to as "narrative" into the discussion of the meaning of revelation. Although he devoted an entire chapter to what he called "the story of our life," Niebuhr never explained precisely what he meant by "story," how revelation or disclosure occurs within Christian narrative, nor how the community serves as the necessary context in which this process of storytelling occurs. What Niebuhr did do was to suggest a clue, a category not previously explored, which subsequently kindled the imagination of many theologians. In recent years numerous theological articles and books have appeared which make use of the category of story or narrative. In some of this material the category of "story" bears little or no resemblance to Niebuhr's use of the term, but in most cases the emerging discussion of narrative theology is deeply indebted to Niebuhr.

In this chapter we will review briefly some recent proposals for the use of narrative in theology, examine some of the problems of method and definition that surround the category, and outline how we will use narrative in Parts II and III to describe the structure of Christian identity and the meaning of revelation.

1. Different Forms of Narrative Theology

In the last few years many people have found the category of "narrative" a suggestive and potentially useful device for addressing perennial theological problems.[1] Unfortunately there is nothing close to a consensus on precisely what the term means. The proposals that have invoked the category are bewilderingly diverse and often there is little or no agreement among them. It is possible, however, to divide the literature on narrative into several broad camps.

a. Introduction to Religion

The first of these we might describe as proposals that employ story or narrative as an introduction to the study of religion in general and perhaps Christianity in particular. Sam Keen's *To a Dancing God*, Harvey Cox's *The Seduction of the Spirit*, Michael Novak's *Ascent of the Mountain, Flight of the Dove*, Robert Roth's *Story and Reality*, John Shea's *Stories of God*, and a collection of essays edited by James B. Wiggins, *Religion as Story*, are recent examples of attempts to describe religion and Christian faith by means of the category of narrative.[2] In each case "narrative" is used to describe and explain the location of religion in human experience and the meaning of "faith" in relation to a person's encounter with other people and the world. The "religious dimension" of human experience is interpreted as having something to do with the narratives people recite about themselves or the narratives they use in order to structure and make sense out of the world. An ambiguity that often emerges in these discussions is whether narrative is the form through which one gets at that reality which is the source of religion in human experience, or whether narrative is not just the form or occasion for an encounter with the sacred but is itself the bearer of the sacred.

One problem that plagues much of this literature is that "story" seems to mean something slightly different in each case. Furthermore it often is not clear precisely what story does refer to in each proposal. In some cases it seems to be a broad category that includes a variety of different literary genres from poems to novels; in others it is used only to refer to a particular literary form, such as the parable. Obvious but difficult questions such as the relation between story and history and the criteria that might be used to assess in what sense a story is true are seldom discussed. A reader often gets the impression that although the announced theme is narrative or story, that category is not the author's real concern and in fact is peripheral to the author's real agenda. Deception in advertising is not found only in the business community. If the category of "narrative" were as important to the project as the author claims, one would assume that it would not remain as ill-defined and undeveloped as it often is, and difficult hermeneutical questions about the problems of interpreting and appropriating a narrative would not be ignored.

A case in point is Gabriel Facre's recent book, *The Christian Story*.[3] The book is subtitled "a narrative interpretation of basic Christian doctrine," and in the introduction Facre attempts to develop a category of "story" that will explain the core meaning of Christian faith. Given this description of the project and the significance that Facre attributes to the term "story," one naturally assumes that he will offer a careful description of the category and an explanation of its critical function, but the reader searches in vain for such a description. Despite Facre's plea that it is of utmost importance that the Christian community "get the story straight," it simply is unclear whether "story" refers to a set of narratives in Scripture, a set of doctrines, the experience of Christian individuals or communities, or a combination of some or all of these. Doctrines such as creation, fall, covenant, Christ, church, salvation, comsummation, and God are described as "the chapter headings of the Christian story." Yet these are not narratives but doctrine, and doctrine, at least as it traditionally has been formulated, does not usually take the form of a narrative.

Equally disturbing is what Facre does with the category of story. Having announced that story will function as the overarching theme for the systematic exposition of Christian faith, it is not clear that the category has any critical significance for him. His interpretation of doctrines such as creation and christology does not differ significantly from the interpretations usually given these subjects. The category of story does not seem to enhance or to alter traditional interpretations of Christian faith, nor does Facre explain how the category illumines perennial theological problems such as the relation of the two natures in Christ or the meaning of "God acts."

A more thoughtful attempt to use narrative or story as a category for understanding and interpreting Christian faith is John

Navone's *Towards a Theology of Story*.[4] Although it is not clear whether Navone thinks "story theology" leads to new insights into traditional Christian doctrines, he clearly believes that the category provides the necessary link between personal experience and religious symbols. Furthermore, he uses contemporary phenomenology (terms such as embodiment and intersubjectivity) to demonstrate the relation between "story" and "religious experience." Similarly, David Baily Harned has tried to demonstrate how the self is constituted by certain "master images" which are embedded in narratives. His *Images for Self-Recognition* examines the images of the self as player, sufferer, and vandal.[5]

The German discussion of the use of narrative in theology began slowly but in recent years it has produced a number of important essays. Initially the topic seemed to be of interest only to American theologians, but, clearly, such is no longer the case.[6] The German discussion, like the one taking place in the United States, has focused on two major issues: the relationship between narrative and doctrinal theology and the reinterpretation of traditional doctrines by means of the category of narrative. One of the issues that quickly surfaces in the question of the relation between narrative and doctrinal theology is whether theology is miscast in its traditional form of discursive argument and whether it should be recast in the form of narrative. We will return to this question in the following section on narrative as a theological category. For the moment we should note that the small volume by Dietrich Ritschl and Hugh O. Jones, *"Story" als Rohmaterial der Theologie*, has made an important contribution to the discussion.[7] Also of significance have been essays by Harald Weinrich and Johann Baptist Metz and a recent book by Josef Meyer zu Schlochtern.[8] Ritschl's essay is particularly important. He briefly discusses the relation between story and human identity, the nature of story, its form and function, and the relation between story and theology.

Given the numerous methodological problems that have

emerged concerning the relation between narrative and theology and the possibility of a narrative theology, it is not surprising that there have been only a few attempts to reconstruct the meaning of Christian doctrines in light of the category of narrative. Three such projects which seem likely to provoke discussion for some time to come are Hans Frei's *The Identity of Jesus Christ*, Edward Schillebeeckx's *Jesus: An Experiment in Christology*, and Eberhard Jüngel's *Gott als Geheimnis der Welt*.[9]

The German discussion has addressed, if not answered, some of the basic problems that the American discussion has avoided. In the first place, in much of the American discussion narrative or story is not clearly defined either as a literary genre or as a critical principle. Secondly, often no explanation is offered of what it is about human experience that makes story or narrative the appropriate and perhaps necessary category for articulating the encounter with the holy, with that which is ultimately real.

b. The Life-Story and Lived Convictions

A second group of theologians has taken up the question of the experiential roots of narrative. Articles by Stephen Crites and books by James William McClendon, Jr., Stanley Hauerwas, and John Dunne offer sophisticated discussions of the meaning of narrative and its relation to human experience. Perhaps the most significant of these is Stephen Crites' article, "The Narrative Quality of Experience," which was one of the earliest pieces in so-called "narrative theology" and has proved to be one of the richest and most suggestive.[10] Regardless of whether one agrees with Crites' interpretation of the nature of religion or with his imaginative thesis about the relation between music and action, his invaluable contribution has been to advance an argument for why narrative is a necessary category in the description of religious experience. He argues that one of the conditions for being human is the possession of the capacity for having a history, and "that the formal quality of experience through time is inherently narrative."[11] That is, the form which active consciousness assumes in its experience of the world is narrative form, which suitably expresses "the tensed unity" of the three modalities of past, present, and future.[12] In order to understand the primordial status of narrative in human experience (and in that sense its "religious significance"), we must concentrate not simply on the "mundane stories" which people recite, stories which are set within a determinate world (*mundus*) and frame of consciousness and by which people explain "where they have been, why things are as they are, and so on."[13] Rather we must also attend to what Crites calls "sacred stories," "not so much because gods are commonly celebrated in them, but because men's sense of self and world is created through them."[14] These are powerful stories which are never directly told because they shape consciousness rather than being an object to consciousness. Sacred stories provide consciousness with a sense of orientation in life and a pre-conscious apprehension of reality. Hence, the "narrative quality of experience," as Crites describes it, has three dimensions: "the sacred story, the mundane stories, and the temporal form of experience itself: three narrative tracks, each constantly reflecting and affecting the course of the others."[15]

Like Crites, both James William McClendon, Jr. and John S. Dunne concentrate on the relation between narrative and experience. McClendon believes that theologians should be concerned not just about belief or doctrine in the abstract, but about "what difference God's being (as well as the belief in it) makes to those who believe or disbelieve."[16] And that means being concerned about Christian beliefs that are "living convictions which give shape to actual lives and actual communities."[17] In order to examine these convictions McClendon suggests that theology "must be at least biography." To that end the biographies or life-stories of specific individuals become the theologian's primary material for investigating the meaning of the doctrines and confessional claims of Christian faith. The biographies of certain

"singular or striking lives" in the Christian community (Mc-
Clendon uses Dag Hammarskjöld, Martin Luther King, Jr.,
Clarence Jordan, and Charles Ives) may provide a perspective on
what Christian faith means by "atonement," for example, which
differs from traditional theological interpretations of the doctrine. If it functions in this fashion, "biographical theology" offers a convincing demonstration that theology never can be finally separated from ethics and that the doctrines of Christian
faith are or should be lived beliefs which have direct consequences
for moral judgments and decisions.

The category of "life-story" is also an important one for John
S. Dunne. His book, *A Search for God in Time and Memory*, sounds
themes that are strongly reminiscent of Augustine, Calvin, and
H. Richard Niebuhr. If we struggle to bring the past into the
conscious present, to "bring time to mind," we may encounter
God, "or at least . . . what God tends to be for us." [18] But bringing time to mind and examining one's life-story is a more difficult process than it might first appear. In order to learn how to
search one's past, Dunne proposes the heuristic use of biography
and autobiography. By a method he describes as "passing over,"
Dunne believes the reader can enter into the lives of others, come
to understand what a "life-story" is and what is distinctive about
the reader's own life-story. By means of this process Dunne thinks
we can enter into the life-stories of Paul, Augustine, and Kierkegaard and discern the different forms a Christian life assumes
and in turn come to a new understanding of ourselves. Furthermore one can do the same thing with modern life-stories. In
language similar to Calvin's, Dunne argues that the result of this
process of passing over is twofold. On the one hand, a person
"discovers the shape of the life story in other ages, the story of
deeds, and the story of experience, and coming back from this to
his own time is how he discovers by contrast its current shape,
the story of appropriation." [19] And in the midst of these life-
stories a person discovers something else—"God's time, the

greater and encompassing time which is that of the stories of God, and he experiences companionship with God in time."[20]

One serious problem in the programs sketched by McClendon and Dunne is the way in which they appear to slight or avoid the hermeneutical issues that loom in the background. McClendon argues that the key to his compelling biographies is "the dominant or controlling *images* which may be found in the lives of which they speak."[21] Yet he does not explain how one knows which images are the appropriate ones to apply to another person's life or to one's own. What if the image of the "atonement" is not the appropriate one to apply to Martin Luther King, Jr.? What are the consequences of that misapplication? So too Dunne's "method" of "passing over by sympathetic understanding to others" seems difficult to justify in light of what we know about the relativity of historical understanding. Whatever "passing over" means, it requires more than simple "sympathetic understanding" for a person in the twentieth century to actually enter the life-story of a Paul or an Augustine. Neither McClendon nor Dunne seem to appreciate the historicity of human experience that is the basis of every individual's life-story. By focusing on the controlling images and the method of passing over they ignore the hermeneutical issues that emerge at the juncture of narrative and human identity.

Stanley Hauerwas' proposal is no less ambitious than McClendon's and Dunne's, but it is formulated with greater precision and is perhaps more modest in its claims. Although he makes much use of the category of "story," Hauerwas denies that he is doing "story theology." His real interest is the nature and formation of Christian character, and he argues that "narrative is a perennial category for understanding better how the grammar of religious convictions is displayed and how the self is formed by those convictions."[22] Hauerwas, like McClendon, believes that the meaning of character is to be found in narratives and that these narratives are a form of explanation. A story "is a narrative account that binds events and agents together in an intelligible pattern," and in so doing offers a description and explanation of why things are the way they are.[23] In Hauerwas' argument, narrative is "a necessary form" for describing the intentionality of human action.[24] He advances the discussion begun by Dunne and McClendon by raising the issue of self-deception and the question of criteria for determining the truthfulness of a story.

c. Biblical Narrative

To many people, discussions such as the ones we have been reviewing seem hopelessly abstract and vague. Story or narrative appears to refer to everything and yet to nothing. The critical reader hungers for a specific example of a narrative and longs to see theories anchored in specific texts. It is not surprising, therefore, that there has emerged a third form of "narrative theology," one that has been produced by theologians and biblical scholars working primarily with Scripture. While other forms of narrative theology may be bogged down in apparently endless discussions about what is and is not a narrative and what it means to say that a narrative is "true," biblical theologians can point to specific texts in Scripture as examples of narrative and move on to the more interesting question of how these narratives function in the life of the communities that understand them to be authoritative for interpreting reality.

The discovery of narrative and its role in Scripture is obviously not a recent development. For some time biblical theologians such as Gerhard von Rad, Oscar Cullmann, and G. Ernest Wright have pointed to the crucial role played by different forms of *Heilsgeschichte* and narrative history in Scripture.[25] Yet it is only recently that the genre of narrative and questions about its function in the context of the whole of Scripture have received concerted attention. Among those who work primarily with the Old Testament the narrative structure of the Pentateuch and the possibility of canonical criticism have been major topics of conversation. Among interpreters of the New Testament, questions about the very nature of "gospel" as a literary genre, and the structure of Mark in particular, have generated a considerable body of literature.

One issue that emerges in practically all of these discussions is the question of the distinctiveness and even uniqueness of biblical narrative. Is "biblical narrative" a distinctive genre in comparison to the literature of antiquity? A related question is: is it possible to speak of a "biblical narrative"? Does not Scripture consist of such a variety of different forms of narrative that it would be impractical if not misleading to speak of one genre called "biblical narrative"? These questions have become particularly interesting in light of recent applications of literary criticism to the Gospels. "The narrative mode," Amos Wilder argued, "is uniquely important in Christianity."[26] If that is true, it would not be surprising that, "When the Christian in any time or place confesses his faith, his confession turns into a narrative."[27] Whether the Gospel is a unique genre among the literature of antiquity is not easy to determine, but in any case the Gospels are clearly a form of narrative, and "whether or not it is 'the proper' form of the Gospel, it is the form of the books called Gospels."[28]

In part this discussion of the nature of biblical narrative is due to a remarkable book in literary criticism that was first published in 1946. In the first two chapters of *Mimesis*, Eric Auerbach compared selected biblical texts (the story of Abraham and Isaac in Genesis 22 and Peter's denial of Jesus in Mark) with literary texts in antiquity and concluded that "A scene like Peter's denial fits into no antique genre."[29] What is distinctive about some biblical narratives, and perhaps what makes them unique in the literature of antiquity, is their style:

certain parts brought into high relief, others left obscure, abruptness, suggestive influence of the unexpressed, "background" quality, multiplicity of meanings and the need for interpretation, universal-historical claims, development of the concept of the historically becoming, and preoccupation with the problematic.[30]

On the basis of his analysis of the style of biblical narrative, Auerbach believes that the text presents the reader with a vision of the way things are, a representation of reality in which Scripture makes an imperialistic claim. The text depicts a world, and it is "not satisfied with claiming to be a historically true reality—it insists that it is the only real world, is destined for autocracy."[31] The challenge the biblical text presents to the reader is not whether the reader can appropriate the text and its claims within the reader's world; the challenge is whether the reader can and will enter into the world of the text; "we are to fit our own life into its world, feel ourselves to be elements in its structure of universal history."[32]

Systematic theologians and biblical scholars have found Auerbach's thesis richly suggestive. Hans Frei, for example, finds in Auerbach's description of realistic literature a clue to the development of theological and biblical hermeneutics in the eighteenth and nineteenth centuries.[33] Examined from the perspective of realism, biblical narrative is not so much history as it is what Frei calls "history-like." The "pre-critical" manner of reading Scripture began to disappear when distinctions were drawn between the text's literal sense—the world it depicted—and its historical referent. Once meaning was separated from reference it was no longer possible to read the text realistically. The modern question became, "I understand what it means, but is it true?" In a more recent book, *The Identity of Jesus Christ*, Frei argues that the New Testament not only depicts a world but it also renders the identity of an agent.[34] The Gospel narratives render the identity of Jesus Christ by means of their description of him. He is who he truly and universally is in these narratives which record the intention-action sequence of his life and his self-manifestation in his Passion.

While Frei concentrates on the Gospel narrative as it emerges from each of the books in the New Testament, Norman Perrin focuses his work on the Gospel of Mark. He too finds Auerbach helpful for understanding biblical narrative, but his reading of Auerbach differs significantly from that of Frei's. As Frei reads Auerbach the text makes imperialistic claims on the reader, and the meaning of the text cannot be found elsewhere than in the text itself. Perrin, on the other hand, finds in Auerbach the basis for a redactionary interpretation of the text.[35] The meaning of the text is not the text itself, not what the text says, but what the text tells us about the author's intentions and theological vision. The real meaning of the text lies outside of it. Its meaning is a secret known only to the author and to the discerning reader. Of course one must attend carefully to Mark's narrative in order to discover these things, but only if one has grasped Mark's theological position is it possible, for example, to understand the role the disciples play in the narrative and the meaning of the centurion's confession in Mark 15:34.

From a different perspective, what has sometimes been referred to as "canonical criticism," the function of narrative in both testaments has been the subject of considerable discussion. The Torah, as James Sanders interprets it, is not just a law code but "essentially a story."[36] It is in the context of the narrative structure of the Pentateuch that Israel's ordinances, commandments, and statutes have their meaning. Hence, in order to interpret the meaning of any piece of Scripture, it is necessary to examine its location and function in the canon as a whole. Such a canonical approach, Brevard Childs insists, does not imply a "non-historical reading of the Bible."[37] To focus on the canon "is an attempt to do justice to the nature of Israel's unique history." Canonical criticism, therefore, "seeks to understand the peculiar shape and special function of these texts which comprise the Hebrew canon."[38] And, in order to do so, it concentrates on the final form of the biblical text rather than on the history of its formation. It

remains to be seen, however, whether canonical criticism is anything more than a methodological tool for working with important but difficult questions such as the relation of historical criticism to the function of Scripture in the church's life. What is not
clear is whether canonical criticism will illumine the church's
understanding of the content of biblical narrative and therein the
substance of its faith.

Yet another group of theologians and biblical scholars has focused attention neither on the canon nor the narrative structure
of the Gospels but on the parable. Parables, they argue, are a
form of narrative and when understood as metaphors they show
us how Christian narrative in its different forms (as poetry, novel,
and autobiography) functions. One of the most interesting attempts at "parabolic theology" is Sallie McFague Teselle's *Speaking in Parables*.[39] She argues that New Testament parables are not
allegories but extended metaphors formed out of the tension between a familiar, worldly setting and a radical dimension within
that setting. In the parable of the Prodigal Son, for example, it
is this other dimension which "provides the context which dis-
rupts the ordinary dimension and allows us to see it anew as reformed by God's extraordinary love."[40] The claim that New Testament parables are extended metaphors and that Christian faith
itself is metaphorical and perhaps requires the learned ability to
see the world metaphorically suggests different ways of understanding theology and its task. But to suggest that the parable is
the primary genre in the New Testament raises a host of critical
problems. In the first place, the parables are not self-contained.
Apart from their setting in the larger narrative of the Gospels
they are susceptible to whatever strong winds of interpretation
happen to be blowing at the moment. And secondly, taken in
isolation the parables have no necessary relation to historical
events. In this sense they resemble Wisdom literature. Whatever
one may think about the relation between biblical narrative and
history, Scripture clearly makes claims about historical events.

Biblical narrative is not ahistorical and enormous problems emerge if one tries to correlate a faith based on the interpretation of historical events with a biblical genre that has no necessary relation to history. Christian faith may well be metaphoric and parabolic but that does not mean that the parable is the primary genre in the New Testament.

2. Narrative as a Theological Category

Because the use of narrative in theology is a relatively recent development, most theologians have reserved judgment as to whether "narrative theology" is only yet another in a series of fads that have emerged in theological discussion in the 1960s and 1970s, or whether the category has real significance for the interpretation and reconstruction of Christian doctrine. By no means is it the case that everyone agrees that "narrative" or "story" should become a major motif in systematic theology.[41] Too many issues have yet to be resolved before a convincing argument could be advanced that narrative should play that role. One of the most important of these is the question of the relation between narrative and theology.

Theology has been and probably always will be an intellectual activity based on discursive argument and rational explanation. One obvious problem that emerges in any discussion of the use of narrative in theology is that narrative seems to have a wholly different structure and logic than do traditional forms of systematic theology. A narrative may be used to explain something, but it is a different sort of explanation than theology usually offers. For example, if someone asked, "What do Christians mean when they say that 'God is Creator'?" one response might be to have that person read the first three chapters of Genesis. That would be one way of explaining what the term "Creator" means for Christian faith. A different response would be to direct that person to a discussion of creation by a systematic or doctrinal theo-

logian. There, too, one would discover an explanation but an
explanation of a different sort than that found in Genesis 1—3.
The issue that emerges here is whether narrative is at best an
introduction or bridge to systematic theology or whether it properly has some role within theology itself.

In much of the literature we discussed in the preceding section narrative is described as a propaedeutic to theology, what
Teselle calls a kind of "intermediary or parabolic theology."[42]
Used in this fashion narrative theology is neither systematic theology nor the first-order religious language of Christian faith.
That is, it is not the language of Christian confession. Rather, it
is something in between the first-order language of faith and the
second-order reflection of systematic theology and serves as a
bridge between them. Christian narratives—poems, short stories, novels, and autobiographies—would be primary resources
for understanding and interpreting the more abstract, discursive
arguments in Christian doctrine and systematic theology.

Another version of this intermediary form of narrative theology is James McClendon's proposal for a "biographical theology."
The biographies or life-stories of particular individuals would become the primary material for explaining the meaning of the
doctrines and confessional claims that make up Christian faith.
Biographies of striking figures in the Christian community
would put flesh and blood on what is otherwise an abstract and
formal doctrine.

In both cases—in "parabolic" and "biographical" theology—
narratives provide the data with which theology works, but in
neither case do the narratives become a principle material for the
systematic elucidation of Christian faith. A narrative may better
enable someone to understand a particular doctrine but narrative
itself does not lead to a reinterpretation or reformulation of the
doctrine. As Teselle and McClendon use them, narratives function as examples of doctrines or as a bridge to systematic theology, but neither uses narrative to reinterpret and reconstruct the

doctrines of Christian faith. And there are good reasons for con-
cluding that the category of story or narrative could not and
should not serve such a function. As it has usually been described, theology is a second-order discipline; that is, it is not
itself the language of faith, the confessional language of the believer. No one needs to have read and studied systematic theology
in order to be a Christian believer. The task of theology is to
reflect critically on the language and life of the Christian community (what we have been calling "first-order" language) in order to assess whether what the community says and does is appropriate to the Christian tradition and whether it is intelligible
to that community's larger world. But if theology is a second-
order discipline and if its primary task is critical reflection on the
first-order language and life of the Christian community, then is
not a "narrative theology" which attempts to be more than a
propaedeutic or bridge to doctrinal theology a confusion of incompatible categories? Is not "narrative theology" a *non sequitur*,
a basic confusion of two incompatible, if not contradictory, forms
of discourse? A narrative is simply not the same thing as a discursive argument and the two should not be confused.

Similarly, in Dietrich Ritschl's discussion of narrative theology narratives may provide "the raw material" mined from the
experience of individuals and communities which the theologian
sorts through, reflects on, and criticizes by means of the Christian
tradition, but the actual process of theological reflection is not
"storytelling" nor does it take the form of a story. The theologian's task is not to tell or repeat stories but to provide criteria or
what Ritschl calls "regulative sentences" for making critical
judgments and comparisons among the different narratives that
make up theology's "raw material."[43] The theologian's task is not
the same as that of the priest or the minister, and while storytelling may be an appropriate means by which the minister pro-
claims the gospel, the theologian has a different agenda that requires different methods.

The positions taken by Teselle, McClendon, and Ritschl represent a formidable argument against the notion that narrative can serve any function other than that of a propaedeutic to theology. But it may be that positions have been taken too quickly and that lines of demarcation have been drawn prematurely, that the dichotomy between first-order faith language and the second-order language of analysis and criticism is not as fixed as it first appears. Indeed, the primary task of theology is not storytelling or the recitation of narratives but the critical analysis of the language and activity of the Christian community. Nor does theology engage in analysis and criticism purely for the sake of intellectual activity itself. Theology is not an end in itself; there is a point to it all. The theologian brings critical analysis to bear on the language and life of the church in order that the church may better understand what it believes, correct its mistakes, and live more faithfully the gospel it confesses. In this sense there is also an important constructive task that theology undertakes. It attempts to construct Christian faith—its beliefs and doctrines—in such a manner that it will be intelligible to the world and the situation that the church seeks to address. It may be misleading, therefore, to draw too sharp a distinction between the "raw material" with which theology works and the intellectual activity of critical reflection. The two should not be confused, but if narrative, for example, is the necessary form for the articulation of personal identity (and if H. Richard Niebuhr is correct, the necessary form for the articulation of faith), then it is not unreasonable to expect that narrative might play a major role in the theological interpretation and construction of the doctrine of revelation.

If narrative does have an almost primordial location in human experience, then every philosophical anthropology, Christian or not, which claims to offer a full description of human being must come to terms with the narrative structure of human identity. Any theological description of Christian identity that does not take into account this narrative structure ignores an essential di-

mension of human experience in the interpretation of faith. The
issue is not simply whether "narrative theology" requires that
theology assume the form of a story. The decisive issue is whether
narrative does indeed play an essential role in the articulation of
personal identity. If it does, then the category of narrative would
seem to be indispensable in any theological attempt to describe
the nature of Christian identity, which as we have seen is closely
related to the doctrine of revelation. Furthermore, it would seem
that narrative has significance not only for the doctrine of revelation but for all the doctrines of Christian faith, in as much as
they are all related to the faith experience of the Christian community. Consequently the theological interpretation and construction of the major doctrines of Christian faith should reflect
the normative importance of narrative in the expression of human
experience in general and Christian faith in particular.

The debate as to whether theology should assume the form of
narrative is miscast and not the most important issue in the discussion of theology's relation to narrative. Of utmost importance
is whether the content of basic Christian doctrines, such as the
relation between the two natures in Jesus Christ, the nature of
God's reality and relation to the world, and the identity and mis-
sion of the church reflect this basic category which appears to be
so essential for an adequate philosophical and psychological description of human being.[44] To claim that theological reflection
should "come to terms with," "take into account," and "reflect"
the narrative structure of existence may mean more than simply
acknowledging that narrative plays an important role in the
expression of human identity. It may mean a thorough reinterpretation of the contents of Christian doctrine.

The real significance of narrative for doctrinal theology is not
that it provides a novel or heuristically useful introduction to
discussions about the meaning of Christian faith. Narrative is an
important theological category because it is essential for understanding human identity and what happens to the identity of

persons in that process Christians describe by means of the doctrine of revelation.

3. Problems of Definition

As we noted in our brief survey of the literature that makes use of narrative in theology, an immediate problem is confusion about what the term means. When used loosely the category is so broad and elusive that it includes practically everything and excludes nothing. Two questions of definition are particularly important: to what kind of genre does narrative refer, and what is the relation between narrative and history?

In the literature on "narrative theology" we have seen that narrative can refer to many different genres. In some quarters narrative refers to a specific genre within Scripture—Auerbach's realistic narratives in Genesis or Mark, Frei's identity narrative in the Gospels, or Teselle's New Testament parables. In other camps narrative refers to a wholly different kind of genre, to something akin to biography or life-story. Narrative is that literary form in which a person's life-story comes to expression, but the relation between that life-story and narratives such as those contained in Scripture remains uncertain, as in McClendon's discussion of the relation between biblical images and exemplary lives.

To what does the term "narrative" refer? Does it refer to a specific, easily discernible literary genre, such as legend or historical chronicle (narratives of very different types but both found in the Bible), and if so what are the generic features of narrative? Or does the term refer not so much to a specific literary genre as it does to a form of human experience (for example, the movement from one stage of life to another) which is expressed in various literary genres and cannot be restricted to any single genre? Hence it is no more likely to take the form of biography or autobiography than it is that of a poem or short story. Or does "narrative" refer to neither a particular literary genre nor a specific type of human experience but to a primordial yet concrete form of human understanding which appears in various literary forms as an expression and interpretation of human experience and identity? In the latter case, even though narrative is understood to refer to a hermeneutical process, a process in which a person interprets and understands, the common features that these different forms of narrative share must still be identified.

There are some generic features which characterize most forms of narrative. There is always "movement," "direction," or some form of "plot" in a narrative.[45] As Crites describes it, the narrative that articulates human experience emerges from "the tensed unity" of the modalities of past, present, and future, and it is this tensed unity which gives the narrative its internal coherence.[46] So too Dietrich Ritschl insists that "Stories have a movement to an end; they have an inner continuity, which is not bound to the use of specific words and sentences."[47] It is the movement or direction from what was to what will be that gives a narrative its dynamic quality and its internal coherence. That is just as true of fairy tales as it is of the factual histories of individuals and peoples, and it is one generic feature which allows us to refer to literary forms as diverse as fairy tale and biography as "narrative." Although it is possible to discover some features that most forms of narrative have in common, we will be using the term "narrative" in a twofold sense—to describe both a literary genre and a hermeneutical process or mode of understanding that takes place in Christian faith.

The literary form we will refer to as "Christian narrative" is similar to a form of religious autobiography or what at one time was called "confession," the classic example of which is Augustine's *Confessions*. We will discover that this confessional form of narrative presupposes and emerges from two other kinds of narrative. It is the product of their integration or what in some cases perhaps is best described as their "collision." The first of these two narratives is what we will describe in Chapter IV as "the narrative form of personal identity." Christian narrative does not differ in its form from other kinds of autobiography.[48] It is universally and primordially the case that the articulation of personal identity assumes the form of a narrative, a narrative that is considerably more subtle and complex than it sometimes first appears. Out of the vast array of events and experiences that make up each individual's life a few are selected, for reasons that may be only partly known, as constitutive of that person's identity. In other words, in order to identify ourselves to another person or persons, in order to explain what kind of person we are and why we are the way we are, we recite a narrative that recounts and interprets personal history.

The narrative of Christian confession or autobiography emerges from the collision between individuals and their personal identity narratives and the Christian community and its narratives. As subtle and complex as is every person's identity, the narratives the Christian community uses to identify itself—to explain how it understands the world and why it lives the way it does—are at least as multi-faceted and complex. In Chapter V we will examine some of the fundamental features of the Christian community's identity narrative. Communities, like individuals, have identities and these identities also assume narrative form, narratives which re-present and interpret the community's history and experience. In Christian communities this identity narrative consists of a "text" which begins with the canonical history Christians call "Scripture" and extends through the community's history into the present. Scripture and the history of the community's attempts to interpret the text and make it intelligible to the rest of society constitute the community's "tradition" and therein its narrative identity.

Christian narrative, therefore, assumes a literary form akin to that of confession or religious autobiography. It emerges from the interaction or collision between the identity narratives of individuals and the identity narratives of the Christian community.

As we will be using the term, "Christian narrative" refers to a determinate genre that has readily identifiable features, and it is a genre that has a history with some notable, classic examples. However, because of the peculiar features of Christian confession it includes other forms of narrative (legends, for example) which do not necessarily share the same generic features of Christian confession except in the broad sense in which all narratives share a few common marks such as dynamic movement and inner continuity. It is these other forms of narrative included in Christian narrative that pose the second problem of definition—the relation between narrative and history.

Obviously not all forms of narrative are interpretations of historical events nor do all narratives even make that pretense. There are numerous forms of "narrative" which are not "history" in either form or intent. These non-historical narratives serve different functions and have an importance in their own right, but they do not attempt to recount and explain what happened in the past. Legends, folk tales, parables, and myths may function as explanations in the sense that they provide an account or a description of a community's origins and behavior, but they also may be told for no other reason than to entertain, amuse, and delight. Simply because a piece of discourse or a literary form is a narrative does not mean that it is history. Christian narrative, however, as a form of confessional narrative, is "history" in that it attempts to interpret the past and to explain what is done in the present and expected in the future in light of the claims made about the past. If it were established that the events narrated in a legend or myth did not really take place such a discovery would not render the myth meaningless or useless. For example, the meaning of the myth of Adam's fall in Genesis 3 has nothing to do with its "historicity," with whether there actually was some figure named Adam who was cast out of some geographical location called Eden. Such is not the case, however, with a historical narrative. If it were established that Abraham Lincoln was secretly in league with the Confederacy to destroy the Union or that Jesus of Nazareth died of old age in Galilee, then those historical narratives that claim to report facts about Lincoln and Jesus would be seriously undercut. At best they would no longer "mean" the same thing that they once did. Historical narratives may share the form and some of the generic features of narratives which are not history, but there are also significant differences between them.

One of these differences becomes apparent when we consider some of the criteria that enable us to say a narrative is or is not true. A historical narrative which distorts or misrepresents the events that it claims to recount and interpret is false because it does not correspond to what we know to be the case. A myth, on the other hand, is not necessarily false because it has no referent in objective history. The Adamic myth is "true" if it reflects and illumines human experience, not if it accurately represents some event from history. Because the conditions for assessing the truth and falsity of historical narratives and mythic narratives are so diverse, not a great deal is gained by insisting on the generic similarities between them. But to point to these differences is not to suggest that myth and history are incompatible literary forms which must be rigidly segregated. In some cases they obviously cannot be neatly separated. Many narratives consist of a mixture of different narrative forms, and it is not unusual to find legends, myths, and history rolled into one narrative frame. The development of form criticism has enabled modern readers to examine a New Testament Gospel, Mark for example, and discern various literary forms in the one Gospel narrative.

Christian narrative is "historical" in that it claims to re-present a person's identity (and therein his or her history, present behavior, and hopes for the future) as it has been constructed from the perspective of Christian faith. But the one identity narrative we encounter in Christian confession is itself the result of the collision between different kinds of narrative, not all of which are history or pretend to be. Symbols and myths which have nothing to do with historical events are commonly used to interpret the meaning of historical experience. While most of the myths in the primeval history in Genesis 1—11 may have no basis in fact (i.e., in history), Israel found them indispensable for interpreting its experience of God, the world, and history. Because it is so difficult to separate "fact" from "interpretation" in any historical narrative the separation of history from myth is at best tenuous if not finally impossible.

Although "Christian narrative" includes many forms of non-historical narrative, all of which play important roles in the larger confessional story, if it could be established that the symbols and myths of the Christian tradition have been used to interpret personal and communal histories in a manner that has significantly distorted them, one would then have to conclude that Christian narrative is not true. It may still be meaningful in the perverse sense in which idolatrous symbols and demonic myths are "meaningful" (i.e., they create a world of sorts and allow one to function in it), but the narrative is no longer true because it misrepresents what it claims to report. The relation of Christian narrative to history and myth is complex, and, as we will see, the line between "alteration" and "distortion" is thin indeed. While the very meaning of "conversion" requires the alteration of the way in which one interprets personal history, alteration is not the same thing as the misrepresentation involved in distortion.

Christian narrative is unabashedly historical. It makes claims about the past, and its judgments about the present (moral, political, and social) and hopes for the future are finally dependent on its interpretation of those events in the past. Christian narrative is "historical" for two reasons. On the one hand, its claims about reality are based on and appeal to certain events in the communal history of Israel and the personal history of Jesus of Nazareth. But secondly, Christian narrative is not recited in order to amuse or entertain. There is an explicit kerygmatic undertow to Christian narrative. It is told for a reason, to make a point, which of course is that the redemption and salvation of personal and communal histories is to be found in this Christian story. Persons and communities cannot be redeemed without their histories, for their identity is inseparable from them.

4. Narrative and Christian Identity

Part II of this book will attempt to develop an intelligible description of Christian narrative in order to see if it offers any assistance in understanding what Christians mean by revelation and what the doctrine of revelation has to do with the meaning of Christian identity. The previous section made the claim that Christian narrative refers to both a literary genre, something akin to religious autobiography, and to a hermeneutical process, an extended act of interpretation and appropriation. Part III of this book will try to clarify some of the fundamental features that are at work in the process of understanding Christian narrative.

Christian narrative emerges from the collision between an individual's identity narrative and the narratives of the Christian community. The metaphor of "collision" is appropriate for describing this encounter because in many instances if a person's identity is illumined and transformed by Christian faith, if revelation takes place, significant disorientation and reinterpretation take place. The subsequent reconstruction of personal identity can be a painful, difficult task, and the Christian confessions of figures such as Paul and Augustine indicate how extensive this process can be. Nor is the process of reinterpretation wholly one-sided, merely a matter of the individual appropriating the faith of the community. Occasionally the impact of an individual's experience and identity on the life of the community is such that it forces an alteration or revision of the community's narrative. Although it is usually the individual's identity that is most seriously altered and transformed in its encounter with the narratives of the Christian community, the two are dialectically related and in any such encounter a degree of reinterpretation takes place in both narratives.

In subsequent chapters we will examine some of the formal features of the genre of Christian narrative as it appears in its confessional form, but our real interest is not the literary genre but the hermeneutical process which is the foundation for Christian narrative. In Christian narrative a specific process of understanding and interpretation takes place which makes possible the appropriation of Christian faith and the reconstruction of personal identity. This appropriation and reinterpretation finally assumes the literary form of autobiography or confession. The literary genre and its formal features are important for our consideration because they give us our only access to the hermeneutical principles at work in Christian narrative and the dynamics of what Christians mean by revelation and confession. It is in those dynamics that we uncover the structure and meaning of Christian identity.

The structure of Christian narrative will tell us something about what is involved in the process of understanding and appropriating Christian faith. Understanding is in part a facility, a learned ability to carry on an activity or to use concepts and ideas. Consequently it is a serious error to conclude that understanding Christian narrative means being able to quote chapter and verse from Scripture or to perform the prodigious feat of reciting Mark's Gospel from memory. So too understanding Christian narrative is not simply a matter of repeating what Paul, Augustine, Luther, and Barth said about the doctrine of justification. To understand Christian narrative properly is to be able to reinterpret one's personal identity by means of the biblical texts, history of tradition, and theological doctrines that make up the church's narrative. The real test of Christian understanding is not simply whether someone knows the content of the Christian tradition and can repeat it on demand but whether he or she is able to use

Christian faith as it is embodied in the church's narratives to reinterpret personal and social existence.

The category of Christian narrative suggests not only that a particular literary genre is of decisive importance for Christian theology but that there is a peculiar form of understanding in the appropriation of Christian faith to which theology must attend. Furthermore it suggests that the meaning of revelation and the nature of Christian identity are intimately related to this process of understanding that takes place in Christian narrative. If theology is faith in search of understanding and if narrative indeed does illumine the nature of the understanding that faith seeks, then narrative may be much more than simply a propaedeutic to theology. Narrative theology may offer a different perspective on basic theological topics such as the authority of Scripture, the relation between Scripture and tradition, the nature of revelation, and the meaning of the term "Word of God." From the perspective of a narrative theology these perennial theological topics may have a slightly different look about them, one which may make them more accessible to the contemporary believer. In any case, the decisive question which must be addressed to any theological proposal, narrative or otherwise, at this point in history is whether it speaks to the identity crisis which now besets the Christian community.

PART II
Christian Identity

Chapter IV
The Narrative Form
of Personal Identity

Any discussion of the nature of narrative theology and its significance for the crisis in Christian identity must begin with a number of preliminary questions, the most important of which is the question of the relation of narrative form to theology and human experience. Is narrative simply an imaginative way of entering into theological reflection, or is there something about the nature of human being and the structure of human experience that makes narrative the appropriate and even necessary form for the articulation of personal identity? If the latter is the case, then attention to the nature and function of narrative provides not only a novel introduction to the discipline of theological reflection but also the necessary context in which to ask questions about the meaning of Christian identity and the sense in which Christian faith transforms self-understanding. Christian theology traditionally has employed confessional language in order to describe this transformation as "redemption" and has insisted that human existence be interpreted by means of the paired realities of grace and sin.[1] If the Christian claim is that faith is a human response to God's grace and that this response entails transformation and redemption, then these theological categories should have visible consequences in the stories Christians tell about themselves.

But before we turn to an investigation of the nature of Christian narrative we first must examine the relation between narrative and personal identity. The primary issues here are philosophical and anthropological. We first must establish what we mean by "personal identity" and then demonstrate why the expression of personal identity takes the form of a narrative. Before the argument for the theological significance of narrative can be advanced a case must be made that narrative indeed does have a primordial locus in human experience. In other words, it must be shown that the expression of personal identity necessarily takes the form of a narrative before we can turn to the question of the nature of Christian narrative and its function in the transformation of personal identity.

In this chapter we first will ask what it is about the nature of human experience that makes narrative the necessary form for articulating personal identity. Then we will examine some of the features of this narrative form and consider a specific example of it. Finally, we will turn to a few of the unresolved issues which lurk in the background of this discussion, such as the problems of distortion and self-deception.

1. The Structure of Personal Identity

The terms "personal identity" and "identity crisis" have appeared frequently in our discussion and are often encountered in casual conversation. Precisely what they mean and the sense in which they are used, however, is a complicated issue. The term "identity" can function in several ways and have quite different meanings. On the one hand it can refer to generic similarity, as in "those men have identical hair color." Or identity can refer to the continuity of a person or object in the passage of time, as in "Jim Smith is no different now from what he was twenty years ago." In this latter sense, as Sydney Shoemaker has observed, "the term 'identity' implies persistence, i.e., the existence of one and the same thing at different times."[2] When dealing with persons what enables us to say that this person at any given moment is the same person as the one we knew in the past and the one we expect to know in the future? Much of our everyday activity, such as making promises, placing trust, anticipating the future, is predicated on our belief that there is continuity of some sort in a person's identity, but precisely what it is that is the basis for that continuity is a difficult philosophical question which has been much debated in the past and continues to puzzle contemporary philosophers.[3]

In addition to the problem of persistence through time there is another sense in which the term "identity" is used. Rather than referring to temporal continuity, "identity" can be used to describe a quality of personhood. In this sense "personal identity" refers to what *kind* of person an individual is or is becoming.[4] "Fred Fox lives in constant fear of his father" tells us something about Fred's identity, something about what kind of person he is.

Each of these different uses of the term "identity" presupposes a basic category common to them all. Without the use of human memory we could not talk about personal identity in any sense as persistence through time or as a quality of personhood. And of course the role of memory in the description of personal identity is by no means a recent discovery. Its roots can be found in Plato's theory of knowledge and in Augustine's reflections on the nature of time. John Locke, for example, described a person as "a thinking intelligent being, that has reason and reflection, and can consider itself as itself, the same thinking thing, in different times and places; which it does only by that consciousness which is inseparable from thinking, and, as it seems to me, essential to it."[5] Furthermore, Locke argued that personal identity refers to "the sameness of a rational being: and as far as this consciousness can be extended backwards to any past action or thought, so far reaches the identity of that person."[6] Although Locke's discussion of the nature of personal identity was couched in terms of the problem of personal continuity, it is important to note that memory played a central role in his analysis. After rejecting the view that there is some substance, such as the soul, which is the same at different points in time and that it is this sameness of substance which constitutes the identity of a person, Locke argued that personal identity is "the identity of consciousness" in a person rather than the sameness of a material or an immaterial substance. In making this move Locke insisted that the "identity of consciousness" is dependent on the psychological faculty of memory:

> yet it is plain, consciousness, as far as ever it can be extended—should it be to ages past—unites existences and actions very remote in time into the same *person*, as well as it does the existences and actions of the immediately preceding moment: so that whatever has the consciousness of present and past actions, is the same person to whom they both belong.[7]

In both the eighteenth century and in contemporary philosophical discussion Locke's use of memory to describe personal identity has been vigorously attacked from different points of view, and Locke's defenders, both then and now, have proposed different revisions of his position.[8] A particularly thorny issue in this discussion of temporal continuity is the question whether there are any criteria which may be used to assess statements about personal identity or whether personal identity is finally a primitive concept which does not readily lend itself to analysis. Many people would agree that personal identity entails reference both to bodily existence and to psychological structure, but whether these are the only two referents and precisely how they are related are complex questions. Does memory, for example, provide a necessary and sufficient criterion for personal identity? Shoemaker argues that it does not, that if bodily identity were not a criterion for personal identity "we could not know the truth of statements of personal identity."[9] But while bodily identity is *a* criterion, Shoemaker insists that it cannot be the sole criterion, because "there is an important sense in which memory, though certainly not the sole criterion, is one of the criteria."[10] Shoemaker does not explain how one should adjudicate conflicts between these two criteria of memory and bodily identity nor does he resolve the extremely difficult issue of the nature of their relation. It is clear, however, that while it may not provide a sufficient criterion for assessing personal identity judgments, memory is still a necessary ingredient in any description of what we mean by "person" and "personal identity," for as Shoemaker summarizes the matter, "Involved in being a person is having a memory, and this involves having the ability to make, without evidence, true statements about one's own past."[11] That would seem to be the case regardless of the context in which personal identity is discussed.

The exercise of memory plays a decisive role in every construction of personal identity. But acknowledging the importance of memory does not resolve the difficult question as to whether there are any criteria other than memory for assessing statements about personal identity. The problems posed by self-deception and distortion, regardless of whether the motives are conscious or unconscious, are serious and we will turn to them in the last section of this chapter. All that we have sought to establish at this point is that memory does indeed play a central role in the construction of personal identity. That discovery leads us to two further conclusions: that memory is of crucial importance because the identity of human beings is inextricably tied to history and that personal identity, in its dependence on memory, is essentially a hermeneutical concept.

Personal identity is a hermeneutical concept because it is primarily an exercise in interpretation. By means of the memory an individual selects certain events from his or her personal history and uses them to interpret the significance of the whole. The claim that human beings are inextricably tied to history simply means that they search for meaning and unity of self in some pattern of coherence in their personal history. An individual's particularity and therein his or her personal history is unique, "unique" in the sense that no two personal histories nor the possible range of interpretations that emerge from them are exactly the same. Personal identity, therefore, is always a pattern or a shape which memory retrieves from the history of each individual and projects into the future. No description of the relation between personal identity and personal history is any clearer than that which Josiah Royce formulated some sixty-five years ago:

> The self comes down to us from its own past. It needs and is a history. Each of us can see that his own idea of himself as this person is inseparably bound up with his view of his own former life, of the plans that he formed, of the fortunes that fashioned him, and of the accomplishments which in turn he has fashioned for himself. [12]

A similar point has been made by Wolfhart Pannenberg. The decisions an individual makes and the things that happen to him or her constitute that person's "history," a history which is "entirely particular and unique." [13] In fact, there is no such thing as personal identity which is not an interpretation of a person's past or what Pannenberg calls "life history."

> Rather, the particular individuality of each person is decisively determined by his course of life. Only this path constitutes the respective concrete reality of this or that individual man. All the events in his life have their particular meaning and their importance only in the context of his life history. [14]

"Life history" is not simply the sum of all those events an individual has experienced, those moments from birth to the present that make up a person's past. "Life history," like personal identity, is an interpretive concept used to bring order out of a person's unstructured past and in so doing to imbue it with a particular significance or worth. The identity of any person is an interpretation culled from that individual's personal history.

From a different perspective a similar description of the nature of personal identity can be found in Erik Erikson's work on the life cycle and the stages in the development of personality.[15] For Erikson the identity of a person is a genetic concept, a reality that is always in the process of emergence and becoming. One of Erikson's favorite terms for describing identity is "configuration." Identity formation is "an evolving configuration—a configuration which is gradually established by successive ego syntheses and resyntheses throughout childhood."[16] The particular identity configuration which is assumed by an individual at any given moment is dependent on the use of memory to recover and reinterpret the past. This dimension of recovery in personal identity, which of course is a Freudian legacy, led Erikson to the conclusion that there are some strong similarities between the craft of psychoanalysis and the work of the historian. In psychotherapy the patient's interpretation of his or her personal history is the object of the therapist's inquiry; "and the way they submit their past to our interpretation is a special form of historicizing, dominated by their sense of fragmentation and isolation and by our method of restoring to them, through the encounter with us, a semblance of wholeness, immediacy, and mutuality."[17] The clinician like the historian is engaged in what Erikson describes as "a restorative act" in which a fragmented past and, consequently, a confused sense of identity receive wholeness, coherence, and meaning. For different reasons both the clinician and the historian pursue the recovery and the reinterpretation of an individual's personal history. Unless the patient is able to exercise his or her memory there can be only a limited recovery of the past and without this personal history there can be neither inquiry into nor restoration of personal identity.

Personal identity is a hermeneutical concept which depends to a considerable extent on the use of the memory for the interpretation of the past. The nature of self-understanding and the understanding one person has of another is intrinsically historical, but precisely because of its historicity personal identity is never a static nor an exclusively private reality. Although understanding itself is always confined to the perspective of a particular situation, the interpretive context that is brought to bear on one's personal history is never wholly the result of individual invention or genius. Just as we never fully understand the meaning of a text or an object of art, so too personal history, the raw material from which personal identity is constructed, is never fully understood or exhausted. The very historicity of personal identity means that persons are in the process of becoming, and, consequently, the interpretation of personal history and personal identity is an unending process.[18] On the one hand, the process is never finished because the future is an open horizon toward which one's personal history is moving. As long as a person continues to have new experiences the identity of that person is in the process of becoming. Secondly, in the course of a single life a person's identity may undergo severe changes. While personal history does not change, the past may be repressed or forgotten. Still, it does not cease to be a reality. What may undergo radical change is the interpretation that is given to personal history. It would be a serious mistake, therefore, to think that one person can easily move from one interpretation to another or that it is possible to assume another person's identity. To step into another person's identity is to assume the constellation of events and experiences that make up that person's past, a personal history which is still in flux and in movement toward a projected future.

Because personal identity is an interpretation of personal history it is extremely difficult to alter one's own identity or to step into someone else's. It is not simply a question of knowing the factual data that make up a person's history. Of even greater importance are the values, categories, goals—the interpretive scheme—that is used to interpret personal history. It is one thing to know something of another person's past, but it is an entirely different matter to understand the values, symbols, and prejudices at work in that person's interpretation of the past. As Hans-Georg Gadamer has pointed out, these "prejudices" should not be shunned for they are important clues to the particularity of every individual and to the "tradition" used to interpret that person's history.[19] The process we have been calling "personal identity" is simply one instance of what Gadamer describes as "the hermeneutical circle," in which "the movement of understanding is constantly from the whole to the part and back to the whole."[20] In this instance personal identity is an interpretation imposed on the whole of a life history from the partial perspective of the moment. Gadamer's interpretation is especially important because it draws our attention to both the part and the whole and reminds us that the movement of understanding and interpretation is indeed circular. The interpretation given to any part is shaped by what is anticipated from the perspective of the whole, and the whole, the anticipatory structure, has emerged from an analysis of the parts. In other words, a person's identity at any given moment is an interpretation imposed on the whole of that person's history, but the interpretation used to interpret the meaning of particular events is always prejudiced by the tradition from which it is derived. As Gadamer describes this process,

> Understanding is not to be thought of so much as an action of one's subjectivity, but as the placing of oneself within a process of tradition, in which past and present are constantly fused.[21]

A person's identity is never static because personal history is always unfolding and there is no self-understanding apart from an understanding of the historical horizon or tradition which serves as the context for the interpretation of identity.

As we have seen, the use of the memory is essential to the process of becoming a person, but remembering is only one moment in the complex act of interpretation. That is but one reason why the problem of self-deception is not confined to the work of the psychoanalyst. To remember what happened when you were ten years old is to engage in interpretation. First the effort must be made to unearth the past or at least that part of it that is sought after. Then some attention must be given to the categories used to interpret what is unearthed, categories which are a part of that moving horizon or tradition in which one finds oneself.[22] To be a person, therefore, is not simply to have a history which can be remembered but also to live within a horizon or tradition which provides the symbols, myths, and categories for the interpretation of that history. No "person" is without a horizon. To be in the world is to be in a situation, to have a standpoint from which one experiences and interprets reality, and the horizon peculiar to each person is not something that individual constructs. Initially one finds oneself in a situation, a tradition, already engaged in numerous acts of interpretation.

The dimension of the "whole" or the "tradition" is essential for a proper understanding of personhood because it reminds us that personal identity is never a private reality. The tradition within which we interpret our personal history and our world represents part of the social and communal dimension of personal identity.[23] "Tradition" is more that situation (in Gadamer's sense) in which I find myself doing a variety of things—making moral judgments, venturing political and economic opinions, affirming some values and denying others—than it is an intellectual stance I have chosen to assume. Our judgments about and assessments of other persons, cultures, and civilizations are influenced by the social nexus in which we live, the social environment where the categories for the interpretation of personal history have been acquired. Personal identity requires the use of memory to interpret personal history, but it also depends on the framework in which personal history is interpreted and that framework is shaped by a person's location in a particular community.

Persons are social beings and their identity is constituted in part by their social relationships. Nearly fifty years ago George Herbert Mead argued persuasively that a person or what he called a "self" is "essentially a social structure, and it arises in social experience."[24] Since Mead's day the social and communal dimension of personal identity has become a commonplace among psychologists and sociologists, and its importance is acknowledged occasionally even by theologians.[25] Tradition, the interpretive horizon within which one remembers, is both a historical and a social reality and is an essential ingredient in the description of personal identity. Without the social dimension represented by tradition there would be no framework for interpretation nor would there be any basis for making judgments about the interpretation of personal history. It is only within the life of a particular social world, which may include various communities, that a person remembers personal history and interprets and constructs personal identity.

Although memory alone is not a sufficient category for the full description of personal identity, it is certainly essential. A person with no access to his or her past may be a "person" in the legal and medical sense of the term (a person suffering from amnesia certainly still has legal rights), but there is a very real sense in which that person has no "identity" and cannot account for what he or she does and what kind of person he or she is. Furthermore, the primacy of memory in the construction of personal identity illumines the sense in which it is a historical and hermeneutical concept. Memory is necessary because a person's identity always entails some reference to that person's history and the recovery of the past is always an act of interpretation. Finally, we have argued that personal identity is neither static nor private.

The very symbols and categories a person uses to articulate his or her identity are evidence of both the processive and social dimensions of personhood. Each of these features is important in describing the nature of personal identity and in understanding why a particular kind of narrative is the appropriate form for its articulation.

2. Narrative and Personal History

It is no accident that when they are asked to identify themselves most people recite a narrative or story. Regardless of the situation—whether it is a new person at work, a first-semester-college student, or a new recruit in the army—people tell stories about themselves in order to identify themselves to other people. Often these narratives are simple and brief and contain only basic data, such as date and place of birth, vocation, family, etc. But with only a little probing it quickly becomes apparent that every person's identity narrative is far more subtle and complex than it first appears. In an individual's identity narrative, what we might refer to as a person's "autobiography," certain events are lifted out of that person's history and given primary importance for the interpretation and understanding of the whole. In every person's history there is a chronological order of sorts, yet no identity narrative includes all or even a majority of the events that have taken place in a single life. For various reasons some events are selected and lifted up in a person's history as disclosive of the meaning of the whole. A person's identity, therefore, is an interpretation of personal history in which the meaning of the whole and hence the identity of the self is constructed on the foundation of a few basic events and the symbols and concepts used to interpret them.[26]

Personal identity necessarily assumes the form of a narrative because it is history that is remembered and only narrative provides the form and structure in which some events may become

the focus for interpreting the meaning of the whole. As Stanley
Hauerwas aptly describes narrative, it "binds events and agents
together in an intelligible pattern," and it is this pattern which
provides the form and meaning for personal identity, because "To
tell a story often involves our attempt to make intelligible the
muddle of things we have done in order to become a self."[27]
Although Hauerwas does not argue that narrative is the only
form for the expression of personal identity, he does insist that
apart from narrative "there is no other way we can articulate the
richness of intentional activity."[28] Some philosophers of history
have tried to make an even stronger case for the necessity of narrative in the interpretation of the past. W. B. Gallie, for example, has argued that history necessarily assumes the form of
narrative, and, consequently, any recounting or interpretation of
the past will be narrative in form.[29] If Gallie's thesis can be sustained it has some important implications for our inquiry into
personal identity, for if history necessarily assumes the form of a
narrative and if personal identity is always an interpretation of
personal history then personal identity must also assume narrative form.

From a slightly different perspective, Stephen Crites, in one
of the most significant and provocative articles yet written on the
religious importance of narrative, takes the position that personal
identity assumes the form of a narrative because "the formal
quality of experience through time is inherently narrative."[30]
Past, present, and future are the "tensed modalities" which are
inseparably joined in every moment of experience. Furthermore,
the unity of these three modalities "requires narrative forms both
for its expression (mundane stories) and for its own sense of the
meaning of its internal coherence (sacred stories)."[31]

But what kind of narrative is it that individuals construct out
of their past in order to articulate their personal identity? There
are at least two different dimensions or levels to personal identity
narratives. One hidden level of that narrative represents the

givenness of a person's social and historical world while the other
level, the more visible and accessible one, is the conscious projec-
tion and interpretation of the first. What we have been describing as a personal identity narrative assumes a form that in most
cases perhaps could be called "autobiography." The first level or
dimension of this narrative we shall refer to as a person's "chronicle" and the second as a person's "interpretation." Both "chronicle" and "interpretation" are necessary for a full understanding
of the structure of a personal identity narrative.

A chronicle is simply the sum of those events and experiences
which constitute an individual's personal history. According to
Robert Scholes and Robert Kellogg, chronicles are the "simplest
forms of historical narrative."[32] While chronicles are not restricted to the personal histories of individuals and may be used
to preserve the histories of states and cultures, our interest is
primarily in the chronicle found in personal histories. Nor does
the chronicle begin only with a person's birth, or first moment of
awareness, or first thoughts.

> The chronicle usually begins at whatever point the chronicler be-
> lieves life to have begun, or his civilization to have been founded,
> and works its way toward the continuous present, at which point
> it merges with the annals, which are simply a yearly record of
> events. This kind of historical writing is to true narrative history
> as a diary or journal is to true narrative biography or autobiogra-
> phy. In records of this kind we usually feel the lack of two elements
> essential to narrative art: selectivity and movement.[33]

In other words, the problem with a chronicle is that it has no
"plot" (defined by Scholes and Kellogg as "the dynamic, sequential element in narrative literature" which makes minimal reference to character). Only when the chronicle is interpreted does it
begin to have plot and become "history." By no means is this
distinction between chronicle and interpretation peculiar to literary criticism. Several philosophers of history have insisted on a
similar distinction and have attributed major significance to it.

W. H. Walsh, for example, draws a distinction between "plain" and "significant" narratives based on the very different forms of understanding and knowledge in each.[34] A "plain" narrative, which resembles what we have been calling chronicle, attempts a form of description while a "significant" narrative not only describes the importance of events but attempts to explain and interpret them.[35]

The chronicle of an individual is made up of those facts, events, and experiences—those things that happened—which are subject to interpretation in biography and autobiography. The distinction between chronicle and history does not mean that the former is free from any taint of interpretation, regardless of what it is that is being chronicled. Every chronicle obviously includes an element of interpretation, but the major difference between chronicle and history (or "interpretation") is one of intent. The chronicler intends only to recount and to describe while the historian intends to explain and to interpret.

There are two formal features of a person's chronicle that are particularly important: the "givenness" of the chronicle, and the social world reflected in the chronicle. In the first place, a person's chronicle is not confined only to those events which the individual can remember. What has happened to a person can be repressed or forgotten, but as long as it is remembered by others or can be recovered by archaeologists of the psyche an event is not "lost." Every moment in a person's history forms a piece of the whole and for this reason among others a person's past is not wholly malleable and not open to every conceivable interpretation. It is this givenness of the chronicle that provides one kind of criterion for assessing the coherence of a person's interpreted history. That a person is a white male, raised in a particular social setting by specific people means that these events and "facts"are the raw data of personal history which cannot be altered. There is a bedrock of sorts to a person's chronicle which constitutes its givenness and its objectivity.

Secondly, the chronicle includes those larger worlds—historical, social, and cultural—that make up an individual's personal and inherited history. A person is a social being and a person's chronicle is unintelligible apart from the social world in which it is formed. Because this social world has a history of its own and includes the racial and cultural features of a particular community, a person's identity is always an interpretation of or coming to terms with those pre-conscious givens, data which form the boundaries and parameters of a person's identity. The struggle for personal identity is the struggle to understand and appropriate the meaning and coherence of the chronicle. Without some minimal conscious relation to that bedrock material we call chronicle, an individual has no personal identity, as is the case with those who suffer from amnesia. The chronicle can never be reduced simply to the personal and the private dimensions of existence but always includes social and cultural influences.

A personal identity narrative, however, includes more than just a chronicle of personal history. In fact, a personal identity narrative is not a chronicle as such but only presupposes it as the necessary condition for "interpretation," the process in which personal identity is constructed.[36] A narrative in the genre of autobiography is a conscious re-presentation of personal identity and as such is rooted in and is an interpretation of personal history or chronicle. From this perspective autobiography is an act of interpretation in which a form or shape or pattern is culled from the chronicle and projected over the whole. While the chronicle provides the material and the parameters for the act of interpretation, it is only in interpretation that personal identity finally emerges.[37] Paul Ricoeur describes the dynamics of Freudian psychoanalysis in similar terms: "the real history is merely a clue to the figurative history through which the patient arrives at self-understanding; for the analyst, the important thing is this figurative history."[38]

It is in the context of this relation between chronicle and

interpretation that other features of personal identity become intelligible. The nature of alienation and conversion and the role of the community in the formation of personal identity are illumined if we examine what happens to that chronicle in the act of interpretation. What is sometimes described as "alienation" is often simply the attempt to live in ignorance of or in flight from all or a part of one's personal history. In this context alienation describes the repression or negation of chronicle in that conscious act of interpretation that yields personal identity. Of course neither a part nor the whole of the chronicle can be destroyed. It can be forced into the unconscious and ignored but it remains a reality and invariably leaves its mark on personal identity. It does not take much of a detective to sift the clues and uncover the trail of that which has been hidden in a person's past.

While alienation entails a loss or rejection of the past, a different dynamic is at work in conversion. In conversion a person's self-understanding or personal identity comes into question and one's personal history must be reworked, reinterpreted, and reappropriated. For most people this process is not easy nor is it something that happens frequently. It occurs rarely, if at all, and is a difficult, often painful, experience. Events in one's personal history that have functioned previously as interpretive centers for the whole chronicle must be reinterpreted and in some cases discarded in favor of other events which have suddenly become more important. Not only is personal identity altered in conversion, but there is also a sense in which the chronicle itself is "converted." The events that make up a person's chronicle are converted when they are viewed from the perspective of a different interpretation or what Peter Berger calls a different "meaning system."[39] In the process of conversion those events in a person's life which are the most important in the interpretation of identity—family background, education, marriage, vocation—may lose their significance and cease to have disclosive power to illumine the meaning of the whole chronicle. Having been raised in a wealthy home, someone who has become vice-president of Richquick Oil Company, earns a hundred thousand dollars a year, and belongs to the most fashionable country club in town may well refer to these personal facts in order to explain who he or she is. In the process of conversion, however, these facts may lose their significance. Other events which previously had played no overt role in the articulation of personal identity because they had been repressed or forgotten in shame, guilt, or fear may become vitally important in the reinterpretation of personal history and the reconstruction of the self. Denial of a parent's love, the disintegration of a marriage, rejection by children, the barely visible contributions made to the lives of other people— these repressed or hidden facts in a person's life may become indispensable for understanding who and what a person is. The prominence of one set of events over another depends entirely on the symbols, myths, and categories that are used to interpret personal history. If the interpretive scheme that one brings to bear on one's personal history is the Horatio Alger myth, a myth that stresses initiative and achievement, then a different set of events will become the basis of personal identity than if one turns to personal history with the symbols and myths of the Christian Gospel, a narrative dominated by the symbol of the cross.

What is really at issue in conversion is the interpretive scheme or vision with which a person turns to the past and looks into the future. As we have noted, the raw data of one's chronicle will not long tolerate an interpretation which has no relation to the events that make up personal history. The dissonance eventually will become intolerable. But within the parameters of the chronicle the issue in conversion is the perspective with which one interprets the past and anticipates the future.

Finally, the role of the community must not be neglected in any description of the process of interpreting personal history. Just as a person's chronicle always reflects the social and cultural worlds which make up its setting in history, so too the interpretation given to any person's chronicle includes social and cultural influences. Every act of interpretation takes place within the horizon of a determinate "situation," what Gadamer describes as "a standpoint that limits the possibility of vision."[40] Interpretation occurs in the context of a particular situation and because the interpreter can never entirely step outside of the situation he or she can be at best only partially aware of the blinders that limit vision. And one of the most significant limitations to every interpretive act is the tradition and community within which the interpretation takes place. The same event may have a wholly different interpretation in one tradition from what it has in another. The social world of the interpreter is a fundamental factor in every act of interpretation. Should the interpreter move into a community with different concepts and categories for interpreting reality the consequences for the interpretation of personal history are extensive.

Our discussion of the nature of personal identity and the role of narrative in the interpretation of personal history has been formal and abstract. In order to put flesh and blood on these formal categories of chronicle and interpretation and to examine how personal identity is constructed and reconstructed we will look at one example of this process. In principle we could turn to almost any autobiographical statement in order to examine the adequacy of our formal description. The autobiography of Malcolm X simply demonstrates the formal categories that are at work in the construction of any person's identity.

3. The Autobiography of Malcolm X

Personal identity is an interpretation of personal history, and, as we have seen, occasionally a person's chronicle contains facts and events that are of such overwhelming significance that they are unavoidable in any interpretation of personal identity. Precisely how those facts are interpreted, however, may vary from one interpretation to another. For Malcolm X the "fact" that is of primary importance in his chronicle is his racial identity. What does it mean to be a black man, and, more importantly, what does it mean to be a black man in a white, racist society? His racial identity is one of the unalterable givens in Malcolm's personal history and much of his struggle for personal identity is a coming to terms with his blackness.

Malcolm was born in Milwaukee on May 19, 1925 and assassinated in New York on February 21, 1965. While he was a boy in East Lansing, Michigan, Malcolm's father was murdered by whites. His mother was harassed by the state social agency and finally committed to a mental hospital. Malcolm and his seven brothers and sisters were parceled out to foster homes and state agencies, but finally Malcolm went to Boston to live with his stepsister, Ella. In Roxbury and later in Harlem he encountered a black culture wholly unlike anything he had experienced in Michigan. For the first time he discovered jazz, zoot suits, conks, and black churches in which people "threw their souls and bodies wholly into worship."[41] After working in Harlem as a waiter, Malcolm became a hustler. He sold drugs, worked in the numbers racket, became a "steerer" for a madam, and organized a burglary ring in Roxbury. He was caught by the police when he took an expensive watch he had stolen to a friend's for repair and eventually sentenced to ten years in prison. Malcolm had not yet begun to shave when he entered Charlestown State Prison at the age of twenty-one.

In his autobiography Malcolm insisted that he was writing openly about his life as a criminal not in order to titillate the reader, but "because the full story is the best way that I know to have it seen, and understood, that I had sunk to the very bottom of the American white man's society when—soon now, in prison—I found Allah and the religion of Islam and it completely transformed my life."[42]

While in prison Malcolm was converted by his brother, Reginald, to the Muslim religion of Elijah Muhammad, and as a result of his conversion Malcolm became a hermit, read everything he could find in the prison library, and was forced to re-examine his past, particularly in light of Elijah Muhammad's claim that white people were the devil.

> The white people I had known marched before my mind's eye. From the start of my life. The state white people always in our house after the other whites I didn't know had killed my father . . . the white people who kept calling my mother "crazy" to her face and before me and my brothers and sisters, until she finally was taken off by white people to the Kalamazoo asylum . . . the white judge and others who had split up the children . . . [43]

In Malcolm's account of the first twenty-one years of his life, prior to his conversion, he assumed various attitudes toward his own blackness and toward white society. On the one hand he took great pride in his sexual conquests of white women, yet he also tacitly assented to the existing structures and institutions of a racist, segregated society. He was a criminal but certainly no revolutionary. He accepted the world white society imposed on him and responded to it by carving out an existence marked by drugs, hustling, and the constant danger of the jungle in the streets. It was only after he became a Muslim that Malcolm learned to hate "the white devil" and to see the institutions of white society as real instruments of oppression and racism. Only then did he come to understand that his blackness was not something to be regretted, not a curse, but a part of his humanity, even a mark of divine favor.

After his conversion to Islam, Malcolm engaged in a thorough reinterpretation of his personal history. It was necessary to remember it all again in order to reinterpret it from the perspective of his new faith.

> I still marvel at how swiftly my previous life's thinking pattern

slid away from me, like snow off a roof. It is as though someone else I knew of had lived by hustling and crime. I would be startled to catch myself thinking in a remote way of my earlier self as another person.[44]

After his conversion Malcolm was no longer able to ignore his blackness, but he did reject any interpretation of himself as a nigger, regardless of whether that interpretation came from whites or from his black brothers and sisters. He did not reject that part of his chronicle in which he had looked at himself as a nigger, at least not in the sense that he excised it from his past, but his conversion meant that it was no longer possible for him to interpret his past and present identity in those terms. As a nigger Malcolm had been willing to assent to a white dominated society, but as Malcolm X, as a Muslim, he became self-consciously a black man and learned to take pride in his blackness and to hate that which oppressed him. The past could not be erased, but the decisive issue was not whether the past could be forgotten. The real issue was Malcolm's interpretation of his personal history and therein the construction of his personal identity.

Once he became a Black Muslim minister, Malcolm's life bore little resemblance to his youth in Roxbury and Harlem, but if we did not have Malcolm's reinterpretation of his first twenty-one years it would be difficult to understand his new personal identity.

> But people are always speculating—why am I as I am? To understand that of any person, his whole life, from birth, must be reviewed. All of our experiences fuse into our personality. Everything that ever happened to us is an ingredient.[45]

As a Black Muslim minister Malcolm did what he had been unable to do in his youth—he accepted and affirmed his blackness, but he rejected a society in which black people were understood to be subservient to whites. His reinterpretation of his blackness culminated in a radically transformed understanding of the past and present, because as Malcolm put it, "I was going through the hardest thing, also the greatest thing, for any human being to do; to accept that which is already within you, and around you."[46]

When he was released from prison, Malcolm returned to a society which was much the same as he had left it. Roxbury and Harlem were the same communities in which Malcolm had lived as a pimp and a pusher, but the Malcolm who returned was not the same Malcolm who had left. Not only did he return with a new understanding of his own blackness, but his understanding of reality and his role in the world had been transformed. The essential fact in his chronicle—his blackness—was no longer a source of alienation from his personal history but the basis for his conversion and his recovery of his past.

The shifts in Malcolm's identity—from country boy to ghetto hustler to Black Muslim minister—were several and dramatic, perhaps more so than is the case for most people. For example, it is remarkable how many names Malcolm assumed during his life: Malcolm Little, "Big Red," "Satan," "Homeboy," Malcolm X, and El-Hajj Malik El-Shabazz. Each of these names represents a distinct interpretation of Malcolm's identity and although there may be little continuity between them they are all interpretations of the one continuous chronicle which was his personal history. These are not only the different names of one man; they represent the different worlds he lived in and the different ways in which he interpreted his world and his place in it. All of these names and the worlds and events they represent make up the one chronicle, the one life, that was Malcolm X.

In Malcolm's autobiography we see at work most of the themes we have discussed in our formal description of personal identity narrative. Malcolm's chronicle is the bedrock, the raw material, out of which he constructs his personal identity. That hermeneutical task required the exercise of his memory, the recovery of his past, and the reinterpretation of his personal history.

But Malcolm's search for meaning in his personal history, his quest for a coherent personal identity, was not finally a private and isolated struggle. The decisive event in Malcolm's life which enabled him to discover meaning and coherence was his conversion to Islam and, more importantly, his life and ministry in Black Muslim communities in Detroit and Chicago after his release from prison. The small community that gathered at Detroit Temple Number One provided the social context for the completion of Malcolm's conversion from nigger to black man.

> I had never dreamed of anything like that atmosphere among black people who had learned to be proud they were black, who had learned to love other black people instead of being jealous and suspicious. I thrilled to how we Muslim men used both hands to grasp a black brother's both hands, voicing and smiling our happiness to meet him again. The Muslim sisters, both married and single, were given an honor and respect that I'd never seen black men give to their women, and it felt wonderful to me.[47]

The small Muslim community provided the necessary social matrix for Malcolm's appropriation of Islam at various levels of his existence, the experiential as well as the intellectual. In an important sense the Detroit Temple served as the mediator of the tradition of Islam to Malcolm in a way that the prison library could not. In this community he could live the faith of Islam and see it at work in a way that he could not in prison.

Of course Malcolm's identity narrative does not end with his conversion to the Black Muslim community. The remainder of the story is fascinating in its own right. Malcolm's understanding of Islam and his view of the black person's position in white society was sharply influenced by a subsequent trip to Mecca, his encounter with traditional forms of Islam, and a series of disagreements with Elijah Muhammad, a conflict that led finally to hostility between the two and to Malcolm's assassination. Throughout these events Malcom's understanding of his own identity and his role in society was continuously being revised.

But if it is possible to speak of a watershed in Malcolm's self-understanding it would have to be his prison conversion to the Black Muslim faith. Although Malcolm would revise his understanding of himself and of Islam, his interpretation of his personal history and his perception of the world would never escape the impact of his encounter with the life and faith of the Black Muslims.

4. Deceit and Self-Deception

Although a person's identity takes the form of a narrative we have seen that the structure and even the content of the narrative often is more complex than it first appears. Indeed, the complexity of this kind of narrative is only one of several reasons we should pause before claiming to have understood the identity of another person. We cannot easily enter another person's identity, and if the concepts by which that person's past is interpreted and the community in which that interpretation takes place are alien to us, then the degree to which we can claim understanding of that person's identity is seriously limited. If both the chronicle and the interpretation of another person's identity are significantly different from our own, then we should be modest in what we claim to understand about that person. Personal identity is not the random ordering of personal history; rather, it emerges in the dialectical tension between chronicle and interpretation. A person's identity is not simply a recitation of his or her chronicle, nor is it an interpretation that has nothing to do with the reality of personal history, but it emerges from the interaction of both chronicle and interpretation. Failure to attend to the nature of this dialectic can result in immodest claims about how well one understands oneself or another person and distorted interpretations of the nature of personal identity.

One example of the problems that develop when the dialectic between chronicle and interpretation is ignored is Michael Novak's book, *Ascent of the Mountain, Flight of the Dove*.[48] In the second chapter, "Autobiography and Story," Novak develops a concept of story (what we have been describing as a personal identity narrative) as the primary motif for describing how one becomes "religious."[49] Novak does not, however, offer a formal description of the nature of this story nor does he discuss the philosophical and hermeneutical issues that beg for attention. Regardless of whether he is correct about the nature of religious experience, what Novak means by the category of "story" is far from clear. He describes "story" as the sum or aggregate of the different "standpoints" a person has assumed in the course of a life. What he calls the "key struggle of life" is the search for psychic transformation or "breakthroughs in the way one perceives events, imagines oneself, understands others, grasps the world, acts."[50] The function of a story, therefore, is not only to link actions together but to link transformations.

A person perceives, imagines, and understands from a "standpoint," which Novak describes as "a complex of experiences, images, expectations, presuppositions, and operations (especially of inquiring and deciding) by which men act out their own sense of themselves, of others, of nature, of history, and of God."[51] But what Novak does not seem to understand is that the standpoint or what Gadamer calls "the situation" in which a person interprets personal history and the social world is not randomly selected. To be a person is to have a particular standpoint or situation, which is by no means fixed and unalterable, but which is not easily shed. A person does not move from one standpoint to another as though shopping in a clothing store, moving from one rack of suits to the next. Because of the dialectical relation between chronicle and interpretation it is difficult, if not impossible, to randomly "try on" stories or to "pass over" into another person's identity.[52] If Malcolm X had attempted to interpret his personal history from the standpoint of a white suburbanite the contradictions would have been far graver than simply that of skin color. The very nature of personal identity and its rootedness in personal history is such that one cannot flit from one interpretation to another like a bee in a daisy field. A person's chronicle is a given and imposes limits on the range of possible interpretations of personal identity.

The effort to understand personal identity demands time, reflection, and a remarkable degree of honesty in order to unearth the different interpretations that form the sediments of the past. The dialectical relationship between chronicle and interpretation obviously does not preclude the alteration and transformation of personal identity but much more is involved in the process than Novak suggests. A person's identity is not simply the sum of those standpoints or interpretations that have functioned in the past, nor can a person's identity be separated from personal history. Although a person may move from one interpretation of his or her chronicle to another without radically altering the interpretation of personal identity, the chronicle is not subject to every conceivable interpretation. Dissonance between chronicle and interpretation often results in a not so subtle form of incoherence in personal identity.

Novak fails to appreciate the relation between chronicle and interpretation and consequently avoids the hermeneutical problem of how standpoints or interpretations are linked together in a coherent narrative that articulates personal identity. He offers no analysis of how one moves from one standpoint to another nor does he explain the hermeneutical principles at work in this linking of standpoints. If a person's "story" is simply a collection of randomly selected standpoints, without any necessary relation to chronicle or personal history, then there is indeed no hermeneutical problem. But if personal identity, as we have described it, is an interpretation of personal history, then it is intrinsically hermeneutical and the distinction between chronicle and interpretation cannot be ignored.

This dialectical relation between chronicle and interpretation is of considerable importance in dealing with the difficult issues of truth and self-deception in the construction of personal identity. Previously we referred to Ricoeur's comment that in psychoanalysis the analyst's concern is not primarily the patient's "real history" but his or her "figurative history," the history the patient has constructed in order to explain why things are the way they are. That figurative history may have little or no resemblance to real history; indeed, one measure of a person's "illness" may be the discrepancy between what did happen and what the patient believes happened. But there is also a sense in which the patient's figurative history is "true." From the patient's perspective the narrative is functionally true; that is, it "works," it provides an apparently coherent description of some if not all past events and explains the nature of the self in the present.

Self-deception, therefore, is not simply a matter of the conscious or unconscious distortion of an event in the past. Self-deception is not so much an event or a deed as it is a description of the incoherent way a person lives in relation to the past and in anticipation of the future. It is not a momentary indiscretion, a lapse of memory, or a mental error, but more like what Herbert Fingarette calls "a 'self-covering' policy," which generates "a more or less elaborate 'cover-story.'"[53] Self-deception is a discrepancy between the past and what a person says about the past, and an incoherence between how a person actually lives in the world and the account that person offers to others. It is not the account or the story itself that is self-deceiving but the discrepancy between the account and what happened or is happening. Because the quest for personal identity is a search for coherence and order in personal history, self-deception, as Stanley Hauerwas and David Burrell have observed, "can accompany this need for unity, as we systematically delude ourselves in order to maintain the story that has hitherto assured our identity."[54]

Self-deception is a form of flight from reality into fantasy, a human experience preserved in some of the oldest and most important religious myths, such as Genesis 3, God's encounter with Adam and Eve after they had eaten the fruit from the tree of knowledge of good and evil. After their eyes were opened and they knew they were naked, Adam and Eve made clothes for themselves, but when they heard God walking in the garden in the cool of the day they hid. Dietrich Bonhoeffer attributed Adam's flight from God to his conscience, which "agrees with God, and on the other hand in this flight it allows man to feel secure in his hiding place." The conscience, therefore, is the source of the creature's self-deception.

> This means that it deludes man into feeling that he really is fleeing. Moreover it allows him to believe that this flight is his triumphal procession and all the world is fleeing from him. Conscience drives man from God into a secure hiding place.[55]

Of course there is no such secure hiding place and God addresses Adam in the midst of his flight, calling him to account ("Where are you?" Gen. 3:9). Self-deception is no single act but a pattern of life. In this case it is the creature's flight from its Creator. Not the tasting of the forbidden fruit nor the making of clothes but the flight itself, the creature's attempt to live apart from its Creator, is the act of self-deception. What follows in the encounter between God and his creatures is only the inevitable consequence of the flight that has already begun. Adam responds to God's question, "Have you eaten of the tree of which I commanded you not to eat?" (Gen. 3:11), by blaming the woman ("she gave me the fruit of the tree, and I ate" [Gen. 3:12]). And not to be outdone, the woman blames the serpent ("The serpent beguiled me and I ate" [Gen. 3:13]). Neither Adam nor Eve can answer God's question because they are already in flight, already engaged in a self-deception that prevents them from hearing or speaking the truth. Neither of them can answer God's direct question ("What is this that you have done?" [Gen. 3:13]). Their self-deception separates them from the original event ("she took of its fruit and ate; and she also gave some to her husband, and he ate"

[3:6b]), and in their flight from the truth neither of them can say, "I have done what was forbidden me and have eaten the fruit from the tree of the knowledge of good and evil." The most their self-deception will allow is "she gave me the fruit of the tree" and "the serpent beguiled me," statements which evade the original event and which are the product of a "cover-story" already at work to justify subsequent behavior.

There can be no guarantees, of course, against self-deception. Inasmuch as self-consciousness is a reflexive, mediated reality there is always a certain distance between experience and a person's conscious awareness and interpretation of that experience. It is here, in the very structure of human consciousness, that self-deception becomes a possibility. Because personal identity is an interpretation of personal history for the purpose, at least in part, of self-explanation and because it is dependent on the exercise of memory for the re-collection of the past, self-deception is always possible. Were there no significant "other" in this process there would be no basis for distinguishing between self-deception and legitimate interpretation. Personal history or chronicle is but one form of this otherness. If the dissonance in a self-deceiving interpretation of what has happened and is happening becomes too extreme, personal identity may disintegrate from within. However, the human capacity for self-deception is so great that it happens only in the most unusual of circumstances. It may be that self-deception is recognized for what it is only when a person is called to some form of accounting by another person or by a community. God said to Adam, "Where are you?" (Gen. 3:9) and to Eve, "What is this that you have done?" (Gen. 3:13). It is only when a self-deceived person is called to account by the reality of the past or by another person that there is any hope that the web of deceit can be broken. The Prodigal Son, for example, continued to deceive himself and to flee from his father until, as Luke put it, "he came to himself" and returned to his home. What the Prodigal "came to" was the intolerable discrepancy between life in his father's home and his self-imposed misery. "How many of my father's hired servants have bread enough and to spare, but I perish here with hunger!" (Luke 15:17). So too Malcolm X's flight from his racial identity ended in prison only when his past was called into question by his brother, Philbert, who offered him an alternative interpretation in the Black Muslim faith. Forced to take stock of his past, Malcolm "came to himself" and was freed from the bondage of his racial self-deception. The encounter with the otherness of one's past or with another person cannot guarantee an end to self-deception. Adam continues to deceive himself, never hears God's call to accountability, and is "sent . . . forth from the garden of Eden, to till the ground from which he was taken (Gen. 3:23)," no doubt still insisting that the real culprit was Eve or the serpent.

The narrative a person uses to interpret his or her identity must illumine the past and it must have something to do with present behavior. Although neither the givenness of the chronicle nor the otherness of the community offers a guarantee against self-deception, they do function as clues and signals that this kind of distortion has become a problem. Of course the problem is not just limited to individuals. Entire communities can suffer self-deception. When this happens the community's only hope is the prophet or the rebel who will point to the massive web of self-deception and force the community to see the discrepancy between reality and fantasy, between what it says about itself and what it is and does. In this encounter between the individual (either prophet, rebel, or both) and the community a collision takes place. In this collision it is usually the community that provides the corrective lens for the individual's interpretation of reality. Occasionally, however, it is the community who suffers self-deception and it is the individual who points to the distortion and calls the community to account. In either case what is at stake is the interpretation of the past, the coherence between that interpretation and present behavior, and the hopes and dreams by which the future is anticipated. In the absence of the "other," be it person or community, there would be no one to listen to and challenge the self-deceiving narrative by which a person interprets the past, acts in the present, and anticipates the future.[56] Not only does the community provide an individual with a tradition and with symbols and categories for interpreting personal history, but the community also listens to how the individual uses the tradition to construct personal identity and it observes how the tradition is lived and enacted. The community with its collective memory serves as a check on every individual's interpretation and appropriation of the tradition and even though the community may not have immediate access to a person's past it can call into question how the tradition is used to interpret personal history and how it coheres with present projects, policies, and forms of behavior.

Personal identity is the interpretation of personal history by means of the exercise of memory. As we have seen, personal identity takes the form of a narrative because of its intrinsically historical nature. Precisely because "the formal quality of experience through time," as Crites argues, "is inherently narrative," personal identity as an interpretation of human experience takes the narrative form of autobiography. People are who they are because of the stories they tell about themselves, and, appearances aside, these stories preserve what is most important in the past and anticipate what is hoped for in the future. In this sense these stories or confessions are intensely personal. Yet they are not intensely private, for every personal identity narrative employs symbols, concepts, and categories of interpretation which have been inherited, appropriated or borrowed from a particular community and its traditions. In order to understand how personal stories are altered, transformed, and in some cased "redeemed," it is necessary that we first examine how the identity of a community, like that of individuals, takes the form of a narrative. Only then can we investigate the collision that takes place between the narrative identity of individuals and the stories of a community.

Chapter V
The Church's Narratives

Communities, like persons, have identities and the phrase "communal identity" has the same range of diverse meanings as does "personal identity." To speak of the "identity" of a particular community might be to refer to the sense in which it is continuous with communities in different historical periods. Or to speak of "communal identity" might be to refer to a specific character or quality in a community, to say something about what *kind* of community it is. In this chapter we will examine the nature of the community and the expression of communal identity by means of a narrative. Then we will turn from these formal considerations to a specific set of communities, those in the Christian tradition, and we will examine the function of narrative in the articulation of the Christian community's identity and the most important features of that narrative.

1. The Structure of Communal Identity

A community is a group of people who have come to share a common past, who understand particular events in the past to be

of decisive importance for interpreting the present, who anticipate the future by means of a shared hope, and who express their
identity by means of a common narrative. What was true of the
identity of persons is also true of that of communities—memory
is a necessary if not sufficient category for the description of communal identity. What distinguishes a community from a crowd
or a mob is a common memory which expresses itself in living
traditions and institutions. Such a description of community and
its dependence on memory is very similar to that which Josiah
Royce formulated some sixty years ago. He insisted that there is
a basic difference between a crowd, "whether it be a dangerous
mob, or an amiably joyous gathering at a picnic," and a true
community. Although there may be a sense in which the crowd
has a mind, it has "no institutions, no organization, no coherent
unity, no history, no traditions."[1] One of the essential features of
a community, therefore, which makes it something other than a
crowd is its shared memory and the common narrative by means
of which it interprets the past.[2] As was the case with the identity of persons, communal identity is both a historical and a
hermeneutical category. The language which the members of
a community have in common is rooted in history and functions as an interpretation of the past and an anticipation of the
future.

The community's common narrative is the glue that binds its
members together. To be a true participant in a community is to
share in that community's narratives, to recite the same stories as
the other members of the community, and to allow one's identity
to be shaped by them. If a person has only a casual acquaintance
with a community's stories and life, it is questionable to what
degree that person is a participant in the community. A person is
a member of a community only when he or she re-members with
the other members, only when the community's common narrative and the past it preserves are appropriated and extended into
the future, both the future of the community and that of the
individual. There is a decisive difference, therefore, between

those persons who participate casually in a community's life and those whose personal identities have been shaped by the community's stories, symbols, and rituals. Unless the community's narrative becomes the context for the interpretation of personal identity a person has not really become a member of that community; or as John Smith has argued, "When we engage ourselves or seek to be incorporated into a community, we at the same time accept certain extensions of ourselves: we identify ourselves with the common past and the common future of that community and accept both as part of our individual history."[3] What is perhaps less clear is how a community's past and the narratives by which it preserves that past become a part of an individual's personal history and identity. As we will see in Chapter VI, it is one thing to say that a person knows a community's narrative identity and something else entirely to say that a person becomes a part of that community's narrative. At issue is the fundamental question of whether redemption is primarily a private or a corporate reality. Does the community's past and its narratives serve as an example or a footnote to what has already been discovered and appropriated in personal identity, or is personal identity altered by the interpretive light which the community's narrative shines on personal history? For the moment our attention is focused on the nature of the community's identity and the narrative by means of which it articulates that identity.

In at least a formal sense there are several similarities between the narrative shape of personal identity and the community's narrative. The categories of "chronicle" and "interpretation" apply in both cases. A community's "chronicle" includes that series of events which is the community's common history. Part of what it means to identify oneself as a citizen of the United States is to acknowledge that the Revolutionary War and the settlement of the American frontier are events which are a part of one's communal history and are important for the interpretation of communal and personal identity. One American is bound to another in some semblance of community if both acknowledge a common history and its importance for the interpretation of their personal histories. In this sense there is a "common memory" and a shared narrative among the members of a community. As we observed in Chapter IV, the distinction between chronicle and interpretation is somewhat artificial because there is no such thing as an uninterpreted fact or event. It would not do to suggest that a community is constituted merely by a common past. It is more accurate to say that a community is constituted by a common memory in which the past is remembered and interpreted. Consequently it is not enough to say that a community is a collection of people who point to the same series of events in history. Of even greater importance are the categories and symbols by which the past is interpreted. Both Egypt and Israel could have understood the crossing of the Reed Sea to be a decisive event in their communal identity, but they could not be a part of the same community because the event has a wholly different interpretation for the Jews from what it has for the Egyptians. The categories of chronicle, history, and memory are as important for understanding the nature of communal identity as they are for interpreting personal identity. For most if not all communities, regardless of their size or structure, it is a common, remembered past which gives the community its distinctiveness and its sense of location in time and space. It is also this same remembered past which must be appropriated in order for any individual to become truly a member of a community and to participate in its common vision of the future, its hopes and dreams.

Although a case might be made that these formal categories of chronicle, history, and memory have a primordial status which makes them universally necessary for a proper description of communal identity, that kind of phenomenological claim is not our primary concern. Our particular interest is not the formal structure of human community but the peculiar nature of those communities that claim to be a part of the Christian tradition. Virtually all Christian communities share certain common features, not the least of which is that each appeals in some fashion to Scripture as an indispensable resource for interpreting its identity and world. Thus in order to describe the narrative identity of the Christian community we must examine the nature of biblical narrative and its function in the Christian community.

2. Biblical Narrative

There is a considerable portion of the Bible that cannot be described as narrative. Most of the Wisdom literature, many texts in the prophetic material, the New Testament epistles, poems, hymns, and creeds are clearly not of the genre of narrative, if categories such as "plot" (what Scholes and Kellogg describe as "the dynamic, sequential element in narrative literature") and "character" are essential features of that genre.[4] The Bible is not, however, primarily a collection of Wisdom sayings or religious propositions, but a proclamation and confession that points to God's grace and presence at decisive moments in the history and pre-history of God's people. The core of Scripture is a set of narratives which serve as the common denominator for the whole of Scripture. These narratives vary in form and content but each of them functions as an explanation for what Israel and the church believe and why they live the way they do. While these narratives or stories do not make up the whole of Scripture, some of the most significant non-narrative material in the Bible is concerned with the hermeneutical questions of how these narratives should be interpreted and how they should function in the life of the community that recites them. Although Deuteronomy is not itself a narrative, it is deeply concerned about the question of the relation between narrative and communal identity. But before we examine Deuteronomy and the function of narrative we must first look at the nature of biblical narrative.

It is difficult to apply one category of narrative to the whole of Scripture and impossible to do so if that is taken to mean that all forms of biblical narrative are cut from a common cloth. The Bible consists of various kinds of narratives and they differ significantly in their form, structure, and function. Some biblical narratives seem to be reports of historical events; that is, they narrate events in the history of Israel and the church which are decisive for faith, events which according to the narratives happened at a particular time and place. The events described in Exodus 14, the encounter between Pharaoh's army and the people of Israel "encamped at the sea, by Pi-ha-hi'roth, in front of Ba'al-zephon" (Exod. 14:9), have a historical reference in the sense that the story of the expulsion of Adam and Eve from Eden in Genesis 3 does not. Both narratives may be "true" but only in different senses of the word. At the heart of Israel's confession of faith (Deut. 26:5 ff.) is a claim about an event in history ("and the LORD brought us out of Egypt with a mighty hand and an outstretched arm" [Deut. 26:8]) and the truth of Israel's faith stands or falls with that claim.[5] The story in Genesis 3 of the "fall" of Adam and Eve may be "true" in the sense that it articulates the human experience of sin as flight from God, the violation of a covenant, but it would be a serious mistake to assume that the story is true only insofar as it refers to an event that happened at a particular moment which, at least in principle, is open to historical investigation.

The problem is that some narratives in Hebrew Scripture do make claims about historical events and others do not. The truth of the former is at least partially subject to the results of historical investigation, but there are other narratives, such as Genesis 3 and many of the patriarchal narratives, which appeal to a different order of truth.[6] The same is true in the New Testament. If it could be demonstrated conclusively that Jesus of Nazareth did not die on a cross in Jerusalem but died of old age in Galilee, then the core claims of Christian faith, such as those in Acts 10:34–43, would no longer be true. They might be true symbolically as statements about what is noble and meaningful in human behavior, but that is a different kind of truth claim than that made by the text in its final form. Because both the Hebrew Scriptures and the New Testament consist of such a rich variety of narratives it is difficult to conclude that there is one genre to which all forms of biblical narrative belong. One of the important contributions form criticism has made to our understanding of Scripture is to draw our attention to its diversity of genre. Some narratives have the form of chronicle or history and clearly make claims about historical events. Other narratives serve a different function and should not be read as historical reports.

But even if one grants that there are different kinds of narrative in the Bible there are still many important, unresolved questions about the nature of biblical narrative. For example, what kind of narrative do we encounter in the creation stories in Genesis 1 and 2? In some circles these texts have been read as "history," as empirical, if not scientific, descriptions of how the universe came into being. In more enlightened quarters these stories are understood to be myths, of the same genre as other ancient Near Eastern creation stories, perhaps functioning as poetic and symbolic statements of the nature of the human condition. Karl Barth, on the other hand, insists that these creation stories are neither history nor myth but what he calls "saga."[7] The creation stories form a "connected history" and do describe specific events, but these events are neither history nor non-history but what Barth designates as "pre-historical history." For theological reasons Barth insists that what we call "history" is from God's perspective not history but pre-history. Genesis 1 and 2 describe the beginning of creation, of human time, but creation is intelligible only in the context of God's covenant of grace; "the first and genuine time which is the prototype of time is not the time of creation but that of the reconciliation for which the world and man were created in the will and by the operation of God."[8] The creation stories, therefore, refer to events in time and space but they are about events which are not in but prior to human history. The stories are not myths, because as Barth understands it a myth does not really refer to "definite times and place" but to "the essential principles of the general realities and relationships of the natural and spiritual cosmos."[9] The stories are not myth but saga, "an intuitive and poetic picture of a pre-historical reality of history which is enacted once and for all within the confines of time and space."[10] Although Barth believes that the narratives in Genesis 1 and 2 are "pure saga," he does not argue that all biblical narratives are of the same genre. On the contrary, he readily admits that in some biblical narratives "we have pure and more or less incontestable 'history.'"[11]

Two difficult problems emerge from Barth's discussion. One concerns the relation among the different kinds of narrative in Scripture and the broader issue of the relation of narrative to non-narrative texts in Scripture. If some biblical narratives are "saga" and others are "history" how are they related to each other? Is there any relation between non-narrative texts, such as most Wisdom literature, and narrative texts? The second problem is related to the first. Are there some biblical texts that lend themselves to one method of interpretation and analysis but not to others? That is, are there some narratives akin to what Barth described as "saga" which do not appear to be susceptible to historical-critical inquiry?

Borrowing from Karl Barth's *Church Dogmatics* and Eric Auerbach's *Mimesis*, Hans Frei develops the thesis that biblical narrative is "realistic." Realistic narrative is not history but what Frei calls "history-like." Realistic narrative renders a world or the identity of an agent or to use Auerbach's phrase it offers a "representation of reality" which cannot be separated from the narrative itself. The subject of the narrative cannot be divorced from the narrative because it is the narrative that renders the subject, and precisely because biblical narrative is realistic, there are appropriate and inappropriate ways of reading it. According to

Frei, a realistic reading of Scripture has become rare because of hermeneutical developments in the eighteenth and nineteenth centuries. In the Enlightenment the literal sense of a text was no longer understood to be identical with the historical or "real" sense of the text, and the result, as Frei describes it, was "the breakup of the cohesion between the literal meaning of the biblical narratives and their reference to actual events." [12] In precritical interpretations of Scripture, those by Luther and Calvin for example, the literal or grammatical meaning of the text was understood to be identical "with the text's subject matter, i.e., its historical reference, its doctrinal content, and its meaningfulness as life description and prescription." [13] But during and after the Enlightenment the nature of hermeneutics underwent a drastic change and the consequences were enormous for biblical interpretation. Quite simply, the categories of meaning and truth were no longer understood to cohere in any realistic text. The meaning of a realistic narrative, its literal sense, could be uncovered by grammatical study, but the determination of the meaning of the text was no longer understood to be the resolution of the question of its truth. Meaning and truth became distinct categories, and the question of meaning no longer cohered with the question of truth. A literal or grammatical reading of a text may disclose its "meaning," which is simply what the narrative depicts, but if the reader wants to know whether the narrative is "true" then it must be determined whether the claim of the text (its "literal meaning") coheres with some referent external to the text, such as a "historical fact." The assumption that meaning and truth do not necessarily cohere, that the world of the text is not the "real" world of historical event, that the truth of a narrative is a matter of the correspondence between its claim and its historical referent make it virtually impossible to read a text "realistically."

With the emergence of the historical-critical method in the eighteenth and nineteenth centuries the realistic reading of Scripture all but vanished from the theological world, with the exception of Barth, who should not be confused with those fundamentalists who eschew everything since the Reformation and continue to pretend they live in the first or sixteenth century. The historical-critical method is both a method and an interpretation of the nature of reality and historical inquiry. Those "methods" which usually are gathered under the rubric of "historical criticism," such as source criticism and form and redaction criticism, share certain common features with each other. Understanding the text means looking behind or outside of the text at its development or formation, historical setting, the theological intentions of the author, and at parallels in other religious or cultural traditions. In every case what one examines in order to interpret and understand the text is something external to the text itself. The historical-critical method has attained such influence in twentieth-century biblical scholarship that figures such as Barth and Frei strike the modern reader as anomalies.

But in the last few years serious questions have been raised about the apparent hegemony of the historical-critical method. The most important of these questions have not been raised by fundamentalists or conservative critics of modern scholarship but by biblical and systematic theologians who have been schooled in the critical methods but who have begun to doubt that these methods provide all that is necessary in order to understand fully every biblical text.[14] Questions about the limits and function of the historical-critical method have been prompted in many cases by two major concerns. In the first place, while critical methodologies illumine *some* dimensions of a biblical text, do they in fact provide the perspective necessary for a full understanding of the text? Are historical-critical methods sufficient in themselves for understanding a text or must they be supplemented by other approaches and methods? Given that most historical-critical methods, perhaps with the exception of redaction criticism, take the text apart in order to examine its sources, parallels, and development, do they also enable the reader to understand the text as a whole, what might be called the final form of the text? In order to understand the text in its final form, as the reader encounters it, some contemporary interpreters have begun to apply the canons and methods of literary criticism. One need not go to an extreme position and argue that literary criticism provides the *only* method for understanding the text, an argument which may be implicit in Frei's position, for that would be to repeat the hubris that may have come to characterize historical criticism. The issue is not whether the reader must decide between historical criticism or a narrative interpretation of the text, but whether the methods peculiar to both perspectives can be utilized for a richer, fuller understanding of Scripture.

The second concern that prompts the reappraisal of historical criticism is the relation between Scripture and the church. Unfortunately it does not seem that historical criticism has enhanced the church's understanding of Scripture or, perhaps more importantly, that many practitioners of historical criticism are even concerned with that issue. It may well be that such a state of affairs cannot be attributed to the method itself but only to those who utilize it. Still, in the enormous mass of literature spawned by historical criticism (consider the *Journal of Biblical Literature*, for example) there is little evidence of a concern for interpreting Scripture in the context of the life and history of the Christian community. Yet the Bible is the church's book and one might expect any critical approach to the text to be concerned at least in part with the question of what it means to interpret the text in the context of the community that uses it to understand and interpret reality. [15]

This twofold concern for the final form of the text and the role of Scripture in the church's history and life has resulted in the emergence of what has come to be known as "canonical criticism." For biblical scholars such as Brevard Childs and James Sanders canonical criticism occasionally resembles that pre-critical approach to Scripture Hans Frei describes as "figural reading," although precisely what is meant by canonical criticism and the nature of its method varies among its several practitioners.[16]

Apart from the legitimate questions that have been raised about the limits and proper function of historical criticism there also seem to be significant hermeneutical reasons for arguing that biblical narrative must be interpreted in its wholeness. One important reason this must be done, as we have noted, is that Scripture plays an indispensable role in the life and self-understanding of the Christian community. While historical-critical methods may tell us much about the development and formation of the text, the understanding and interpretation of Scripture may entail additional questions about the role of the text in the life of the community.

This latter form of understanding does not imply that the Christian reader can or should dispense with historical-critical inquiry. Precisely because of the essential role that Scripture plays in the Christian community, genuine concern for the text in its wholeness, what might be described as a theological reading of the text, demands that the reader employ historical-critical methods of interpreting the text. There are two basic reasons for that demand. In the first place, one of the great benefits of historical criticism has been that it constantly reminds the reader of his or her distance from the text. By exploring the text's relation to the religious and cultural influences of the ancient world historical criticism reminds the reader of the strangeness and alien character of Scripture and in so doing makes it difficult for the reader too quickly to embrace and domesticate the text. It is the very "otherness" of the text which creates and sustains dialogue between the text and the reader, and in part (but only in part) this otherness is due to the historical and cultural "alienation" of the reader from the text. Those "story theologies," therefore, which describe a smooth encounter between the reader's identity ("my story") and Scripture ("the story") do a serious injustice to

Scripture and to the complexity of the reader's relation to the text. The encounter may eventually involve some degree of appropriation on the reader's part, but a more appropriate metaphor for describing the initial encounter between reader and text is that of "collision." Historical criticism, when properly used, warns the reader that the text may not conform easily to the reader's world and expectations. Indeed, the text may stand over against the reader and make claims that the reader would prefer not to hear, such as in Amos 5:21–24 and Matthew 25:31–46. It is this "otherness" in the text uncovered by historical criticism which serves as a check on the reader's idolatrous impulses. Historical criticism does not allow the reader to "claim" the text too quickly, and that is one reason some interpreters believe that historical criticism is a hermeneutical consequence of the Reformation doctrine of justification.[17] Both the doctrine of justification, as an interpretation of the meaning of the cross, and historical criticism function as critical principles which stand in judgment of all human forms of idolatry, all attempts to replace faith and dependence on God's grace with some form of human achievement, be it a theological system or a particular interpretation and appropriation of Scripture.

Secondly, the Christian reader must use historical criticism because when all is said and done Christian faith and Scripture refer to historical events and historical criticism enhances the reader's understanding of Scripture's witness to those events. Certainly not all texts in Scripture refer to historical events, just as not all texts in Scripture represent some form of narrative, but most passages, including sagas and realistic narratives, presuppose a narrative core which is based on the interpretation of specific historical events. That does not mean that historical criticism can give the reader a full understanding of the text and its claims about reality. As Barth and Frei have ably demonstrated, there are some biblical texts which require a different approach than that presupposed by historical criticism if their claims are to be properly heard and understood. The narratives about the patriarchs and much of the material in the Gospels require both historical-critical investigation and a theological reading. Regardless of the nature of the narrative, historical-critical inquiry is indispensable because biblical narrative and Christian faith are based finally on claims made about historical events, such as the creeds in Deuteronomy 26:5–9 and 1 Corinthians 15:3–7 demonstrate. Historical criticism enables the reader to understand better how Scripture interprets these events.

At the center of Scripture is a set of narratives and these narratives are the frame around which the whole of Scripture is constructed. Apart from these narratives the Prophets would not be intelligible and without the frame of the Gospel narratives it would be difficult to understand the full meaning of the parables, epistles, creeds, and hymns of the New Testament. It may be that there is something distinctive about the way in which a person perceives the world from the perspective of Christian faith and that this distinctiveness is due to the parabolic or metaphoric character of faith itself, but while faith may be parabolic the parable is not the primary genre in the New Testament.[18] The narrative frame of the Gospels provides the necessary context for the interpretation of the parable and without this narrative frame the parables could be read simply as aphorisms.[19] Set as they are in a narrative frame parables illumine the meaning of the Gospels, but apart from their narrative context they would be open to several interpretations.

The most intriguing question is why narrative is such a primary genre in Scripture. We have suggested that there are two basic reasons why this is the case, one philosophical and sociological, and the other theological. The identity of a community like that of a person requires the interpretation of historical experience, and narrative seems to be the appropriate literary genre for articulating and interpreting the past. Narrative embodies the shared memory and communal history which binds individuals together into a community. Secondly, the faith of Jews and Christians is radically thisworldly and historical. Redemption and salvation are not just images or ideas but realities which are understood to be rooted in events that happen in the past and realities which continue to unfold in the present and future. It is no accident, therefore, that the structure of the Pentateuch, as James Sanders observes, "is not that of a law code but rather that of a narrative."[20] One need not argue the extreme position of Amos Wilder that narrative "is uniquely important in Christianity" in order to grant his conclusion that Christian confession always takes the form of a narrative.[21] It does so not simply because narrative is the primary genre in Scripture but because the very nature of what it is that the Christian wants to confess requires narrative as the necessary literary form. The Christian confession refers to events that have taken place in history, events which are understood to have redemptive and transforming significance, events which "live" in the sense that they continue to imbue the present with meaning and evoke hope in the future.

The Christian community gives expression to its identity by means of a narrative that begins, "A wandering Aramean was my father" (Deut. 26:5), culminates in the confession "that Christ died for our sins in accordance with the scriptures, that he was buried, that he was raised on the third day in accordance with the scriptures" (1 Cor. 15:3–4), and continues in the narrative history of the church through the ages as it witnesses to the coming kingdom of God. This narrative which binds the church together and links it to other Christian communities in the past and other Christian traditions in the present begins with but is not limited to the narratives of Scripture. Christian narrative, as we will see, begins with biblical narratives but it also includes the history of their appropriation by previous Christian communities and the interpretation of that tradition in the present. In this sense Christian narrative is a living tradition and is always "open" to reinterpretation regardless of whether the biblical canon is open. Because of its function in this larger narrative, what we will describe in Chapter VIII as its "authority," biblical narrative plays a normative and indispensable role in every Christian community's attempt to appropriate the Christian story and extend it into the personal and social existence of those who make up the community. If we examine Scripture itself we discover that it acknowledges the primacy of narrative and provides us with clues as to how the narrative should function in the interpretation and appropriation of Christian faith. In order to understand better the nature of biblical narrative and its function in the Christian community we will look briefly at Deuteronomy and the Gospel of Mark.

3. Narrative and Torah

The book of Deuteronomy is not itself a narrative, but it has much to say about the function of narrative in Israel's faith and life. The religious and theological issue in Deuteronomy is nothing less than the question of Israel's identity. Most of Deuteronomy is written in the form of a sermon by Moses and consists of a list of "statutes and ordinances." The people of Israel will find their true and proper identity in the covenant with Yahweh if they keep the commandments of the covenant. The covenant between Yahweh and the people of Israel is not just something that happened once in the distant past, but is a living reality in the present. "The LORD our God made a covenant with us in Horeb. Not with our fathers did the LORD make this covenant, but with us, who are all of us here alive this day" (5:2–3). Hence the life and faith of the people of Israel are bound up with a narrative which recounts the salvific history of Israel's relation to Yahweh, a narrative which appears in the abbreviated form of a creed in Deuteronomy 26:5–9:

"A wandering Aramean was my father; and he went down into Egypt and sojourned there, few in number; and there he became a nation, great, mighty, and populous. And the Egyptians treated us harshly, and afflicted us, and laid upon us hard bondage. Then we cried to the LORD the God of our fathers, and the LORD heard our voice, and saw our affliction, our toil, and our oppression; and the LORD brought us out of Egypt with a mighty hand and an outstretched arm, with great terror, with signs and wonders; and he brought us into this place and gave us this land, a land flowing with milk and honey."

Neither this text nor a similar passage in Joshua 24:2 ff. are narratives as such. They are more akin to a creed or a confession of faith, but as confessions they do formally summarize and presuppose an oral narrative about decisive events in Israel's history. Creeds do not appear *ex nihilo*, and in this instance Israel's creed obviously is a carefully constructed summary of oral and perhaps written narratives which rehearse Israel's history and are the basis of Israel's religious faith and cultic activity.

There is a clear relation between creed and narrative in Israel's faith. The creed presupposes and summarizes a narrative and in turn is interpreted by the familiar narratives of the Pentateuch. As von Rad rightly observed, "If we imagine a considerably greater advance still in this process of connecting a narrative to the old pattern and widening its theological range by means of all kinds of traditional material, then we find ourselves face to face with the work of the Yahwist or the Elohist."[22] The narratives of the Pentateuch are theological expansions of the faith summarized in the confessional formula, but the creed itself is a summary or recapitulation of "the main events in the saving history from the time of the patriarchs (by the Aramean, Jacob is meant) down to the conquest, and they do this with close concentration on the objective historical facts."[23] While there may be those who would question von Rad's description of these events as "objective historical facts," still the creed does refer to and is based on a series of interpreted historical events which from the beginning of Israel's existence no doubt assumed the form of a narrative.

The function and content of these creeds suggest several obvious facts about Israel's faith. First, it is clear that Israel's faith is not primarily a philosophy about life nor a cosmic, mystical speculation about the structures of the universe. Israel's faith is earthy, tangible, and concrete. It refers first and last to specific historical events in its collective past in which it believes Yahweh has been decisively and redemptively at work. The arena of human history is the only context in which Israel can articulate and confess what it believes. Secondly, because the Hebrew Scriptures refer repeatedly to a series of historical events, summarized in these early creeds, the genre of narrative is both formally and materially indispensable for a proper understanding of Israel's faith. The reference to historical events explains why the genre of narrative is of such overwhelming importance to Israel, why the Pentateuch is built on a narrative frame rather than that of a law code or a collection of wisdom sayings. As we have seen, history necessarily assumes narrative form in its recounting and interpreting of what happened. At the material level, narrative directs our attention to several features of Israel's faith—its belief that Yahweh is encountered in the midst of the earthy events of the everyday world, that the God it worships is encountered not just in Israel's past but also in its present and future, that this God has "covenanted" with Israel. Thirdly, not only does Israel's faith refer to historical events, and not only does narrative become the decisive form for Israel's confession, but Israel's faith does not and cannot survive if it is cut off from or forgets this narrative.

A theme that resounds throughout Deuteronomy and indeed throughout Hebrew Scripture is that Israel's faith cannot be extricated from its narrative of salvation history. Israel must not forget nor forsake that narrative, not simply because it is an intrinsically worthwhile narrative, but because apart from the narrative with which Israel confesses its faith what it says and does as a community is unintelligible. Nowhere is this more apparent than in Deuteronomy 6. At the center of what Israel believes about Yahweh is the "shema" in Deuteronomy 6:4–5:

> "Hear, O Israel: The LORD is our God, the LORD alone; and you shall love the LORD your God with all your heart, and with all your soul, and with all your might."[24]

Of all the testimonies and the statutes and the ordinances which govern Israel's life and prescribe its behavior this is the most important, and it is these words which Israel is commanded to carry in its heart, to teach to its children, and to write "on the doorposts of your house and on your gates" (Deut. 6:6–9). Yet as important as this commandment is, if Israel's faith rested only on these words it would not long endure. The commandment to love God with all one's being is neither self-explanatory nor self-sustaining. The writers of Deuteronomy are acutely aware that in a culture where various religious faiths contend for allegiance or in a nation that has grown fat and prosperous it is not self-evident why one should love God, why one should honor Yahweh ("You shall fear the LORD your God; you shall serve him, and swear by his name" [6:13]) rather than pursuing other gods ("the gods of the peoples who are round about you" [6:14]). The temptation to "forget the LORD your God, who brought you out of the land of Egypt, out of the house of bondage" (8:14) cannot be resisted simply on the basis of an apodictic commandment.

The simple questions children ask are the same ones that lie hidden in the routine with which adults smother their doubts. Why should one love God with all one's heart and soul and might (Deut. 6:5)? Or, as the writers of Deuteronomy put the question in the mouths of children, "What is the meaning of the testimonies and the statutes and the ordinances which the LORD our God has commanded you?" (6:20). The answer to those questions cannot be an appeal to the intrinsic authority of the command itself. The point here is that one does not love God because it is

the right thing to do or because that is what the child's parents
have always done and custom dictates that the child do the same.
As far as the writers of Deuteronomy are concerned, the "because"
that answers the child's question is a narrative that begins, "We
were Pharaoh's slaves in Egypt; and the LORD brought us out of
Egypt with a mighty hand" (6:21). The meaning, function, and
authority of the testimonies, statutes, and ordinances are intelligible only if we understand their setting in relation to this narrative by which Israel confesses its faith and articulates its communal identity.

What the writers of Deuteronomy fear most is the possibility
of Israel's apostasy, that having occupied the promised land Israel
will forget whose she is and whence she came and will trust in
her own strength and righteousness or turn to the graven images
of local deities. That path clearly will lead to Israel's destruction,
but it need not be Israel's future as long as she remembers the
narrative history of her faith.

> "And if you forget the LORD your God and go after other gods and
> serve them and worship them, I solemnly warn you this day that
> you shall surely perish."
>
> (8:19)

With each succeeding generation, however, Israel's creed recedes
into the past and becomes more difficult to appropriate. In fact,
the problem for the writers of Deuteronomy was how new generations were to appropriate a narrative in which the saving
events had become ancient history.[25]

The Deuteronomists' solution is the oft repeated injunction
that Israel "remember and not forget" its narrative history. But
memory for the Deuteronomists is not simply a matter of "calling
to mind." Remembering for the Deuteronomists, as Brevard
Childs has argued, occurs "when the worshipper experiences an
identification with the original events."[26]

No longer has Israel direct access to the redemptive events of the past. Now memory takes on central theological significance. Present Israel has not been cut off from redemptive history, but she encounters the same covenant God through a living tradition. Memory provides the link between past and present.[27]

In remembering, Israel "actualizes" its past, but the process of actualization is subject neither to mythical nor to historical analysis. When Israel remembers and in so doing actualizes the past it does not and cannot return to the events themselves. They happened once and for all at a given point in history and cannot be repeated, although they may be re-presented. Yet the redemptive events in Israel's history are not lost to the contemporary generation. They are redemptive events and as such they are accessible to later generations, for when Israel "responded to the continuing imperative of her tradition through her memory, that moment in historical time likewise became an Exodus experience."

> Not in the sense that later Israel again crossed the Red Sea. This was an irreversible, once-for-all event. Rather, Israel entered the same redemptive reality of the Exodus generation.[28]

The God to whom Israel is related in the covenant is known only in and through Yahweh's redemptive activity in Israel's history. Memory, therefore, serves an indispensable twofold function. It is the basis of everything Israel knows about Yahweh and it provides Israel access to the redemptive power of Yahweh's mighty acts. It is not surprising that from the Deuteronomists' perspective the greatest mistake Israel could possibly make would be to forget, to cease to remember.

Furthermore, there is a dialectical relationship between the narrative of redemptive history and the testimonies, statutes, and ordinances which govern Israel's life. On the one hand, the Deuteronomists believe that Israel's narrative history is the necessary context for understanding and obeying the law, be it the law at Sinai (5:6–21), the Shema (6:4–9), or the various statutes in chapters 12—25. The writers counsel Israel to teach its children the meaning of the Torah by retelling Israel's redemptive history. Even the commandments of the decalogue (Deut. 5:7–21 and Exod. 20:3–17) are prefaced by the reference to Israel's redemptive narrative, "I am the LORD your God, who brought you out of the land of Egypt, out of the house of bondage." The Deuteronomists argue clearly and unequivocally that apart from this narrative history Israel's testimonies, statutes, and ordinances have no meaning and will soon be discarded. On the other hand, although this narrative is the necessary context for understanding the meaning of Israel's Torah, the other side of the dialectic is that the narrative cannot be recited casually and disinterestedly. It is a narrative that demands to be embodied and lived and Israel's statutes provide the context for the enactment of the narrative. By honoring its covenant with Yahweh and obeying the statutes and ordinances Israel remembers its redemptive history, for the most important recital of the narrative is not simply its retelling but its enactment and embodiment by each generation.[29] Part of what it means to obey Yahweh's commandments is to recite Israel's redemptive history, and to remember that narrative is to honor and obey its statutes and testimonies. To refuse to worship other gods ("the gods of the peoples who are round about you" [6:14]), to obey the first commandment ("You shall have no other gods before me" [5:7]), is to enact and embody Israel's redemptive narrative. The two go hand in hand and the one is unintelligible apart from the other.

Later generations of Israelites participate in the Exodus when they observe the statutes and testimonies. The Deuteronomists are concerned that these new generations know how to respond to their children's questions simply in order to preserve the Torah. The statute itself is neither sacred nor inherently meaningful. The Deuteronomists' concern is that the dialectic between statute and narrative be preserved because that is the only way in which subsequent generations can actualize Israel's narrative history and participate in its redemptive power.

> And Moses summoned all Israel, and said to them, "Hear, O Israel, the statutes and the ordinances which I speak in your hearing this day, and you shall learn them and be careful to do them. The LORD our God made a covenant with us in Horeb. Not with our fathers did the Lord make this covenant, but with us, who are all of us here alive this day."
>
> (Deut. 5:1–3)

4. The Identity of the Crucified One

The theme of "identity" is not the peculiar concern of the writers of Hebrew Scripture. In different forms it is a major theme in most of the literature of the New Testament as well, although the sense in which identity is understood has been significantly altered. In the Hebrew Scriptures the identity of the individual Jew is to be found in the narrative history of Yahweh's people, in the covenant narrative that describes Israel's relation to Yahweh. In the New Testament, on the other hand, an important reversal takes place and it is in the narrative history of one individual Jew that the community discovers its identity.[30] The Gospel narratives identify who Jesus of Nazareth really is and in so doing also identify the community of those who are a new creation in him. Perhaps the most illuminating example of how the identity question emerges in the New Testament is the Gospel of Mark.

For some time Mark's Gospel has fascinated and intrigued readers of the New Testament. Taken strictly as a piece of literature it is a puzzle to most interpreters. The Gospel narrative loosely weaves historical incidents, sayings, myths, and parables into one tapestry which succeeds in leading the reader, in T. S. Eliot's memorable phrase, "to one overwhelming question" almost in spite of itself. The narrative seems at times disjointed and lurches from one setting and incident to another without reason or explanation. In the midst of the unfolding narrative certain themes appear so often they could be interpreted as the heavy-handed work of a clumsy editor. Repeatedly the reader observes Jesus perform some demonstration of unusual authority— a healing miracle or an encounter with demons—and hears Jesus instruct the person healed to keep what has happened a secret; "See that you say nothing to any one; but go, show yourself to the priest, and offer for your cleansing what Moses commanded, for a proof to the people" (1:44). Although this motif of the "messianic secret" was not invented by Mark and probably was present in earlier tradition, still Mark clearly uses the motif for his own literary and theological purposes.

On another level the reader notices a tension in the titles attributed to Jesus in Mark's Gospel. Except for his encounter with the demons (in 3:7–12 and 5:1–13, for example) and the centurion's speech in 15:39, Mark does not let Jesus identify himself as "the Christ" or "the Son of God" or allow others to identify him by that title. He speaks of himself in terms of the title "Son of Man," and a mysterious tension builds in the narrative between these two titles and the christologies that stand behind them.[31]

In addition to these puzzling themes in Mark's narrative there is the crucial question about the purpose of Mark's Gospel. Is it a narrative, a story of sorts, or is it more properly described as a sermon, a piece of kerygma addressed to a community in a specific situation in the first century, or perhaps a summons for the community to engage in missionary activity? Or is Mark's Gospel a polemic designed to refute perverse interpretations of the Christian faith? Or is it not so much a story or a sermon or a polemic as it is a didactic piece of literature written for the instruction and edification of the reader? It is difficult if not impossible to confine Mark's narrative to any one of these categories. Clearly Mark's Gospel includes many of these themes and it is not sur-

prising that there is no consensus among Mark's modern interpreters about the book's real purpose. According to Nils Dahl,
Mark is not "presenting the solution to something which has
been an unanswered riddle; he is emphasizing the mysterious
character of something with which his readers are familiar."[32]
Mark's purpose is paraenetic, to instruct his readers, who are already believers, in the true meaning of the gospel. Mark reminds
them of the mystery at the heart of the gospel in order to warn
them "against self-sufficiency and ambitious striving."[33] The
church Mark addresses is "in danger of taking the Gospel for
granted."[34]

Norman Perrin reads Mark's narrative somewhat differently.
He understands Mark to be a "realistic" or mimetic narrative
which has the remarkable power to draw the reader into the story.
Mark's real genius, according to Perrin, is his ability to create a
narrative which involves the reader "in the gospel story as a whole
rather than in some particular part of it."[35] Like most other interpreters of Mark, Perrin believes the geography of the narrative
discloses something about its structure and meaning. "Mark's
purpose is to catch the attention of his readers and lead him from
Galilee through Caesarea Philippi to Jerusalem and the empty
tomb, and to the realization that he, the reader, is being challenged to discipleship in the context of the prospect of the coming Jesus as Son of Man."[36]

Regardless of whether one agrees with Perrin's interpretation
of Mark's "realism" or with his description of the role of the disciples and the conflict between the christologies represented by
the two titles "Son of God" and "Son of Man," Perrin, like Dahl,
focuses our attention on the whole of Mark's Gospel. At the center of Mark's Gospel is the question that serves as the fulcrum for
the narrative—the question about Jesus' identity: who is Jesus of
Nazareth and what does it mean to call him "the Christ"? Not
only does Mark confront the reader with this question, but he
poses the question in such a manner that it cannot be answered

disinterestedly. He poses the question that way because the issue of Jesus' true identity is finally inseparable from the question of what it means to be a disciple of him. Hence Mark's Gospel is an "identity narrative" in a twofold sense. It is a narrative that identifies who Jesus is and in so doing raises the question of whether the reader is truly a disciple of him.

Mark's Gospel can be divided into three parts, which correspond to the shifting geography of the narrative.[37] The first part, following the introduction in 1:1–13, extends from Mark's summary of Jesus' ministry in 1:14–15 to a more detailed description of his activity in Galilee (1:16—6:13) and in the country beyond (6:14—8:21). Chapter 4 in this section is one of the two passages in Mark's Gospel that appears to come from the tradition of Jesus' sayings.[38]

Two themes run through this section and hold together the various smaller units that make up the whole. The first of these, the question of Jesus' true identity, is prompted by the authority that Jesus exercises in the narrative. Of all the characters in the story, including members of Jesus' family and his disciples, only the demons know who he really is. "What have you to do with us, Jesus of Nazareth? Have you come to destroy us? I know who you are, the Holy One of God" (1:24).[39] The question of Jesus' identity is intensified by the issue of his authority. The whole of Jesus' ministry—his exorcisms, teaching, association with tax collectors and other undesirables—and the wonder it evokes raise questions about his authority. "Why does this man speak thus? It is blasphemy! Who can forgive sins but God alone?" (2:7). It is the authority with which Jesus acts—what he says and does— that lends urgency to the question of his identity. The messianic secret is the device Mark uses to link the question of Jesus' identity to his exercise of authority. Jesus is only properly identified following those incidents in which he demonstrates remarkable authority. Mark's use of the secrecy motif suggests to the reader that the tension between who Jesus is and what he does awaits some future consummation and should not be prematurely resolved. To link Jesus' identity with his healing ministry would mean that the authority that he exercises is supremely and magnificently human. Even here, in the earliest sections of the narrative, the reader senses the foreboding shadows of later events, events which disclose that the authority Jesus exercises is not simply magnificently human.

The second theme, closely related to the first, is the inability or unwillingness of all the characters in Mark's story, except the demons, to understand who Jesus is. In the face of repeated acts of healing and exorcism Jesus' family can come only to the conclusion that "He is beside himself" (3:21). And the scribes concur, "He is possessed of Be-el'zebul, and by the prince of demons he casts out the demons" (3:22). No matter what Jesus says and does those closest to him appear unable to understand what he does and who he is. Appropriately this section of Mark's narrative concludes with an incident which summarizes the preceding events. In 8:1–10 Mark describes Jesus' feeding of four thousand people from seven loaves and a few small fish, a story similar to the feeding of the five thousand people in 6:30–44. In 8:14–21 the disciples are in a boat with only one loaf of bread, and they worry about whether they will have enough to eat. Jesus reminds them of the baskets of food left over after the feedings of the five thousand and the four thousand, and asks, "Do you not yet perceive or understand? Are your hearts hardened? Having eyes do you not see, and having ears do you not hear? And do you not remember?" (8:17–18).

The second section of Mark's Gospel, 8:22—10:52, is an interlude that separates Jesus' ministry in Galilee and the surrounding country from his journey to Jerusalem and his Passion. This section is bracketed by two healing stories (8:22–26 and 10:46–52) in which Jesus restores the sight of a blind man at Bethsaida and repeats the miracle at Jericho with the blind beggar, Bartimaeus. In light of what takes place in this section Mark's selection of these two stories about Jesus' healing of blindness may seem somewhat heavy-handed.

This brief section poses the major questions and sounds the dominant themes in Mark's narrative. Mark gives us three similar stories (8:27–33, 9:30–32, and 10:32–34) in which Jesus predicts the events that await him in Jerusalem and tries to prepare the disciples for his crucifixion. In each case the disciples either do not believe or fail to understand. Jesus then speaks to them about the meaning of discipleship (8:34–38, 9:33–37, and 10:35–45). Here Mark clearly links the question of who Jesus is—what it means to be the Christ—with the question of the meaning of discipleship. The one entails the other; it is not possible to separate the question of what kind of Christ Jesus is from the question of what is involved in being a disciple of him.

The major event in this section is Jesus' encounter with Peter at Caesarea Philippi (8:27–38).[40] Indeed this incident serves as the fulcrum for all of Mark's Gospel. The overwhelming question which Jesus addresses to Peter is the same question Mark's narrative asks of the reader; "But who do you say that I am?" (8:29). And apparently Peter answered correctly. "Peter answered him, 'You are the Christ.' And he charged them to tell no one about him" (8:29–30). But to call Jesus the Christ is only to attribute a title to him and titles can have various meanings. Whatever Peter understood by the title "Christ" it had little to do with what was about to happen to Jesus. Mark has Jesus explain to the disciples that the Son of Man must suffer at the hands of the chief priests and be killed, and Mark tells us that Jesus "said this plainly." Hearing this prediction Peter rebukes Jesus. Apparently his Christ is not one who suffers and dies. Jesus' response to Peter is a refusal to be what others expect him to be. "Get behind me, Satan! For you are not on the side of God, but of men" (8:33).

In the following verses, 8:34–38, Mark links the identity of Jesus as the Christ to the meaning of discipleship. What it means to be a disciple of Jesus ("If any man would come after me . . .")

is to be a disciple of the crucified Christ. Such a discipleship is not one of power and glory but a discipleship of suffering and death ("let him deny himself and take up his cross and follow me").

The third and final section of Mark's narrative, 11:1—16:8, consists of Jesus' entry into Jerusalem, the apocalyptic discourse in chapter 13, and the story of the Passion in chapters 14 and 15. Just as Jesus' encounter with Peter at Caesarea Philipi is the fulcrum for Mark's Gospel and sets the stage for what is to follow, so the culmination of the narrative is Jesus' crucifixion, the cry of dereliction in 15:34, and the centurion's confession in 15:39. Of all the figures in Mark's narrative the centurion presumedly knew Jesus less well than any of the others, certainly not as well as Jesus' followers and disciples, all of whom at this point in the story have disappeared. "And they all forsook him, and fled" (14:50). Yet it is the stranger, the centurion, who is given the final word, "Truly this man was the Son of God!" (15:39). Mark gives him the final word because the centurion "stood facing him," stood facing the cross. The Son of God is the crucified Jesus of Nazareth and it is only as one comes face to face with the stark reality of that fact that it is possible to know who Jesus is and what it means to call him "the Christ."

Clearly Mark has addressed his narrative to a community that faces specific problems and questions. Given the emphasis he places on the significance of the cross for understanding Jesus' identity and what it means to call him the "Christ," and the significance of the cross for understanding Christian discipleship, Nils Dahl may well be right when he concludes that Mark's Gospel is "addressed to a church in danger of taking the Gospel for granted."[41] Discipleship, for Mark, is not an easy road and certainly not something that fits comfortably into normal daily existence. "For whoever would save his life will lose it; and whoever loses his life for my sake and the gospel's will save it" (8:35). A question that naturally emerges here is whether Mark's narrative has been so shaped to address the specific situation of a Christian community in the first century that it is applicable only to that community. If that were the case then one might conclude that while Mark believed that discipleship entailed a willingness to suffer and die by Christians in that situation not every situation is necessarily similar and Christian discipleship may mean different things at different points in history. To draw that conclusion, however, one would have to argue that Mark's emphasis on the crucifixion as the decisive event for understanding not only discipleship but also Jesus' identity is equally arbitrary. If it is the cross that is the decisive event for understanding who Jesus is and what it means to call him the "Christ," then it is also the cross that determines what it means to be a follower of the crucified one.

Although Mark's Gospel is addressed to a church facing specific problems it is possible to distill from the narrative several hermeneutical principles, like those in Deuteronomy, which seem to have a binding significance for every Christian community. In the first place Mark clearly demonstrates that one cannot know who Jesus is apart from the narrative of his personal history. While it appears that Mark may not be as dependent on a tradition of Jesus' sayings as were Matthew and Luke, still there is evidence, especially in chapters 4 and 13, that Mark did weave sayings of Jesus into his narrative. If Mark's Gospel, or any Gospel for that matter, consisted only of sayings or teachings of Jesus, the reader might know something about what Jesus thought but that in itself would not be enough for understanding Jesus' identity. Only when the reader observes what Jesus says and teaches in the context of those events that make up his narrative history does the reader have some sense of who Jesus is.

To try to understand Jesus' identity in terms of the titles attributed to him is just as inadequate as the sole use of Jesus' sayings and teachings. A major issue in Mark's Gospel is what it means to be the Christ. Mark shows us that the title can mean

many things, but that it does not mean what it did for Peter—
that God's chosen one, Israel's hope and redeemer, was a Messiah
immune to suffering. Although the title has a clear meaning in
the history of Israel, Mark shows the reader that it is not the title
that gives Jesus his identity. Rather, it is Jesus in the concreteness
of his narrative history that defines the meaning of the title
"Christ." Jesus' overwhelming question, "But who do you say
that I am?" (Mark 8:29) cannot or at least should not be answered
by the reader apart from the events of Mark's narrative history. It
is the Gospel narrative that provides the context for interpreting
Jesus' parables, sayings, and teachings, and it is the same narrative that gives Jesus his true identity.

Secondly, Mark's narrative is more than a simple recounting
of events in the life of Jesus of Nazareth. Mark's narrative forces
the reader at some level of his or her existence to respond to the
same question Jesus addresses to Peter, "But who do you say that
I am?" Not only is the question of Jesus' identity the dominant
motif in Mark's Gospel which provides the narrative its dramatic
tension, but it is also Mark's way of drawing the reader into the
narrative and bringing the reader, as Perrin puts it, "to the realization that he, [the reader], is being challenged to discipleship
in the context of the prospect of the coming of Jesus as Son of
Man."[42] What we see here is the strange reversal we noted at the
beginning of this section. How the reader responds to the question Jesus puts to Peter is just as much a statement about the
identity of the reader as it is a statement about Jesus' identity. It
is now the narrative history of a single individual, Jesus of Nazareth, that impinges on the identity of all those who encounter
him and it is this narrative history that evokes an answer from
the reader concerning Jesus' identity. In answering the question
about Jesus' identity the reader simultaneously makes a decision
about his or her personal identity. It is no longer a corporate
narrative that gives the individual his or her identity. Now the
identity narrative of a single individual gives the community and

all those who participate in it the narrative frame in which they must with fear and trembling discover their own salvation.

Thirdly, Mark's narrative so effectively links the question of Jesus' identity to the meaning of discipleship that it is not possible to separate them. Not only does Mark's narrative force the reader to answer the question about Jesus' identity, but if the reader agrees with the centurion's conclusion the reader also knows what it means to become a disciple of Jesus. The genius of Mark's Gospel is that it is not possible to read it, agree with the confession "'Truly this man was the Son of God!'" (Mark 15:39) and then ask what discipleship means. The reader may find the answer to that question unpleasant or unacceptable but Mark leaves little doubt about what discipleship means.

Mark's answer to both questions—the question about Jesus' identity and the question about the meaning of discipleship—is neither a treatise on christology nor a doctrinal discussion of discipleship. The answer is the narrative, the story itself. What it means for Jesus to be the Christ is answered by a narrative in which his identity emerges from those events that make up his personal history. And the meaning of discipleship is not a list of rules and commandments. At no point does Mark have Jesus instruct his followers in the do's and don't's of discipleship. To be a disciple of Jesus a person must "deny himself and take up his cross and follow me," and "following me" is not so much believing certain things about Jesus as it is a form of life, a way of being in the world, in which the cross becomes the primary symbol and one seeks to be "last of all and servant of all." The cross is the decisive reality for understanding who Jesus is and what it means to be a follower of him, but as Mark demonstrates for us, the cross is first and last an event in the identity narrative of Jesus of Nazareth and not a doctrine. Part of the church's responsibility in proclaiming the gospel is to reflect theologically on what the cross means, but any theological statement which turns the cross into an abstraction that has no necessary reference to its original and proper setting in gospel narrative runs the high risk of distorting the cross' meaning. Such a move is well received in some Christian communities because it enables those who call themselves Christians to separate questions about christology from the issue of discipleship. In Mark's Gospel, however, such a separation is not possible.

5. Scripture and Interpretation

Both Deuteronomy and Mark are important parts of the Christian community's identity narrative, but neither separately nor together are they the whole of it. Nor is all of Scripture the Christian community's identity narrative. The narrative that any Christian community recites in order to explain to itself and its surrounding culture how it understands reality and why it does the things that it does certainly includes Scripture. Indeed Scripture's symbols and stories are the means by which the community constructs and interprets its own identity narrative, but that narrative includes more than just Scripture. It is made up of various layers and perhaps is best described by the category of "tradition," for the Christian community's identity narrative is a form of tradition.

At one level the community's narrative includes those texts we call Scripture, and these are crucially important, in part because these texts provide some form of continuity between Christian communities at different points in history. There is a continuity of sorts among them because they all appeal to one Scripture as the means by which they structure and interpret their world. Admittedly these different communities appeal to Scripture in vastly different ways. They disagree about what is most important in the text and even when they agree on the importance of a particular text more likely than not they disagree about what it means. Still, it is possible to examine Christian communities in Alexandria in the fourth century, in Geneva in the sixteenth century, and in Narobi in the twentieth century, and despite their many differences also identify them as belonging to one tradition. They may differ radically in their understanding of the figure of Adam in Genesis 3 or in their interpretation of the meaning of the cross, but they all use these symbols and the narratives in which they are found in order to make sense out of their respective worlds. These shared symbols and narratives, if nothing else, provide a basis for conversation.

A second level of the community's narrative is what might be described as the history of interpretation which has been handed down to the contemporary community. No Christian reads Scripture as though it were a pristine text. For every community Scripture is tainted by time, place, and circumstance. Christians in the twentieth century cannot read Scripture as though it were a recently written text. The Christian community's interpretation of Scripture is shaped by how previous communities in the Christian tradition have interpreted the text. Hence "the horizon of interpretation" that any Christian community brings to the text is affected by the preceding history of interpretation. If we accept Gerhard Ebeling's description of church history as the history of the interpretation of Scripture, then Christian narrative cannot be limited to biblical narrative but extends through the narrative that recounts how in the past the church lived in the world by means of Scripture and how it does so in the present. The narratives in the Pentateuch and Mark are the final form of a "traditioning process," but that process does not cease with the formation of the canon. It continues in the subsequent attempts of successive Christian communities to make sense out of their world by means of Christian faith.

A third level, then, in the Christian community's narrative is its final and most visible form. While the symbols and myths the community uses for interpretation may be taken from Scripture, the community does not cling to these merely to preserve them. The community tries to bring this narrative history to bear on its contemporary world in order to interpret and understand better the present in light of the resources of the past. There is a point and a purpose to the community's identity narrative, and that narrative is not properly understood unless one looks carefully at the world and the cultural situation in which the community finds itself. The twists and turns in the Christian tradition and the idiosyncrasies that characterize each community of Christians are partially due to each community's unique situation in history. Although each community may appeal to a common Scripture and may use the same symbols and narratives, the situation the community must address and the world in which it lives will decisively shape its use of those symbols and narratives.

The identity narrative of the Christian community is the story it tells at any given moment in order to explain its beliefs and its behavior in the world. The narrative is never quite the same, appearances aside. Each new situation and each new moment in the community's history require a subtle but significant shift in the identity narrative. The dynamic that prompts this constant change in the community's narrative is its incessant need for interpretation. Simply because a community's predecessors found that Christian narrative enabled them to make sense out of their world and their behavior in it does not mean that subsequent communitites can use the same interpretation of the narrative to make sense out of their world. What these communities have in common may be a shared disposition, a similar way of looking at reality, shaped by a commitment to the Exodus and the Cross as the decisive clues for understanding reality. That does not necessarily mean that they will agree on what role women should exercise in the life of the community or how the community should respond to homosexuality.

It is the need for and the dependence on interpretation that is the dynamic force in the Christian community's identity narrative. Interpretation emerges from the dialogue between "tradition" and situation. Without the tradition and the different narratives that constitute it there would be nothing to interpret and no guide for interpretation. The community would be forced to find its way on purely utilitarian grounds. Without some appreciation for the questions and demands in each new situation a community would simply repeat its familiar narratives and live in the world in splendid isolation and irrelevance. Repetition is not the same thing as interpretation. To live in the Christian community and to participate in its common life is to share a commitment that its traditions and its narratives are more appropriate than those of other communities and other traditions for making decisions and interpreting the world.

The identity narrative that emerges from the encounter between tradition and situation may take various forms, as is apparent from a brief examination of church history. Yet in the midst of the diverse ways in which Christian communities have interpreted the Christian tradition there are some features that most of these identity narratives have in common, features which are the result of hermeneutical principles rooted in Scripture. For example, the task of interpretation is demanded by Scripture itself. As we have seen, the writers of Deuteronomy fervently believed that Israel must cling to those narratives which report the events that are the basis of Israel's faith. Life itself depends on whether Israel will "remember and not forget." To cease to remember leads to an aimless and confused situation in which Israel will surely "go after other gods, or the gods of the peoples who are round about you" and fall into apostasy. But to remember what God has done in the past is not simply to repeat mindlessly a confessional formula. To remember is to "actualize" the past and "actualization" is one form of interpretation. To actualize the past is to bring its redemptive power and significance to bear on the present situation. Only if the community successfully remembers, actualizes, and interprets the past can it hope to make any sense out of the statutes, ordinances, and commandments which give the community its structure and order. Interpreting the tradition is absolutely essential if future generations are to make sense out of their existence by means of the narrative that begins, "A wandering Aramean was my father."

At any given moment the actualization of biblical narrative may assume various forms. The task of interpretation is to actualize the tradition in the present, to enable the contemporary community to experience the power mediated by redemptive events. If and when that happens there is a collision that takes place in the encounter with Scripture. In Deuteronomy it is the community's narrative that provides the individual the occasion and the context for reinterpreting personal identity. That basic principle is also true of the New Testament. The Gospels reflect the faith and the experience of Christian communities; they have been written by individuals who have been transformed by what they call God's grace as it has been mediated to them in the faith and life of the "ecclesia." But, as Mark's Gospel demonstrates, this transformation is often painful and costly.

In Christian faith it is not just that the individual discovers his or her personal identity in the narrative history of the community. In Christian faith both the individual and the community look to the narrative history of Jesus of Nazareth in order to discover the true meaning of their respective identities. It is Jesus of Nazareth in the uniqueness of his personal identity who reveals the meaning of Christian faith and in so doing establishes the identity of those communities who witness to him. It is this Jesus, as he is identified in the Gospel narrative, who is lord and judge of what takes place in the ecclesia. He is not only the mediator of God's grace but also the critical principle by which the community understands its faith and what it is called to be and to do. The identity of Jesus of Nazareth, as it is revealed in biblical narrative, stands over against the identity of every community and every individual. To enter the Christian community and participate in its faith and life is to encounter those biblical narratives which can never quite be identified with any community's interpretation of them. Precisely because they demand that they be remembered and not forgotten and precisely because they pose the overwhelming question concerning Jesus' identity these texts must be interpreted. But every interpretation is at best provisional and can never be labeled the final meaning of the text.

And the same must be said finally of Scripture itself. Although the Christian community has no other access to Jesus except through the Scriptures that narrate his identity and witness to God's presence in him, biblical narrative is also provisional and the Jesus who was and is to be is not the captive of the written word. He stands over against it too just as he stands over against every human confession of who he is, including Peter's.

Chapter VI
The Narrative Structure of Christian Faith

Revelation becomes an experienced reality at that juncture where the narrative identity of an individual collides with the narrative identity of the Christian community. This "collision" may be experienced by a stranger to the Christian community, someone who is unfamiliar with its faith and life and encounters it for the first time. Or the encounter may take place between the community and a person who has lived all of his or her life in the church but who has never been able to appropriate Christian faith or use it for the interpretation of personal identity. In the latter case a person may live in the community but not be of it. When either the stranger or the native comes up against the narrative identity of the community, a collision takes place and decisions must be made. In this collision we learn something about the nature of revelation and the meaning of what Christians call conversion.

In order to examine this encounter we will look at a classical example of it, Augustine's *Confessions*, which is a paradigm of what revelation looks like in its final form—when personal identity has been reconstructed by means of the faith of the Christian community. Finally, we will see if Karl Barth's discussion of the dynamics of faith enables us to understand the relation between revelation and identity and what is involved in a person's experience of "coming to faith."

1. The Collision of Narratives

At that point where a person encounters the Christian community with its narratives, common life, and faith claims about reality, there is the possibility that the individual will begin the lengthy, difficult process of reinterpreting his or her personal history in light of the narratives and symbols that give the Christian community its identity. At that moment there is the possibility for what Christians describe as revelation—the experience of redemption and the beginning of the process called "faith." It is at this point that identities, even worlds, may be altered and reality perceived in a radically new way.

Sociologically this encounter can be described without recourse to theological language. In his essay, "The Stranger," Alfred Schutz offers a compelling description of the encounter between a community and anyone that community considers to be a "stranger" or "outsider."[1] By "stranger" Schutz means "an adult individual of our times and civilization who tries to be permanently accepted or at least tolerated by the group which he approaches." One example of this social situation is the immigrant, who is a "stranger" in relation to a community or social group for several reasons, one of the most important of which is that "he does not partake in the vivid historical tradition by which it has been formed."[2] Even though the community's history may be accessible to the immigrant in the sense that it can be examined, studied, and learned, as long as that cultural history is not part of the immigrant's biography it cannot be claimed and appropriated.

> The stranger, therefore, approaches the other group as a newcomer in the true meaning of the term. At best he may be willing and able to share the present and the future with the approached group in vivid and immediate experience; under all circumstances, however, he remains excluded from such experiences of its past. Seen from the point of view of the approached group, he is a man without a history.[3]

Unless the immigrant can participate in the community's history it remains alien and unappropriated, and as long as that history is not the immigrant's the group will remember, interpret, and "actualize" a past which the immigrant does not share. The immigrant's personal history and therein his or her personal identity will be unrelated to that of the community.

For various reasons the stranger may desire to become a part of this new community, but the process is never an easy one. The stranger carries an interpretive scheme which he or she has acquired from past experience and from a "home" community and that scheme for interpreting reality is not easily or quickly discarded; nor is the new one immediately appropriated. Schutz compares the process to the difficulty of learning a foreign language. One has not really become a participant in the new community until one thinks and interprets by means of its categories, symbols, and language, and can take part in its distinctive forms of life. "It is the difference between the passive understanding of a language and its active mastering as a means for realizing one's own acts and thoughts."[4]

Of course the case of the stranger is not the only example of the encounter that takes place between an individual and a community. There is also the case of the person who returns to a community which at some time in the past was "home." The situation of the "homecomer" is significantly different from that of the stranger in that the latter knows that the community is unlike that which was originally home. But the homecomer anticipates a community "of which he always had and—so he thinks—still has intimate knowledge and which he has just to take for granted in order to find his bearings within it."[5] Examples Schutz gives of the homecomer are the returning veteran and "the traveler who comes back from foreign countries, the emigrant who returns to his native land, the boy who 'made good' abroad and now settles in his home town."[6] In each case a peculiar set of problems emerges in the encounter between the individual and the community, problems which are not quite the same as those that characterize the encounter between the community and the stranger. In the case of the homecomer the primary problem is that both the homecomer and the home community must be disabused of the belief that neither has really changed. In fact both have changed and the relation between the community and its former member will remain confused until both come to some conscious realization of the differences time has created. As Schutz describes the situation of the homecomer, "the home to which he returns is by no means the home he left or the home which he recalled and longed for during his absence."[7] Both the home and the homecomer have changed in the course of time and experience, and just as the homecomer is not the same person who left so the community is no longer identical with that which was left behind.

Regardless of whether one is a stranger or a homecomer when either encounters the Christian community a serious collision takes place, and it is within the dynamics of this encounter that Christians understand revelation to occur and the process of conversion to begin. To the stranger the Christian community consists of an unfamiliar array of symbols, stories, and rituals which seem to cohere in some form of ordered existence that is not quite intelligible to the stranger. The community shares a common history and even a common memory, and within the community individuals make decisions and interpret contemporary events by means of a shared faith. To the homecomer the problem is even more difficult, especially if the homecomer does not consider himself or herself ever to have "left" the community. The home-comer's experience, as Schutz describes it, is bewildering because the Christian community with its familiar narratives and faith appears to the homecomer to have changed, or the homecomer, without perhaps consciously realizing it, is no longer the same person who once lived in the community. In either case, that of the stranger or the homecomer, a jarring collision occurs when either individual encounters the Christian community. Both individuals experience significant disorientation, a sense that the world as they know it is coming apart, that their understanding of reality no longer quite coheres with their experience, and the result is confusion about what the world looks like from the perspective of Christian faith.

One obvious response is for either the stranger or the homecomer to withdraw from the encounter. The stranger can attempt to return home or seek an environment that better resembles the community left behind. The homecomer can consciously repress the differences that exist between the present shape of the community and its previous form, or the homecomer can attempt to become what he or she once was and ignore the changes created by intervening time and experience. In other words the encounter between the stranger or homecomer and the community need not necessarily lead to a collision or to that process in which an individual begins to reconstruct his or her personal identity by means of the community's narrative history.

However, if the collision between the stranger or the homecomer and the community results in the individual attempting to become a part of the community's life, then the difficult task of reconstructing personal identity by means of the community's narratives and symbols becomes unavoidable. In the context of the Christian tradition revelation refers to that event in which a person or a community encounters what is ultimately real and interprets that encounter by means of the narratives of the Christian community. The individual's decision to see and live in the world by means of that narrative is what Christians call "faith" and the process by which the community's faith and narratives become the individual's is what Christians refer to as "conversion." In spite of the fact that it was written sixteen hundred years ago Augustine's *Confessions* remains one of the clearest examples in Christian literature of the meaning of revelation and the process of conversion.

2. Augustine's Confessions

Augustine wrote the *Confessions* in 397–8, when he was forty-three, ten years after his baptism and six years after his ordination as priest. The first nine books of the *Confessions*, which make up the strictly autobiographical section, cover the first thirty-three years of Augustine's life, from his birth in 354 to his baptism and the death of his mother, Monica, in 387. It is significant that the *Confessions* were written ten years after Augustine became a participant in the Christian communion. Although the events of the first thirty-three years of his life were interpreted from the perspective of Christian faith, a faith to which Augustine clearly has committed himself fervently and wholeheartedly, the *Confessions* is his sober attempt to come to terms with his personal history and identity by means of Christian faith. It is not the overzealous testimony of a recent convert. In terms of the categories we have been developing, the *Confessions* is Christian narrative in its final form. If one examines the book carefully it is not difficult to separate the different sediments of narrative we have discussed previously. At one level there is a personal history and a series of interpretations of that history which gave Augustine his identity prior to his acceptance of Christian faith. This pre-Christian narrative history is then reworked in the *Confessions* by means of the narratives and symbols which Augustine has appropriated from his participation in the Christian community.

For Augustine the writing of the *Confessions* and the recon-

struction of personal identity is itself an act of confession. It is
not so much a statement about his conversion or his appropriation of Christian faith as it is the performance of the act itself. In
one sense the *Confessions* is Augustine's search for God in his personal history, in "time and memory" as John Dunne describes it,
but it is not just that. The book is written in the form of a prayer,
a dialogue between Augustine and God and as such it is not just
an attempt to understand God. As is the case with most dia-
logues it is an attempt on Augustine's part to reach self-understanding through the mediation of the other. Hence Augustine's
plea to God, "Let me know you, for you are the God who knows
me: *let me recognize you as you have recognized me*," is a twofold plea.[8]
On the one hand it is a plea for knowledge of God, but on the
other hand it is also a plea for self-understanding. For Augustine
the one seems to entail the other. As the *Confessions* ably demonstrates, all true knowledge of God impinges on how a person
understands his or her identity and personal history, and the final
meaning of the events that make up personal history can be determined only in light of what one knows about that ultimate
reality who is Creator and Redeemer of everything that is. "But
where was I when I looked for you? You were there before my
eyes, but I had deserted even my own self. I could not find myself, much less find you."[9]

In the first nine books of the *Confessions* Augustine rehearses
those events he understands to be important in his personal history. He describes his relation to his parents (with a great deal of
attention to Monica, his mother), his early education, his development as a teacher of rhetoric, his infatuation with the
Manichaeans, his friendships, his relationship with his mistress
and their son, his encounter with Ambrose and the Christian
community at Milan, and, finally, his conversion to Christian
faith. In addition to these formative events he also includes a
number of other incidents which are not important in themselves, but which are included because of what they suggest

about the meaning of the whole. An example is Augustine's well known description in Book II of his participation when he was sixteen in "a band of ruffians" who stole pears from a neighbor's tree. Out of all the events that make up Augustine's adolescence it perhaps is surprising that he would mention this one. In itself the event does not seem terribly significant. It is not, however, the event itself which is important, but Augustine's interpretation of the event in the context of what he understood (as a forty-three-year-old Christian) to be the waywardness of his youth; "I loved my own perdition and my own faults, not the things for which I committed wrong, but the wrong itself." [10]

The autobiographical section of the *Confessions* is a continuous circular movement between events in Augustine's personal history and the interpretation he brings to bear on those events. Augustine moves back and forth between a straightforward description of events and direct discourse in prayer with God. "O Lord my God, is this not the truth as I remember it? You are the Judge of my conscience, and my heart and my memory lie open before you." [11] Everywhere, in every event, Augustine sees the mysterious working of God's providence. "The secret hand of your providence guided me then, and you set my abject errors before my eyes so that I might see them and detest them." [12] What prompts the selection of certain events, such as the theft of the pears, for inclusion in the autobiography is not necessarily the intrinsic significance of the events themselves, but the sense in which the events illumine the interpretation that holds them together. Similarly if the categories that are used to interpret personal history do not illumine the meaning of what are understood to be constitutive, formative events, even in their noncoherence, then serious questions must be raised about the intelligibility of the interpretive scheme.

The latter problem was at least partially responsible for Augustine's break with Manichaeanism. For nine years Augustine had been a follower of the Manichaeans, but as he reports in

Books IV and V, he was finally unable to reconcile certain facts
and events with a Manichaean interpretation of reality. For example, Augustine was troubled by the conflict between Manichaean cosmology and the new scientific theories which were able
to predict with great accuracy eclipses of the sun or moon. The
two appeared to contradict each other and Augustine could not
escape the conclusion that the Manichaean position consisted of
"tedious fictions about the sky and the stars, the sun and the
moon." [13] But the conflict was not just confined to cosmology. At
issue were larger problems about the nature of evil and God's
relation to the world. When Faustus, the famed Manichaean
bishop, visited Carthage, he was unable to answer Augustine's
questions, and Augustine's interest in and commitment to Manichaeanism began to ebb.

> So it was that, unwittingly and without intent, Faustus who
> had been a deadly snare to many now began to release me from the
> trap in which I had been caught. For in the mystery of your provi-
> dence, my God, your guiding hand did not desert me. [14]

Of course that is not necessarily how Augustine would have interpreted the situation at the time of his encounter with Faustus.
What he gives the reader is an interpretation of these events from
the perspective of his Christian faith. Had he attempted to interpret these events when he was twenty-one rather than forty-three
the picture no doubt would have been quite different. For example, at the beginning of Book IV Augustine briefly summarizes his relation to Manichaeanism.

> During the space of those nine years, from the nineteenth to
> the twenty-eighth year of my life, I was led astray myself and led
> others astray in my turn. We were alike deceivers and deceived in
> all our different aims and ambitions, both publicly when we ex-
> pounded our so-called liberal ideas, and in private through our
> service to what we called religion. In public we were cocksure, in
> private superstitious, and everywhere void and empty. . . . These
> were the objects I pursued and the tasks I performed together with

friends who, like myself and through my fault, were under the same delusion.[15]

If Augustine had written an autobiography when he was twenty-nine, that is not how he would have described himself or his recent history. At the time it is unlikely that he considered himself "deluded" or proud, vain, and superstitious. That judgment and that interpretation of his involvement with Manichaeanism are intelligible only in light of his commitment to Christian faith.

Not only does Augustine see God's providence at work in every nook and cranny of his personal history, but there is another, less obvious theme in the *Confessions* that is equally important. Practically every page of the *Confessions* includes a reference to a biblical text or at least an allusion to a biblical theme. Augustine frequently refers to the Psalms, and it is not unusual to find three or four quotations from the Psalms on a single page of the *Confessions*.[16] What is worth noting is not simply that Augustine knew his Bible or that he found ample occasion to use it; rather what is important is why and how Augustine does use Scripture. At first glance it might appear that Augustine simply is using Scripture as religious window dressing, as a form of "proof-texting," in order to add the weight of Christian authority to his argument and self-analysis. Occasionally that may be true, but in many cases that would not be an accurate interpretation of the role of Scripture in the *Confessions*. For Augustine the interpretation of personal history and the use of Scripture are closely intertwined. The quotations from Scripture are not so much authoritative proof texts as they are crucial interpretive clues to the meaning of people and events. The biblical texts are not used simply as warrants or further evidence to buttress prior conclusions about the significance of people and events in Augustine's personal history. Scripture is the primary basis for the interpretation given those events, and in this sense the biblical texts represent the visible collision in the *Confessions* between Augustine's personal history and the narrative identity of the Christian community. Scripture represents the presence of the Christian community in the *Confessions*—not just its passive presence but the active, necessary role that the faith narratives of the community play in the reconstruction of Augustine's personal identity.

Augustine's use of Scripture also raises another important question about the *Confessions*, one which has long puzzled the book's many readers. The first nine books are not the only place in the *Confessions* where Augustine uses Scripture. In the last four books, Books X-XIII, Scripture is employed with equal frequency, although apparently not for the same purpose as in the first nine books. As we have seen, the first nine books constitute something like a religious autobiography, but the last four books differ dramatically from the first nine both in form and in content. The last four books do not resemble the autobiographical form of the first nine books. Although still cast in the form of a prayer, they are theological and philosophical reflections on the nature of memory, time, form, and matter. Their subject matter appears to differ so completely from the autobiographical concerns in Books I-IX that many readers have wondered why the last four books were included in the same volume with the first nine books.

Several theses have been proposed concerning the relation of the two "parts" of the *Confessions*. One critic believes that the last four books are Augustine's attempt to explain the meaning of what he has constructed in his life-story in the first nine books; "in other words, who he is with respect to the end, conversion, and Christian faith."[17] Having recited the basic facts of his life history Augustine proceeds to offer a theological interpretation of what it all means.

> Before, his language achieved meaning upon the horizon of contrast between lacking Christian belief and gaining it. When he finishes telling of the gain from the standpoint of the lack, that

is, when he ends his story, he asks about the meaning of the story. Having come into faith, he asks about what it means to have faith. [18]

But, as we have seen, such a distinction is not tenable, not even within the first nine books of the *Confessions*. The autobiography is not written from the perspective of someone who lacks faith, but from the point of view of a faith that has had ten years to mature. In fact, Augustine's frequent use of Scripture suggests, among other things, that the meaning of his life story is not something that can be abstracted from the narrative and discussed independently of it. The meaning of the narrative is discovered in the writing and reading of the narrative and nowhere else.

What then is the relation between the autobiography in the first nine books and the theological reflections in the last four books? One possibility is that regardless of whether Augustine intended them as such, the last four books are a theological grammar for the assistance and instruction of the reader. The meaning of the life story is to be found in the narrative in the first nine books, but if the reader wants to understand the categories, concepts, and symbols at work in the construction and interpretation of the life-story, then it is necessary to consult the extended glossary in Books X-XIII. Again we see the circular relation between event and interpretation in the *Confessions*. Books I-IX are by no means a bare recitation of events. The reader listens as Augustine describes his personal history, but that description takes place in the context of his conversation with God. The events described in Books I-IX are interpreted from the perspective of the faith that is then discussed discursively in Books X-XIII. It should be noted that while Augustine does not use Scripture in Books I-IX in proof-text fashion, he does allow the biblical text, the core narrative of the Christian community's identity, to function as the means by which he interprets his personal history. Books XI-

XIII are a straightforward theological exegesis of the opening chapters of Genesis. The reader watches Augustine put Scripture to work existentially in Books I-IX and then examine it discursively in Books X-XIII. From this perspective one might describe Books X-XIII as an interpretation of the faith of the Christian community and Books I-IX as Augustine's reinterpretation of his personal history by means of his appropriation of that historical, communal faith.

Because of this circular relationship between the two parts of the *Confessions* it is not necessary that the reader begin with Book I in order to understand the text. Indeed, it might be argued that a reader who first has read Books X-XIII could better understand the perspective from which Augustine interprets the events reported in Books I-IX. In any case the *Confessions* is probably not fully understood until the reader has worked through it several times. It is necessary to know the events reported in Books I-IX in order to understand the application of the theological themes discussed in Books X-XIII, and the interpretation given to the events in Books I-IX is not entirely clear until the reader has worked through the theological discussion in Books X-XIII.

Two examples of this circular relationship are Augustine's discussion of the problem of evil and the question of God's corporeality. In Books I-IX both of these issues are discussed in some detail, not simply as abstract theological topics, but as questions which have a clear reference to events in Augustine's personal history. Augustine attributed much of his mental anguish to his mistaken view of reality; "my misconception of spiritual things prevented me from seeing the truth, although it forced itself upon my mind if only I would see it." [19] At that time in his life Augustine understood God to be a form of substance, "a bright unbounded body," and as such "a fiction based on my own wretched state." [20] Because he conceived of God as a bodily substance he also understood evil to be "some similar kind of substance." "All my other sacrilegious beliefs were the outcome of this first fatal mistake."[21] And of course the problem was not just that Augustine held to "sacrilegious beliefs"; those beliefs were the basis of his understanding of his world and his behavior in it. In Book VII Augustine describes how, with the help of the Platonists, he came to understand that God, as perfect goodness, might exist and might be infinite "though without extent in terms of space either limited or unlimited."[22] However, in order to understand fully how Augustine interprets God's being the reader must carefully examine the theological reflections in Books XII and XIII. "Within me I hear the loud voice of Truth telling me that since the Creator is truly eternal, his substance is utterly unchanged in time and his will is not something separate from his substance."[23]

In a slightly different way the same point can be made with regard to Augustine's famous discusson of time and memory in Book X. The first nine books are nothing else if they are not an exercise of Augustine's memory for the sake of interpretation. "Allow me, I beseech you, to trace again in memory my past deviations and to offer you a sacrifice of joy."[24] "Look into my heart, O Lord, for it was your will that I should remember these things and confess them to you."[25] The very act of confession is itself an exercise of memory. To confess is "to trace again in memory" that personal history which has been redeemed by God's grace. And the first nine books represent the performance of that task. They are the visible result of Augustine's use of his memory to reconstruct his personal history by means of Christian faith. In Book X Augustine no longer exercises his memory but reflects on what memory is, what takes place in "the vast cloisters of my memory" that makes possible the activity of confession. The memory is not just a collection of sense data.

> In it I meet myself as well. I remember myself and what I have done, when and where I did it, and the state of my mind at the

time. In my memory, too, are all the events that I remember, whether they are things that have happened to me or things that I have heard from others.[26]

The memory that is exercised in Books I-IX is the object of reflection in Book X. Purely on the basis of what Augustine does with his memory in Books I-IX it would be difficult for the reader to know how Augustine understands the memory. Yet if the *Confessions* were written not simply in order to gratify Augustine's personal needs but also to encourage others when they read of "those past sins of mine" not to "lie listless in despair, crying 'I cannot,'" then Augustine must also instruct the reader on the nature and use of the memory. One may disagree with the sharply Platonic interpretation that Augustine gives to memory, but apart from Book X it would be difficult for the reader to know what Augustine understands memory to be.

To confess is at least in part to remember, and the relation between these two activities is relevant to an important question that is often asked about the *Confessions*—namely, where does Augustine's conversion take place? The common answer to that question is that Augustine's "conversion" is described in the well-known passage in Book VIII. In the previous book, Book VII, Augustine describes how he came to understand, at least intellectually, how God might be a substance unsusceptible to corruption, and that evil, the reality that obsessed him, might be "not a substance, because if it were a substance, it would be good."[27] Yet even when Augustine was able to see the weaknesses in Manichaeanism and grasp the alternative offered by Christian faith, he was unable to accept the Christian vision and could not "persist in enjoyment of my God."[28] Not until he experienced the events recounted in Book VIII was Augustine able to accept Christian faith.

The story is well known. While in the garden of a friend's home, overcome with emotion and in "an agony of indecision,"

Augustine heard a child say, "'Take it and read, take it and read.'" Since he had been reading Paul's epistles, Augustine opened the book to Romans 13:13–14, and then "as I came to the end of the sentence, it was as though the light of confidence flooded into my heart and all the darkness of doubt was dispelled."[29] What he had assented to intellectually but had been unable to accept at some other level of his being now became his faith.[30]

Certainly in one sense of the word this event in the garden in Milan could be described as Augustine's "conversion." It was that moment in which the world turned around and Augustine experienced it in a way he previously had not. But in another sense this event is not really Augustine's conversion. If conversion is not really conversion until it issues in confession, then the events described in Book VIII and his baptism in Book IX do not represent Augustine's conversion. Rather, his conversion is best understood as the act of writing the *Confessions*. It is only as Augustine engages in the process of reinterpreting his personal history and reconstructing his personal identity that the pilgrimage of Christian faith actually begins. Conversion means not just a turning from but also a turning to, and it is only in the *Confessions* that Augustine explains to his world and perhaps to himself what he has been and what he is in the process of becoming. It may well be that prior to the writing of the *Confessions* Augustine could not have described to the reader or to himself what Christian faith meant in the context of his personal history. This personal appropriation of faith is a necessary step in the ongoing process of conversion, and, consequently, Christian confession as it is exemplified in the *Confessions* is something like what J. L. Austin once described as a "performative utterance."[31] Apart from the performance of confession, which includes the reconstruction of personal identity, faith is incomplete and not fully a reality.

3. Acknowledgment, Recognition, and Confession

One way of examining the relation between conversion and confession in the *Confessions* and the relation of both to revelation is by means of Karl Barth's insightful discussion of the dynamics of faith in the *Church Dogmatics*.[32] Barth divides his discussion of faith into two parts: the object of faith and the act of faith. Consistent with the rest of his theology Barth insists that one must first speak of the object of faith, the *fides qua creditur*, before examining its subjective expression, the *fides quae creditur*. The object of faith is Jesus Christ and this "object" is the center of faith. It orders the full range of a Christian's existence and as such "concerns him necessarily and not incidentally, centrally and not casually."[33] Secondly, as the object of faith Jesus Christ is the basis of faith. Because Jesus Christ is faith's "basis" there is an important sense in which faith is not produced by human initiative; rather, faith "is also the work of Jesus Christ who is its object."[34] Faith, Barth insists, is a free human act, but its human possibility has as its presupposition "the will and decision and achievement of Jesus Christ the Son of God that it takes place as a free human act, that man is of himself ready and willing and actually begins to believe in Him."[35] Thirdly, Jesus Christ, as the object and basis of faith, also constitutes the Christian subject; that is, in the act of faith "there begins and takes place a new and particular being of man."[36] But as the Christian individual is created anew by faith in Jesus Christ he or she is not driven into isolation. Indeed, the very meaning of faith in Jesus Christ is that the Christian "can believe only in and with the community, only in the sphere and context of it, only in the limitation and determination set by its basis and goal."[37] It is for these reasons that any discussion of Christian faith must begin by examining the object of faith, for it is faith's object, Jesus Christ, who determines what faith is.

> The first thing is that Jesus Christ is, in fact, just for me, that I myself am just the subject for whom He is. That is the point. That is the newness of being, the new creation, the new birth of the Christian.[38]

Christian faith must always be examined first in terms of its object, but that perspective does not fully exhaust the description of faith. Faith is also a free human act—Barth describes it as *the* act of the Christian life—and because it is a human act it can be examined and analyzed. It is subject to inquiry and investigation. Faith is "active knowledge" and can be separated into "three mutually related terms": acknowledgment, recognition, and confession. These three dimensions of the one human act of faith illumine the structure of Augustine's *Confessions* and enhance our understanding of the inner dynamics of Christian narrative as it takes the form of confession.

As a human activity Christian faith is a form of acknowledgment, *Anerkennen*. By "acknowledgment" Barth does not mean what classical theology described as *assensus*, the assent to certain dogmas or the acceptance of propositions in or about Scripture. As the first moment in the human act of faith acknowledgment "is not the subservient acceptance of any reports or propositions, irrespective of whether they are biblical or churchly or modern."[39] Acknowledgment is acceptance of and obedience to faith's object, Jesus Christ, and no dogma or Scripture can be identified with him. Here Barth simply repeats the distinction we examined in Chapter II between the first form of the Word of God, Jesus Christ, and those human words which may become the occasion for God's Word.[40] "Obedience" and "compliance" are the basic features of acknowledgment, but it is the reality which is obeyed that makes acknowledgment something other than assent. Faith's object is not a doctrine or a proposition but a person and as far as Barth is concerned that is a fact of fundamental importance. "This truth is either denied or hopelessly obscured in a conception of faith which involves as its basic act the acceptance of certain statements which attest and proclaim Him, which does not, therefore, consist in simple obedience to Himself."[41]

The second "moment" in the human act of faith is recognition, *Erkennen*. Recognition is not a "second moment" sequentially because acknowledgment necessarily includes it. In other words, acknowledgment is not blind obedience. There is something that is known in the obedience and compliance that characterizes acknowledgment and what is known is Jesus Christ in his authentic form. "It is in this authentic form that from the very first, with the very first step, He becomes to everyone who comes to faith, and is obedient to Him, the object of his recognition."[42] Hence recognition is the second moment in the act of faith in that it is "included in that obedient and compliant taking cognisance."[43]

A correct recognition by the believer does not necessarily mean that there can be only one interpretation of Christian faith and its object, Jesus Christ. On the contrary, because no human word about Jesus can be identified with Jesus ("His form is inexhaustibly rich"), Christian faith will assume many forms. Barth does insist that all forms of recognition must occur within certain limits, within that circle which is defined by the three forms of the Word of God. Knowledge of Jesus Christ "is possible only within this definite sphere," a sphere constituted by the witness of Scripture and the proclamation of the church.[44]

What is distinctive about recognition is that it is not just objective knowledge about faith's object and obedience to it. It is knowledge of Jesus Christ but it includes "from the very first a knowing about the believer himself."[45] What the believer recognizes in the act of faith is that Jesus Christ is *pro me*, and as "my Lord" he determines the believer's identity and self-understanding. Recognition describes the sense in which what is known in faith is "existential knowledge," the subjective determination of the life of the believer by what is an objective reality in Jesus Christ. What the believer recognizes is that his or her self-understanding is altered by the acknowledgment of what God has accomplished in Jesus Christ. Of course the term "self-understanding" is a touchy one for Barth and he carefully distinguishes his interpretation of the subjective dimension of faith from that of Rudolf Bultmann. Also, Barth denies that recognition means that the history of Jesus Christ is re-enacted in the history of the believer. Faith is always a human act, even though it is the Spirit of Jesus Christ that makes it possible. Faith is a recognition of what has taken place in Jesus' history but it is not the repetition of it. "The being and activity of Jesus Christ needs no repetition. It is present and active in its own truth and power."[46]

A faith that sees no distinction between what God has accomplished in Jesus Christ and the believer's personal act of faith is perverse and impoverished. The believer who identifies his or her act of faith with what God has done in Jesus Christ always runs the risk of making the human act of faith rather than the activity of a gracious God the means of salvation. At the same time a faith that does not see any necessary relation between what God accomplishes in Jesus Christ and the believer's self-understanding and existence is equally impoverished. It is a faith that too quickly lapses into a spiritual apathy that avoids repentance and conversion. Neither of these positions is acceptable to Barth. The proper interpretation of faith for him is a form of analogy. As the object of faith Jesus Christ is the *analogans*, and the life of the believer, his or her personal identity, is the *analogatum*. The believer's recognition of faith, that Jesus Christ is *pro me*, means that the believer's self-understanding, in all its brokenness and sinfulness, is altered and becomes a "likeness," a murky reflection, of the grace of God. What the believer recognizes in faith is that his or her personal identity has been determined by that redemptive event which is Jesus Christ.

> When as a member of the community, I confidently recognise that it took place and was manifested for me, I must at once relate it as

well to the community and the world. In it, in the world reconciled with God in Jesus Christ, I recognise as in a mirror myself as
a reconciled man. And I, for my part, have to recognise and understand and conduct myself as the mirror of its reconciliation.[47]

The third moment in the act of faith is that of confession,
Bekennen. As a human act faith is not complete unless it issues in
confession. Faith that is only an acknowledgment of the lordship
of Jesus Christ and a recognition that the believer's redemption is
to be found in him is not fully faith. Unless acknowledgment and
recognition lead to confession the human activity of faith is not
fully a reality, or as Barth puts it, "A Christian who simply acknowledges and recognises without confessing is not a Christian."[48]
As Barth describes it confession is not only the final moment in
the human act of faith; it is also the realization of revelation, for
"There is nothing concealed which shall not be revealed, nothing
hid which shall not be made known."[49] And confession is that
"moment" when the individual believer, supported by the community, is able to reconstruct personal identity by means of what
is acknowledged and recognized to be the truth about Jesus
Christ. Confession is not something the Christian may or may
not do. It is the necessary, irresistible consequence of true faith,
because

> where anyone believes as a Christian a history is enacted: a history
> of the heart, which, as such, is audible and visible in world-his-
> tory; an individual history which, as such, calls for impartation
> and communication; a secret history which, as such, has a public
> character and claim; . . . a history of immeasurable dynamic be-
> cause it takes place in the light of the great history of God.[50]

Confession is the necessary completion of the act of faith because it is intrinsically public and communal. To insist that faith
is not finally faith unless it issues in confession means that faith
can never be understood as a private affair between the believer
and God. "To exist privately is to be a robber."[51] Barth's analysis
of faith takes place in the context of his discussion of the work of

the Holy Spirit, and confession represents the fulfillment of faith when, as in baptism, the believer ceases to live out of his or her own resources and as a new creation lives in the body of Christ. Confession is never a private act and is always "communal" in several senses. In the first place, confession is a public act. It is an activity that one person performs before others, not in addition to the private act of faith but as the fulfillment of that act. Faith not only drives the believer into community, into the body of Christ, but there is something in the internal dynamic of faith that demands that the gospel be proclaimed before all people. That is one reason why acknowledgment and recognition do not by themselves fully describe faith. Secondly, it is the community that provides the context for faith, and confession is simply the enactment by the individual of the community's faith. The work of the Spirit, as Barth describes it, is to "awaken faith" in the individual, but this is not something like a "private revelation." It happens "by the mediatorial ministry of the community which is itself in the school of the prophets and apostles, that a man comes under the awakening power of the Holy Spirit and therefore to faith."[52] Confession is not only an act that happens in the Christian community; it is an act that the community facilitates, an act that is performed in the world before all people.

Acknowledgment, recognition, and confession are each necessary moments in the one human act of faith. If faith never becomes anything more than acknowledgment then it may never be anything other than assent to a creedal authority. If what faith acknowledges—its basis in Jesus Christ—remains only an authority to be obeyed, then faith will always remain external to the believer and the religious dimension of life will be more a duty to perform than a joy to celebrate. It is the process of recognition that saves faith from this fate. In the act of recognition the believer discovers that what is acknowledged in faith is a reality that illumines the believer's existence. What is known in acknowledgment is recognized to impinge on the believer's identity. Knowledge of God in Jesus Christ leads the believer to true

self-knowledge. The Jesus Christ whom the believer acknowledges to be the basis of faith is also recognized to be the believer's
source of hope and joy, because the believer knows that Christ is
pro me, "my Lord." Acknowledgment "precedes" recognition in
that it provides the objective basis that is personally appropriated
in recognition. But unless acknowledgment leads to recognition
it remains sterile and unrelated to the believer's identity.[53]

Similarly unless acknowledgment and recognition lead to
confession faith remains a private, secret affair in the believer's
life. Unless faith is confessed publicly, before all people, what is
acknowledged and recognized in faith can be isolated and separated from other aspects of the believer's existence. A private faith
is something that can be compartmentalized and is vulnerable to
distortion and manipulation by the believer. Confession is that
final moment in the act of faith when what has been acknowledged and recognized is publicly proclaimed in the context of the
community's faith and life. Baptism, therefore, is one part of the
process of confession because it is a public statement on the part
of the believer or the believer's sponsors that the grace of God has
incorporated the believer into the body of Christ and its visible
representation in the Christian community. Baptism is a confession that faith cannot be lived privately but must be lived and
celebrated communally. Baptism is a confession, or perhaps it is
more accurate to say that it is the beginning of confession. In
Augustine's life baptism is the culmination of the events narrated
in Books I–IX of the *Confessions*, but it is the writing of the
Confessions, the reconstruction of personal identity by means of
the faith of the Christian community that is the true performance
of the act of confession. That act is possible only after the believer
has lived within the Christian community, only after the believer
has been nurtured in its piety and has learned to see and understand the world as the community does.

Admittedly, Barth's analysis of the dynamics of faith is not
quite the same as the model we have been developing by means

of narrative theology. By acknowledgment Barth does not mean a human act that is purely objective and by recognition he does not mean sheer subjectivity. Both acknowledgment and recognition have objective and subjective dimensions. Acknowledgment, for example, is more than assent to objective reality in that it is characterized primarily by trust. And recognition is not something purely subjective because it has an object and a content—namely, Jesus Christ. More importantly, the primary emphasis in Barth's discussion of confession as the culmination of faith is the distinction between private and public faith. By confession he means that which is done publicly, before the world, and which can never remain a private reality. Our emphasis on confession has stressed not so much its public dimension, although that is an essential feature, but the sense in which confession is a form of understanding, the final appropriation and integration of what has been acknowledged and recognized as the truth about Jesus Christ. Although our use of confession differs from Barth's, what is significant about his analysis is the structure of faith and the interrelations between acknowledgment, recognition, and confession.

Although faith is a human act, Christians believe it is not possible apart from the work of the Spirit. Barth analyzes the three "moments" of faith in the larger context of his discussion of the work of the Spirit. It is the Spirit who awakens faith and apart from the work of the Spirit acknowledgment, recognition, and confession are not possible; that is, they are not possible as faith. Confession is indeed a human activity, but finally, ultimately, it is a statement of Christian faith only by the grace of God and the communion of the Spirit.

4. Confession and Revelation

As the final moment in the act of faith confession is also the culmination of the process of revelation. The objective reality of

revelation is that series of events that constitutes Israel's cove-
nantal history and the life history and personal identity of Jesus
of Nazareth as the Christ. But revelation is not just an objective
historical event. Revelation also has its subjective dimension,
which becomes a reality in the believer's act of faith, in the believer's acknowledgment, recognition, and confession that what
is objectively true—that Jesus of Nazareth is the Christ—also
has overwhelming, history-shaking, world-shattering consequences for the believer and his or her personal identity. Confession, therefore, as the final moment in the human act of faith,
becomes a reality when the *Credo* of the Christian faith, the faith
of the believing community, becomes the prism through which
the believer's history and personal identity are refracted and reconstructed. Hence confession necessarily assumes narrative
form, but it is a narrative that cannot be identified with that
narrative which recounts the believer's personal history prior to
conversion, nor with that narrative which articulates the faith of
the Christian community. The confessional narratives of Christian
believers are the result of the collision between the faith narratives of the Christian community and the believer's personal history. To confess faith in Jesus Christ is to reconstruct that personal identity narrative in light of the community's *Credo*.

Alfred Schutz's categories of "the stranger" and "the homecomer" describe two possible situations in which individuals
might encounter the Christian community. Although the dynamics of each encounter are different, there are also some striking similarities in the two situations. Both encounters result in
a "hermeneutical crisis," a crisis in understanding and interpretation for both the individual and the community. In the case of
"the stranger" the hermeneutical crisis is whether the individual
can appropriate the faith and life of the community and successfully reinterpret his or her personal identity by means of them.
For the community the crisis is whether it can recognize its collective faith after it has been appropriated and reinterpreted in

the context of the stranger's personal identity. In the case of "the homecomer" a similar crisis emerges if the individual returns to the community in search of a nostalgic ideal fabricated from the past. The community, on the other hand, must be willing to acknowledge that the homecomer is not the same person who once lived in the community and must recognize the significance of the interval in the homecomer's history and personal identity.

In each of these cases the dynamics of confession and revelation differ. As the final moment in the act of faith, confession for the stranger is a matter of fusing his or her personal history with the Christian community's faith narratives, so that the stranger's personal identity is transformed by the latter. Revelation, for the stranger, is not just the detached, objective acknowledgment of the truth of the community's faith; it is also the recognition that that faith bears on the stranger's personal existence, a recognition that does not reach fruition until it culminates in confession.

For the homecomer, confession is a more complicated matter. If the homecomer lived in the Christian community without ever becoming a participant in its corporate life, then confession may not differ significantly from what it is for the stranger, unless the homecomer brings to the Christian community preconceptions of the community's faith, perhaps residual images from childhood, which bear little or no resemblance to how the community understands its faith. But if the homecomer was at one time a participant in the community's life, then confession becomes more complicated. Depending on why and when the individual left the Christian community, confession may entail the reinterpretation of an initial faith which either was undeveloped or distorted, but confession will always require the interpretation of that period in the homecomer's personal history which was lived apart from the community. An example of the complex nature of confession would be a person who grew up in a rigidly conservative Christian church, left that community soon after adolescence, but at some point later in life returned to a different Christian community. Part of the difficulty in this situation is the question of whether different churches, especially churches from different locations on the theological spectrum, can be said to belong to the same "community." In light of our discussion of community at the beginning of this chapter there is perhaps a broad sense of community in which that claim can be made. In any case the faith that will be used to interpret the homecomer's personal history will be significantly different in the community he or she joins in middle-age, and the process of confession must include a reinterpretation of the homecomer's initial faith, which has either been discarded or significantly reinterpreted.

The Augustine of the *Confessions* is more like the "homecomer" than the "stranger," although it is not clear that Augustine in his youth was ever enough of a participant in the Christian community to be said to have left it. Augustine certainly had a strong impression of what constituted Christian faith, and his struggles in his youth, both intellectual and emotional, were in part a coming to terms with what Christian faith did and did not mean. The *Confessions* are important, however, not simply because they preserve Augustine's personal history, but because they tell us a great deal about the nature of confession, its relation to revelation, and the narrative structure of Christian faith. Whatever else they may be the *Confessions* are an exercise in interpretation. Augustine's personal history is the "object" to be interpreted and the faith of the Christian community is the context, the means by which Augustine reconstructs his personal history. As we have seen, not only is the book "confessional" in its literary form, but, more importantly, it is the process of reinterpretation the reader observes in the text that makes the book a confession. A collision of sorts takes place between the *Credo*, the faith of the Christian community as it is sketched by Augustine in Books X–XIII, and Augustine's personal history, the autobiographical material in Books I–IX. The former "text" provides the concepts, categories, symbols, and myths which are used to structure and interpret the latter narrative. In the collision between these two narratives light is shed on Augustine's personal history and the writing of the *Confessions* is Augustine's act of faith, his acknowledgment, recognition, and confession of what the objective reality of God's grace means for his subjectivity—that is, who he is and what kind of person he is in the process of becoming.

If Christian faith were merely a matter of acknowledging the objective reality of revelation then it would indeed take the form of "belief," and would be nothing more than an act of intellectual assent to a series of propositions. But in this form faith has to do with only one dimension of human being—the cognitive—and the other facets of human being are at best only indirectly affected. As an act of assent to revealed propositions this description of faith ignores the essential historicity of Christian faith—that is, the roots of Christian faith in the reinterpretation of particular historical events and the sense in which the confession of Christian faith is an acknowledgment and recognition that an individual's personal history (and therein his or her personal identity) has been redeemed by Jesus Christ. It is the historical referent at the base of what Christians mean by revelation that gives faith in its final form as confession its narrative structure. Any theological analysis of faith which ignores this essential structure runs the risk of reducing faith to only one of its moments—either acknowledgment or recognition—and reinterpreting confession as simply the recitation and acceptance of an external authority or the wholly subjective expression of emotions and feelings that have no basis apart from the believer's personal experience. The act of reciting the community's *Credo* is not itself an act of confession. Nor is an individual's recitation of his or her personal identity necessarily a confessional act. Confession takes place and revelation becomes a present reality only when those narratives which are the basis for the community's *Credo* are used to reconstruct and reinterpret an individual's personal history.

Faith is indeed a human act, and confession is the final performance of that act. The meaning and structure of Christian identity is to be found in the act of confession, for Christian identity, as we have described it in the last three chapters, is not something that accrues to a person by right or by inheritance. It cannot be passively acquired, and it is not something that one possesses because of one's race, religious tradition, or family background. In the Christian community one of the things that one person cannot do for another is confession. The community is the necessary context in which confession takes place, but the reconstruction and reinterpretation of personal history which constitutes the act of confession is something that can be performed only by the individual who has lived that narrative history and whose identity is constructed from it. A description of Christian identity as that confessional narrative which emerges from the collision between the *Credo* narratives of the Christian community and an individual's personal identity narrative has important implications for what Christians mean by revelation, faith, confession, and conversion. That formal claim, however, does not describe what happens in this narrative encounter that makes it possible for confession to take place. In order to get at this set of issues we must turn our attention to the question of the hermeneutical principles at work in the act of confession.

PART III
The Hermeneutics
of
Christian Narrative

Chapter VII
Understanding
Christian Narrative

To confess Christian faith is to engage in a hermeneutical activity—an exercise of reason and intellect that entails interpretation and understanding. The narratives of personal identity and
Christian faith not only must be interpreted but also understood,
and these two activities of interpretation and understanding, although interrelated, are not the same. The process of reconstructing personal identity in the context of the faith narratives of the
Christian community is a hermeneutical activity, a venture as
human as faith itself, and it requires the full exercise of the intellect. Although this activity is an exercise of reason, it also
involves dimensions of human being other than reason. It involves the whole person, including emotions, feelings, and that
vast reservoir of material stored in the unconscious. The reconstruction of personal identity, like every hermeneutical act, also
involves the imagination. If in the act of confession the faith
narratives of the Christian community are employed in the reconstruction of personal identity, then confession requires the use of
the imagination in the reinterpretation of personal history.

Having formally described how revelation takes place in the Christian community and how it culminates in that narrative form we have been describing as "confession," we must now turn our attention to the hermeneutical questions implicit in this description. Precisely what takes place in the human activity of the confession of Christian faith? What does it mean to "understand" personal history by means of Christian faith, and how does "understanding" take place in that process? These hermeneutical questions are the subject of this chapter. We first will examine the nature of understanding and its implications for what we have been describing as confession. Then we will take the doctrine of justification as an example and ask what it means to understand justification within the context of a narrative theology. Finally, we will turn to two related hermeneutical issues: the relation between knowing and doing in the process of understanding and the question of what meaning and truth refer to in Christian narrative.

1. The Nature of Understanding

What is involved in the process of understanding a text or a conversation with another person? When a person says, "I understand what you mean," what is being said? This question has obvious significance for a narrative description of revelation because confession, among other things, is an act of understanding. To confess Christian faith is to say in effect, "I understand who I am in the light of and by means of the faith narratives of the Christian tradition." The actual performance of confession in either its public liturgical form or its personal practice is an exercise in understanding. Confession is not a discourse about what it means to understand Christian faith; it is not language about faith but the language of faith, language that emerges out of the narrative encounter between the individual and the Christian community. Confession is first-order religious language. Confession is an act of religious understanding that is deeply relational, the basis for the intercourse between an individual in his or her transformed personal identity and that personal reality called "God" encountered in the faith narratives of the Christian tradition. In Augustine's description of revelation and conversion the process of understanding is inseparable from memory and confession. "Look into my heart, O Lord, for it was your will that I should remember these things and confess them to you." [1]

In revelation the process of understanding is not simply a matter of meditation and self-discovery, but an event and an activity in which the individual stands in relation to an "other" called "God." In the context of this relation the individual is freed from the bondage of sin by something called "grace." Sin has many manifestations and cannot be reduced to one aspect of human being, such as the will or the intellect, and one of its most important manifestations is the oppressive weight of a disordered and meaningless personal history. The narrative history of the Christian community provides the context in which the individual encounters God and experiences the grace that makes possible the process of understanding involved in reinterpreting personal history.

But what does it mean to "understand"? Understanding is both an event and a learned or acquired ability. Understanding refers both to a facility, something that a person is able to do, learned in relation to specific activities and social contexts, and an event in which transformation takes place, transformation that results from the encounter with another person or text. Hence there are two dimensions to the process of understanding and both are necessary for a full description of it. On the one hand understanding is a learned skill. To understand is to be able to enact concepts. But it is not just that. This learned facility is acquired in an event, the encounter that takes place between different horizons of interpretation.

Understanding is not quite the same thing as knowing, at

least not what we usually mean by knowing, and the distinction is an important one. A person can know something, like the answer to a question, without necessarily understanding what is known.[2] Of course this may be simply a matter of information. For example a child may have memorized multiplication tables and may be able to determine the product of four times four. In the sense in which we are using the term, the child "knows" the answer to the question. It is not self-evident, however, that the child "understands" how to multiply numbers. Similarly, a person may have memorized the rules of a game—baseball, for example—and may be able to state how many strikes constitute an out, but *knowing* the rules of a game and being able to answer questions about those rules does not necessarily mean that one *understands* how to play the game. Understanding implies more than just knowing. To be sure, understanding includes a cognitive dimension, but simply knowing that something is the case is not in itself evidence that one understands what one knows.

One significant test of understanding is whether a person can engage in the activity that knowing describes. The child may know the correct answer to the question about the product of four times four, but it is possible that the child has simply memorized the correct response to the question and does not understand how to multiply other numbers. A bystander may have learned some or all of the rules that govern a baseball game, but knowing those rules is not evidence that the bystander understands how to play baseball. In each case we would say that the child and the bystander understand multiplication and baseball only if they are able to engage in the activity, only if the child can demonstrate that it has not simply memorized the correct response to questions but understands how to multiply numbers, only if the bystander can actually take the field and play the game. Understanding does not refer to a mental process, something that happens in the mind; rather it is a learned skill or ability. A person understands when he or she is "able to go on," when that person is able to continue multiplying numbers or playing baseball. One criterion, therefore, of understanding is not whether a person knows the proper answer to questions about multiplication or baseball but whether he or she is able to engage in these activities. The real test is not just whether they know the rules that govern the game, but whether they can use and apply the rules, whether they can engage in the game itself. Another piece of evidence for determining understanding is whether a person can improvise on established rules and concepts. That is an important criterion because it suggests that it is the activity that has been understood and not just formal principles that have been memorized.

To describe understanding in these terms implies that language is closely related to life, that language is rooted in different activities and that understanding words and concepts and sentences means understanding them in terms of their function and their setting in life. Ludwig Wittgenstein argued this basic point by insisting that "to imagine a language means to imagine a form of life."[3] That is, to think about a particular use of language is to consider an activity, for the meaning of a word or a rule or a concept is not something inherent in the word. Its meaning is its use or its function in the context of a particular activity. As Wittgenstein described it, the use of language is similar to the playing of a game. One understands the meaning of a word or a language when one is able to use it, to employ it appropriately. In comparing the use of language to a game, Wittgenstein was not implying that the use of language is a frivolous activity. What he did intend to demonstrate is that language is a social phenomenon and that understanding a language involves the ability to use it in its own appropriate social setting. "Here the term 'language-game' is meant to bring into prominence the fact that the *speaking* of language is part of an activity, or of a form of life."[4]

Wittgenstein's categories illumine many of the dynamics that have been at the center of our description of life in the Christian community and the nature of Christian identity. For example, it is difficult to determine the meaning of Christian language unless one has observed that language at work in the Christian community. Understanding Christian language is not simply a matter of knowing appropriate definitions. At a more significant level it is a matter of knowing what is and is not appropriate to that language in the forms of life that are enacted in the Christian community. It is one thing to know what the members of a particular Christian community believe about the nature of God; it is something else to understand what the use of that language entails in terms of behavior in the community and life in the world.

One problem, of course, with this application of Wittgenstein's philosophy to Christian language is whether it is possible to describe Christian faith or the life of the Christian community as *a* form of life or even as a collection of forms of life. A strong case can be made that there are various forms of life in every Christian community and that each of these activities has its own rules and internal logic.[5] But even if one grants that it may not be possible to describe Christian faith as one language game, that Christian faith and life consist of various overlapping yet distinctive language games, Wittgenstein's fundamental points still hold and illumine some of the more elusive aspects of the nature of revelation in the Christian community. Revelation that does not culminate in confession is not really revelation, because if revelation is nothing more than acknowledgment and recognition it may be a form of *gnosis*, some kind of knowledge, but it is not truly revelation. Only when the process culminates in confession does revelation become a reality, and, as we have seen, confession involves more than just knowledge. In other words, if revelation does not lead to faith then from a Christian perspective it is not revelation. More so than acknowledgment and recognition, confession requires the exercise of understanding. In terms of the categories we have been using that means that the understanding

that characterizes confession involves more than simply knowledge about faith. Confession is an understanding of Christian
faith which includes the learned capacity to engage in those activities and forms of life which are inseparable from the language
of Christian faith. Hence to understand Christian faith is to be
able to engage in its language and life at a level that is deeper
than that of "knowing about."

Wittgenstein's discussion of the nature of meaning points to
the importance of the social context in which language is learned.
That insight is of particular importance for any examination of
the nature of Christian language and the fundamental differences
between knowing and understanding that underlie confession as
the final moment in the human act of faith. But while Wittgenstein's analysis of the nature of language provides clues for com-
prehending "understanding," there are important dimensions of
understanding that he ignores. While he accurately describes the
sociality of language and the inseparable relation between understanding and "form of life," Wittgenstein does not give adequate
attention to other dimensions of the act of understanding—
namely the historicity of language and hence of understanding
and the sense in which both are embedded in tradition. This
equally important dimension of language and the process of understanding is a major theme in the hermeneutical tradition represented by figures such as Wilhelm Dilthey and Hans-Georg
Gadamer. The nature of language and the process of understanding is not merely social; it is also historical.

Perhaps one reason Wittgenstein fails to give adequate attention to the historicity of understanding is that the primary metaphor he uses to interpret language and understanding is that of
a "tool."[6] Words do not have an intrinsic meaning. Their meaning is their use in relation to a specific function and form of life.
Consequently "meaning" is a functional category for Wittgenstein. But there is more to language than its social function and
its setting in life. Symbols, words, and concepts have histories

and those histories are essential features of the forms of life in which they are rooted. Whether all words are embedded in tradition is a complicated question, but for language that is transmitted from one generation to the next by the ongoing life of a community, such as is the case in the Christian community, the historicity of the language, or what we might refer to simply as "tradition," is an essential feature in its interpretation.

Wittgenstein's metaphor of the tool obscures the historicity of language and therein the sense in which language is not just a detached object standing over against me, but in a very real sense a "thou" with whom I am drawn into conversation. The historicity of language, or what Gadamer calls "tradition," is not something that is "understood" only in the sense of being mastered, as one learns how to "master" a tool, because "tradition is not simply a process that we learn to know and to be in command of through experience; it is language, ie it expresses itself like a 'Thou'."[7] According to Gadamer, understanding is not so much a matter of mastering the use of a linguistic tool as it is the discovery of the reciprocal relationship that characterizes a conversation. To understand, therefore, is not just to "be able to" use language; it is a learned capacity that takes place within the living, dynamic encounter between an interpreter and a text. Gadamer describes tradition as "the horizon of the past" and in every act of understanding there is a merger of the horizon of the tradition (which is itself never fixed) and the horizon of the interpreter. "Thus the horizon of the past, out of which all human life lives and which exists in the form of tradition, is always in motion."[8]

Like Wittgenstein, Gadamer understands application to be an essential ingredient in the process of understanding. Accordingly, understanding for Gadamer is not a matter of translating from one language or realm of discourse into another. "Where understanding takes place, we have not translation but speech."[9] For Gadamer the real test of understanding is not the ability to translate, because "you understand a language by living in it," and it is this "living in it" which Gadamer describes as "an accomplishment of life."[10] On this basic point Wittgenstein and Gadamer take similar positions. Speech, not translation, is evidence that understanding has taken place and speech includes the capacity for application. Where the interpreter's horizon has merged with that of the text conversation occurs and understanding may take place. For both Wittgenstein and Gadamer understanding language is not just a matter of describing and analyzing a particular form of life, as one would describe an object. To understand is to find one's self immersed in conversation with a tradition and engaged in that form of life which the tradition has assumed. Understanding is not just knowledge about a particular realm of discourse and its attendant forms of life. It is not just knowledge about language, but is that "knowledge of" language which comes with participation in the activity and social setting in which the language lives. In this sense to understand, for both Wittgenstein and Gadamer, is to engage in speech. This first-order form of language occurs only when the speaker—or in our case "the interpreter"—does not simply move back and forth between competing realms of discourse but is immersed in the use of a particular form of language. But speech is not just the mastery and use of language. Language has its own history, its own tradition, and in that sense lives a life of its own. While the act of understanding requires that the interpreter be able to engage in the activities appropriate to the use of a particular language, it also requires that the interpreter be aware of the historicity and the horizon in which the language is embedded.

These two foci in the act of understanding—function and historicity—provide clues as to what constitutes a "mistake" in the encounter between an interpreter and a text. On the one hand the interpreter "misunderstands" the text if he or she is unable to engage in the activity or the world which the text depicts. Misunderstanding is not just a matter of getting the wrong answer but of being unable to use a language, being unable to employ the language in its appropriate setting. And misunderstanding commonly occurs because the interpreter ignores the historicity of the text. If a language or a text is used in a manner that has little or nothing to do with the text's historicity that is just as much a violation and hence a misunderstanding of it as is its improper application. And in point of fact the two usually go hand in hand. A misinterpretation or misunderstanding of a text is usually the result of the interpreter's inability to utilize the text, and more often than not that "inability" is a consequence of the interpreter's failure to attend to the text's historicity.

Obviously this interpretation of the nature of understanding is significant for our attempt to describe the hermeneutics of Christian narrative. We have argued that Augustine's *Confessions* is a paradigm of the process of revelation, that "moment" in which acknowledgment and recognition lead to confession. The first nine books of the *Confessions* are not just a "translation" (in Gadamer's sense) of the symbols and concepts of Christian faith, but a form of Christian speech itself. The hermeneutical issue is the question of the nature of understanding and its function in Augustine's reinterpretation of his personal identity narrative by means of Christian faith. As we have seen, confession is not just language about Christian faith; it is the language of faith itself, and in this sense it is "Christian" speech. As the apex of the human act of faith, confession is a hermeneutical activity; it is an exercise of understanding, the utterance of Christian speech. What Gadamer described as a "fusion" of the horizons of the text and the interpreter, we have described as a collision between the faith narratives of the Christian community and the identity narrative of the individual. The language of "collision" is preferable to that of "fusion" because although the latter correctly recognizes the sense in which understanding takes place in the encounter between historically different horizons of meaning, it does not capture an essential feature of Christian understanding—namely, the sense in which fusion demands extensive reinterpretation and reorientation, what we have referred to religiously and theologically as conversion. The confession that emerges from the collision is yet another form of narrative forged in the encounter of these different narratives. Yet in the narrative that is peculiar to Christian confession, the narrative we have described in Chapters IV through VI, it is possible to identify several features of the process of understanding which we have seen described by Wittgenstein and Gadamer. These features of the process of understanding are particularly important for uncovering the dynamics in revelation and Christian narrative.

In the first place, understanding is not simply a matter of repeating or reconstructing language. Understanding is interpretation, and, consequently, it is not a matter of "translation," if translation is interpreted in its pejorative sense as the wooden, mechanical search for equivalent expressions. For the Deuteronomists understanding is not simply a matter of the mechanical repetition of a creed. Understanding for the Deuteronomists is the extension of the faith narratives of the people of Israel into the community's and the individual's present existence. The actualization of these narratives is not simply repetition or reconstruction but a matter of interpretation. So too for Augustine, if we take the *Confessions* as a paradigm, to understand Christian faith is not simply a matter of knowing what is meant by the claim that God is Creator, not simply a matter of the proper interpretation of the nature of evil. If that were the extent of understanding then Augustine would not have needed to write anything other than the last four books of the *Confessions*. Understanding, however, is not simply "translation" in the form of repetition or reconstruction; it is "speech" and to speak is always to interpret. As speech, understanding means that what is spoken is not a lifeless object but a living word which assumes ever new forms when it is merged with the life of the speaker. When the faith narratives of the community are "spoken" by new communities and appropriated by the individuals in them they take on a new and ever changing narrative form we have called "confession."

Secondly, in the context of Christian narrative—in its confessional form—understanding points to the inseparability of language and life. To understand Christian faith is to know what forms of life are appropriate to it. Furthermore, understanding is not just knowing something about faith, but more importantly it is knowing what faith means in the context of one's personal history and existence. For the Deuteronomists to understand Israel's faith is not simply to be able to repeat the Decalogue. Understanding has something to do with being able to locate the Decalogue in its proper setting in Israel's narrative history. Israel's continued existence and her future identity are bound up in the interrelation of the narrative history of her faith and the distinctive life and activity of each new generation. Similarly, for the writer of Mark to understand Christian faith is not just to acknowledge and recognize that Jesus is the Christ. To understand is to be able to speak and Christian speech is finally a matter of confession. To confess that Jesus is the Christ is both to understand what it means to be a disciple of him and to be confronted with a decision as to whether one will pursue a life of discipleship. Understanding the narrative identity of Jesus Christ is knowing what it means to confess him as Lord, and that confession includes the forms of life that go along with Christian discipleship. David Burrell argues that a similar interpretation of "understanding" undergirds Augustine's *Confessions*. "What Augustine helps us to see is that understanding certain things— things which bear upon our own existence—also means going on to live in a manner every bit as consistent and consequential as is our ability to speak about them. Language is a way of life, and a confident use of language demands a consonant way of living." [11]

Finally, understanding Christian narrative in its confessional form includes yet another dimension in addition to significant speech and the interrelation of language and life. Because the final form of Christian faith is that of confession, understanding is not just a matter of acknowledgment and recognition. If Christian faith were nothing more than acknowledgment and recognition, then understanding Christian narrative might be nothing more than knowledge about Christian faith. In its form as confession, however, understanding Christian narrative means that knowledge about faith is inseparable from self-understanding. The very nature of confession is that the faith narratives of the community are appropriated by the individual. What distinguishes confession from recognition, therefore, is the exercise of significant speech. Personal history and personal identity become the fabric that is reworked in the context of the community's faith and its identity narratives. The horizon of the individual is fused with that of the community and the result is that confessional narrative in which revelation is appropriated and faith enacted.

The new self-understanding that emerges from this narrative collision includes more than just self-knowledge. Precisely because a person is more than just intellect, the self-understanding that is at work in Christian confession is not simply reflection or insight. It is a relational form of understanding, for self-understanding in Christian narrative always involves a relation between the self and a significant other—that community which recites and lives the narrative and, finally and ultimately, that reality called "God" who is the narrative's true subject. Furthermore, the relational structure of understanding in Christian narrative includes not just the intellect but also the will and the remaining dimensions of human being. Hence an event of understanding in Christian narrative is not just a moment of insight, although it may include that, but also, and perhaps more importantly, an event of grace in which the individual is no longer in bondage but is free to claim the freedom and identity of those who live in Christ by means of the Spirit.

2. Justification: A Test Case

Although confession may take the form of a narrative, the doctrines of Christian theology do not necessarily assume a similar form. Christian doctrines serve an important, critical function in the church's life; they provide the church with the critical principles it needs in order to understand and to enact its faith. Hermeneutical questions, such as the ones we examined in the previous section, are important for understanding the dynamics in a confessional narrative. But they are also important for understanding the relation between doctrine and faith. In their broadest form the questions of hermeneutics are about the process of understanding at work in the encounter between an individual and the faith narratives of the Christian community. In a narrower but equally important sense hermeneutical questions concern the relation between the confessional narrative and the symbols and doctrines that have been used to construct that narrative. In Chapter VI that issue emerged when we inquired into the relation of the last four books of Augustine's *Confessions* to the first nine. The identity of the community, like that of the individual, takes narrative form, but in the community's narrative history and its interpretation of its identity one discovers the raw material for the symbols and doctrines the community employs to explain its identity—who it is and why it lives the way it does. The major doctrines of Christian faith—creation and covenant, sin and redemption, for example—are not simply abstract concepts but are interpretations of the narrative history of Israel and the church.

As we noted in Chapter I, two symptoms of the identity crisis in the contemporary church are loss of tradition and the absence of theological reflection. The result has been the development of an ahistorical fundamentalism in the church. Christian narrative is simply identified with the life and faith of a particular community—often one in the first or the sixteenth century—and the symbols and doctrines of Christian faith are repeated rather than interpreted and appropriated. No real "fusion of horizons" takes place because the categories and the realities of "history" and "tradition" have ceased to function. Churches attempt to repeat or restore the first century but not to interpret the meaning of faith in the twentieth century. The symbols and doctrines of Christian faith become artifacts that are to be displayed at appropriate occasions, but they no longer "live"; they no longer force a reinterpretation of personal identity and are seldom referred to in the community's life because true Christian speech, rather than religious rhetoric, is heard only infrequently if at all.

An important example of the hermeneutical crisis in the church's understanding of its symbols and doctrines is its use of the doctrine of justification by faith. John Calvin described the doctrine of justification as "the main hinge on which religion turns," and Paul Tillich insisted that it is "the article by which Protestantism stands or falls." [12] In fact Tillich considered justification to be of such overwhelming importance for understanding the Protestant interpretation of Christian faith that he referred to it as "not only a doctrine and an article among others but also a principle, because it is the first and basic expression of the Protestant principle itself." [13] One of the tragedies in Protestantism has been that the doctrine of justification, the "hinge" on which Protestant faith turns, has ceased to be a living part of the church's faith and life. One rarely hears it referred to in the life of the church and when it is mentioned it is invoked as a venerable doctrine that has historical importance but is no longer relevant or intelligible.

The church has not always looked upon justification in this fashion. At one time the doctrine of justification was a powerful statement of the Protestant understanding of grace. The doctrine pointed to the sinfulness of every human being and claimed that in as much as every person is in rebellion against God he or she deserves only God's wrath and rejection. One side of the doctrine of justification was its understanding of sin. Because of the universality of the condition of sin, human beings are so infected by this disease that they are incapable of living righteously. The other side of the doctrine was its understanding of grace. God graciously imputes to the sinner the righteousness of Jesus Christ, who was without sin and was obedient unto death. The righteousness of Christ's sacrificial death on the cross is then imputed to sinners by God with the result that Christians do not cease to be sinners (and hence deserving of God's wrath) but because they are "in Christ" they are "made righteous" in God's sight. Only by God's grace and not by their adherence to the law or by any human achievement are sinners "made righteous." Hence the classical formula for the doctrine of justification is *simul justus et peccator*. Those who live "in Christ" are "simultaneously" both justified ("made righteous") and yet still sinners. They are forgiven sinners—forgiven and as such acceptable to God, but still sinners. The key to the doctrine of justification is the *simul*. It preserves the dialectic that is necessary for a proper interpretation of the doctrine. If it is lost the doctrine degenerates into either something approaching deification (the individual is indeed *justus* and not really still a sinner) or at the other end of the spectrum it degenerates into a task individuals have yet to achieve (and faith becomes something that one must *do* in order to become righteous).

This classical statement of the doctrine of justification has fallen on hard times in the life of the church. Of course there are good reasons why the doctrine appears to be irrelevant or unintelligible to many people. Traditionally it was formulated in juridical language and those concepts are difficult for twentieth-century Christians to understand. Even if the modern Christian decides to skip the tradition and return directly to Scripture the task of interpreting and understanding justification is no less difficult. Classical texts such as Paul's letter to the church in Rome ("For we hold that a man is justified by faith apart from works of law" [Rom. 3:28]) and his letter to the church in Galatia ("a man is not justified by the works of the law but through faith in Jesus Christ" [Gal. 2:16]) cannot be understood without a careful exegesis of what Paul meant by "law."

And the modern Christian encounters the same problem if he or she turns to the Reformers or to the early Protestant confessions for guidance. As Calvin describes it justification is a righteousness that is "imputed" to sinners by their union ("engrafting" was a term Calvin often used) with Christ. Hence the justification of the sinner is the imputing to him or her of the righteousness that belongs solely to Jesus Christ because of his obedience and his sacrificial death. Justification, for Calvin, means "the acceptance with which God receives us into his favor as righteous men. And we say that it consists in the remission of sins and the imputation of Christ's righteousness." [14] To be justified means both to be reconciled to God, to have one's sins forgiven, and to be made righteous by the imputation of Christ's righteousness.

Unfortunately much of modern Protestantism interprets Christian faith—both in word and in deed—in a manner that contradicts what has historically been its most important theological principle. To be fair, one would have to add that the sins of the recent generation are not without precedent in the sins of those who have gone before. In many cases the Reformers' emphasis on the principle of justification by faith has disappeared from the modern church's understanding of Christian existence, and faith has become a matter of believing the correct doctrines or assenting (at least publicly) to specific forms of morality. The church's failure to appropriate the doctrine of justification in its interpretation of Christian faith is yet another example of the crisis in Christian identity and the consequences of the loss of tradition and the absence of theological reflection in the church's common life. The result is a misinterpretation of Christian faith and life that has been compounded many times over. Faith is interpreted not in terms of grace but in terms of things one must believe and do, and the things that must be believed and performed often have no necessary relation to the reality at the center of Christian faith. For Calvin justification and sanctification must not be confused, but they are inseparable.[15] In Christ the believer receives a "double grace"—forgiveness of sins and imputation of righteousness on the one hand and regeneration (or sanctification) on the other. If sanctification is separated from a proper interpretation of justification, then there is nothing to prevent the identification of "the Christian life" with the social and moral convictions of any given culture.

One of the many reasons justification has fallen on hard times in Protestantism is that the church has been unable to provide an idiom for interpreting justification other than the juridical language in which the doctrine was first formulated. One such attempt, of course, was Paul Tillich's use of the quasi-psychological category of "acceptance." By means of that idiom Tillich was able to emphasize one side of the doctrine of justification— its understanding of the otherness of grace—but when he was finished it was not clear that Tillich had been able to preserve the inseparability of justification and sanctification.[16] Although anxiety and guilt are no doubt realities in modern life, it is not clear that they are the equivalent to what the Christian tradition means by "sin." Although the Christian community has tried in various ways to address the modern experience of guilt by means of the doctrine of justification, it has not been very successful, perhaps because guilt is primarily a subjective category and justification is intelligible only if guilt is interpreted in its relation to the objective, ontological reality of sin.[17] If the church addresses itself only to the modern experience of guilt it may have considerable difficulty in making the doctrine of justification intelligible. In Franz Kafka's *The Trial*, for example, there is no tribunal, no judge, only the subjective reality of the accusation of guilt. In Christian faith, however, justification speaks to the experience of guilt only in so far as that subjective reality is understood in relation to the objective reality of sin. The objectivity of sin is its relational character. Sin is not the breaking of a rule—moral or religious—but the violation of a personal relationship which the Christian community describes by means of the category of "covenant." [18] If sin, the violation of this personal bond, is not a reality, then guilt has no other referent than the subjective experience of responsibility but not responsibility to someone. Without the objective reality represented by sin guilt is utterly irrational and terrifying. Its source is faceless and anonymous.

Guilt separated from sin leads to anxiety but not to fear. And the church's doctrine of justification—at least in its traditional forms—insists that guilt must be understood in relation to sin, that the experience of guilt has its source in the violation of a personal relationship. The doctrine of justification, therefore, has played a prominent role in Protestant interpretations of Christian faith, and we have good reason to suspect that any resolution of the identity crisis in the contemporary church will entail a recovery of the significance of this "article by which Protestantism stands or falls."

Justification is an important example of the hermeneutical issues that surround the understanding of Christian faith and the resolution of the crisis in Christian identity. In the sense in which we have been using the term "understanding," the crisis in Christian identity is in part the result of the church's misunderstanding of the doctrine of justification. If we examine this claim in light of the features of understanding we discussed in the preceding section we may see something of the full dimensions of the problem and perhaps clues to a solution.

In the first place, it will not do simply to search for an appropriate "translation" of what Paul meant by "law" or what Calvin meant by the "imputation of righteousness." If justification by faith is an important category for interpreting Christian faith, then it should be a resource for understanding Christian speech. Although justification may not be what is spoken about—the object of faith—in first-order Christian language, it should be reflected in the way Christians reinterpret their personal identity in the narrative mode of confession. A person understands justification if he or she is able to do more than simply talk about what justification means. The decisive criterion is whether that individual is able to use the doctrine in the process of reconstructing personal identity.

We have seen that understanding refers to something that one is able to do. Furthermore, understanding takes place as a result of a collision of narratives or fusion of horizons. Both aspects are necessary for a proper interpretation of justification. It is not sufficient simply to know what Paul said in Romans and Galatians about justification or how Luther and Calvin interpreted the doctrine in the sixteenth century. If a person's understanding of justification is limited to this "historical" knowledge of the doctrine, then it is unlikely that justification will ever become a part of that person's significant speech. That person can talk about justification, perhaps even discuss its historical development with some sophistication, but if he or she is unable to use the language of justification in the interpretation of personal history and personal identity then Christian faith has not been understood.

On the other hand, the mere use of the language of justification by faith is not itself evidence that a person has understood the doctrine. If justification is truly understood, then it will be used with some discrimination, some awareness of what constitutes a proper and an improper use of the doctrine. Justification cannot be used in whatever manner the speaker wants to employ it, at least not if it is to be a "Christian" use of the doctrine. And the limits for a proper use of justification are mediated by the historical tradition in which it is embedded. Without an ongoing conversation with the theological tradition that includes Paul, Augustine, and the Reformers, the church would have no criteria

for determining what is and what is not a proper use of the doctrine in any individual's reconstruction of his or her personal
identity. That does not mean that the doctrine of justification is
a fossil which retains the same form in every age, but it does
mean that there are limits within which the language of justification can be used and that these limits are established by the
tradition in which the doctrine has its function and life. It may
be necessary for the church to find an idiom other than the juridical one in which justification was originally formulated, but
whatever new idiom is proposed it cannot suggest that justification is something that accrues to a person as a consequence of
faith. Any such interpretation degenerates into a form of "works
righteousness," and although such an interpretation may be used
consistently and coherently in the interpretation of personal identity, it is a mistaken interpretation of Christian faith and does not
represent a fusion of personal identity with the horizon of the
Christian tradition.

Secondly, the nature of Christian understanding is such that
language has a clear correlate in visible forms of human activity
or "forms of life." A proper understanding of the identity of Jesus
Christ goes hand in hand with the question of discipleship. To
understand who Jesus Christ is means that one must come to
terms with the cross that gives him his identity and characterizes
the nature of Christian discipleship. Such is also the case with
the doctrine of justification. Justification by faith is not simply a
set of theological convictions but language that refers to a specific
way of being in the world. The forms of life that are the correlates
of the doctrine of justification are not prescribed forms of behavior but a disposition, a posture or stance in life, that is informed
by the principles and convictions in the doctrine of justification.
Interpreted in this fashion, justification cannot be reduced to
holding certain beliefs. Using more traditional theological language justification should not be confused with sanctification,
but there also can be no question that justification is one dimen-

sion of the Christian experience of grace and that any attempt to separate it from the Christian life impoverishes and distorts what Christians mean by grace. That is only one reason why the letter of James has a proper place in the canon of Christian Scripture as a correction of any misinterpretation of Paul's theology. "But he who looks into the perfect law, the law of liberty, and perseveres, being no hearer that forgets but a doer that acts, he shall be blessed in his doing" (James 1:25).

Finally, because the doctrine of justification is a part of significant Christian speech, understanding it is not just a matter of being engaged in the tasks of interpretation and appropriation. Christian faith and language, as we have seen, are relational. They are rooted in that relation the Christian tradition describes as a "covenant"—the conviction of a people that their life comes from the hand of that personal reality who is the source of life itself—and that their existence is lived out before God (*coram Deo*). Hence the doctrine of justification, like the rest of the language used to explicate Christian faith, is not primarily moral, although it has moral implications, nor metaphysical, although it includes metaphysical claims. Justification is a concept that describes the relation between God and those people gathered and bound together in a community that recites a common narrative about God's grace. It is this narrative which mediates the relation between God and the people of the covenant, and the God of Christian faith cannot be known apart from this narrative. Justification by faith, therefore, is a relational concept; it refers not only to the proper interpretation an individual should have concerning his or her personal identity, but more importantly it refers to the meaning of one's personal history in relation to the narrative history of God's gracious activity. It is in the context of this narrative history that justification has its proper setting and function, for in this narrative, self-understanding is inseparably linked to an understanding of God.

3. Sanctification and Christian Identity

The Christian tradition has never been satisfied with the doctrine of justification as an exhaustive description of grace and the meaning of the Christian life. While justification is certainly an essential part of the Christian life it is by no means the whole of it. Paul does indeed have a great deal to say about the significance of the righteousness of faith, how justification takes place not "by works of the law but through faith in Jesus Christ" (Gal. 2:16). But Paul also insists that those who are justified by grace through faith are a "new creation." They live "in Christ" and walk by the Spirit, and this new life in Jesus Christ is characterized by a distinctive kind of freedom which manifests itself not in what Paul calls "the desires of the flesh" but in "the fruit of the Spirit," which Paul describes as "love, joy, peace, patience, kindness, goodness, faithfulness, gentleness, and self-control" (Gal. 5:22–23). In no sense is the Christian life a static, fixed reality, oriented only to a past event and an accomplished fact. Paul is equally concerned that his Christian sisters and brothers continue to grow in Jesus Christ, "so that he may establish your hearts unblamable in holiness before our God and Father, at the coming of our Lord Jesus with all his saints" (1 Thess. 3:13).

The Christian life is characterized by freedom, love, and righteousness, but Christian righteousness is, as we have seen, twofold. As Martin Luther described it, Christian righteousness consists on the one hand of "alien righteousness," so-called because it is a righteousness that is not intrinsic to the person but is given or bestowed from outside. By "alien righteousness" Luther meant "the righteousness of Christ by which he justifies through faith."[19] By faith in Jesus Christ, "Christ's righteousness becomes our righteousness and all that he has becomes ours."[20] It is this first form of righteousness—alien righteousness—which we discussed in the preceding section as "justification by faith." But there is also a second form of righteousness which Luther referred to as "our proper righteousness . . . that manner of life spent profitably in good works."[21] These two forms of righteousness are inseparable but not identical. The latter, proper righteousness, Luther described as "the product . . . its fruit and consequence," of alien righteousness.[22] It consists in "crucifying the desires with respect to the self . . . love to one's neighbor . . . meekness and fear toward God."[23]

This second form of righteousness—proper righteousness—has been described by various terms in the Christian tradition, terms such as conversion and discipleship, but probably the most familiar is "sanctification." Instead of proper righteousness John Calvin used the terms repentance and regeneration. Like Luther, Calvin thought it possible to describe the shape or structure of regeneration. It consists, he argued, of mortification on the one hand—"sorrow of soul and dread conceived from the recognition of sin and the awareness of divine judgment"—and on the other hand vivification—"the desire to live in a holy and devoted manner, a desire arising from rebirth."[24] The object of regeneration, as Calvin interpreted it, was not to increase the virtue or goodness of believers, but "to manifest in the life of believers a harmony and agreement between God's righteousness and their obedience."[25] And if the Christian life were to be summed up in a single phrase Calvin thought that "self-denial" was its most adequate expression. By self-denial he did not mean either Stoicism or masochism but a way of being in the world in obedience to Jesus Christ, what he described as a life of cross-bearing. By no means did Calvin think suffering was good for people as an end in itself. He did believe that those who confess Jesus as Lord and attempt to manifest obedience to God's righteousness will "undergo the offenses and hatred of the world." Consequently, "I say that not only they who labor for the defense of the gospel but they who in any way maintain the cause of righteousness suffer persecution for righteousness."[26]

One of the many interesting features of Calvin's discussion of regeneration or sanctification is his claim that self-denial and cross-bearing are at the very center of the Christian life. What Luther called proper righteousness and what Calvin terms regeneration cannot be reduced to moral categories. It is a great tragedy, therefore, that in the history of many Protestant traditions who count Luther and Calvin as "church fathers" sanctification became little more than a code of morality dressed in religious rhetoric, and, to make matters worse, a form of morality which had little to do with the Christian gospel and a great deal to do with the social, racial, and economic convictions of Western, middle-class people. For Luther and Calvin sanctification was not a moral code, a list of moral do's and don't's, but a way of being in the world, a religious disposition and posture which, to be sure, had serious and immediate moral consequences.

Like the doctrine of justification, sanctification also has fallen on hard times in the Christian community. In part that is because of the unfortunate tendency in the church's history to reduce sanctification to nothing more than a series of moralisms. But that is not the sole reason why sanctification has been misinterpreted and misunderstood. Several problems usually surface in any discussion of sanctification, but two are especially important. The first is the difficulty of finding an appropriate contemporary idiom for sanctification, and the second is the question of the precise relation between justification and sanctification.

Although sanctification is not mired in legal concepts and language as are many traditional interpretations of justification, still contemporary theologians have searched for an idiom which would make the doctrine intelligible to modern Christians without reducing sanctification to the parochial moral beliefs of a particular social class. Paul Tillich, for example, in addition to suggesting that "paradox" and "acceptance" were appropriate interpretations of justification also suggested that "process" was the appropriate idiom for sanctification.[27] And the process of sanctification, he argued, could be described in terms of four principles—increasing awareness, increasing freedom, increasing relatedness, and increasing transcendence.[28] Another theologian, Hendrikus Berkhof, has argued that the most appropriate term for making sanctification intelligible is "effort."[29] Neither "process" nor "effort" are entirely satisfactory idioms. The first suggests something that is almost automatic in its development, while the second (despite Berkhof's clear intentions to do otherwise) does not reflect the freedom that characterizes Christian existence. Numerous idioms have been suggested, but these two illustrate the dilemma theologians encounter in discussions of sanctification. While many theologians have recognized that sanctification must not be reduced to moral categories, they also have been aware that sanctification is a theological category with a clear referent in Christian existence. A major problem has been how to speak of sanctification in clear and precise language without reducing the doctrine to a moralism.

A second major problem concerns the relation between justification and sanctification. The classical problem has been how to describe the relation between justification and sanctification so that sanctification is not understood either as something that follows automatically from justification or as a doctrine that has no necessary relation to justification. If the first path is chosen then justification may become the exclusive focus of the Christian life with sanctification understood as its inevitable outgrowth. The second path leads to various misinterpretations of Christian faith. If there is no necessary relation between justification and sanctification, then Christian faith may be reduced to justification alone. This can lead to a life of religious apathy. Or justification may be understood to be a reality only if sanctification is realized, and this of course is a thinly veiled form of works righteousness.

The dialectical character of the relation between justification and sanctification is difficult to maintain, but perhaps the most successful attempt in twentieth-century theology has been Karl

Barth's. Barth rejected the description of the relation between justification and sanctification as a temporal sequence (as the *ordo salutis* has been interpreted by some theologians). Rather, Barth argued that the relationship between justification and sanctification must be understood in analogy with the deity and humanity of Jesus Christ; "Thus, although the two belong indissolubly together, the one cannot be explained by the other."[30] Barth insisted that justification and sanctification "both take place simultaneously and together."[31] In response to the difficult question of whether one is prior to the other in terms of the structure of Christian faith, Barth responded that "In the *simul* of the one divine will and action justification is first as basis and second as presupposition, sanctification first as aim and second as consequence; and therefore both are superior and both subordinate."[32] Barth's deft handling of this question is masterful, but he runs the risk of being too clever and too subtle. The dialectic is so tightly constructed that it is sometimes difficult to determine why some topics in his theology are discussed under justification and others under sanctification.

In the context of narrative theology the same problems emerge in the discussion of justification and sanctification that surface in classical treatments of the two doctrines, but because of the narrative context the problems assume a slightly different form. As in the classical discussions it would be possible in narrative theology to restrict sanctification to moral categories. Such a reduction, however, would be a mistake of misplaced concreteness. In narrative theology Christian doctrines are never "abstract" in the sense that they have no clear empirical referent. Their referents or the "raw material" out of which they are constructed are the identity narratives of the Christian community. What is redeemed and sanctified in Christian faith is the "person" of Christian individuals and communities and that "person," whatever else it may include, refers to the narrative histories that are the basis of Christian identity. The primary referent for sanctification, therefore, is not a moral attribute but the personal identities of those who have been justified and redeemed by God's grace in Jesus Christ. "Bearing the cross," as Calvin understood it, may well be the deepest sign of sanctification, but bearing the cross, like the term "discipleship," directs our attention to the narrative identity of the Christian believer. It is in this context that "biographical theology," especially as James McClendon has sketched it, offers fresh insights into what Christian faith means by sanctification.

Secondly, in narrative theology the question of the relation of justification to sanctification must be discussed in relation to the narrative history that constitutes individual and communal identity. When the question is raised in these terms, it is clear that justification and sanctification cannot be interpreted in some temporal or sequential order. In other words, justification does not refer to some part of a person's narrative history and sanctification to some other part. In Christian faith it is the whole person in all of his or her brokenness who is justified and ultimately sanctified, and that means that it is a person's narrative identity in its entirety that is the subject matter for understanding both justification and sanctification. Furthermore, because it is a person's narrative history that is the proper context for this discussion, justification and sanctification do not refer primarily and certainly not exclusively to isolated events in that narrative history. One cannot talk about the whole without referring to the parts, but it is the Christian narrative in its final form as confession to which one looks in order to understand the meaning of justification and sanctification and that confessional narrative is something other than the sum of its parts or what we have referred to previously as a "chronicle."

The object of justification is the "person" and that includes all of his or her narrative identity. Justification does not mean that a Christian's past history is annulled or forgotten. Justification refers to the extension of God's grace through Christ's cross to the narrative identity of individuals and communities. Justification does not mean that only particular events are forgiven but the whole narrative and the whole person. Similarly, sanctification does not refer only to a person's moral or spiritual development but to a narrative identity which is continually being reworked and conformed to Jesus Christ.

Finally, the very structure of Christian narrative in its confessional form suggests that some of the arguments about the relation of justification to sanctification are unnecessary. In its confessional form Christian narrative permits neither the identification nor the confusion of justification with sanctification. They represent two distinct but related interpretations of the nature of God's grace. Justification directs attention to the grace that the Christian is unable to generate from within but only able to receive, a grace that makes possible freedom and the reinterpretation of personal identity. Sanctification directs attention to that ongoing, unfinished task of reinterpretation as the Christian attempts to live in the world in witness and conformity to Jesus Christ.

4. Knowing and Doing

A fundamental feature of the hermeneutics of Christian narrative is the relation between knowing and doing. From various perspectives we have seen that understanding Christian narrative in its confessional form cannot be reduced to knowledge about faith. Understanding entails confession—the reinterpretation of personal identity—and participation in the forms of life that attend confession. Understanding Christian narrative includes both the knowledge that comes from the encounter with the Christian tradition and the participation in those activities that make up the life of the Christian community. What one knows in Christian confession cannot be separated from what one does and how one lives. In the hermeneutics of Christian narrative, theology and ethics are two sides of the same coin. Theological reflection that does not lead to questions about Christian moral decisions in both the personal and the social realms of life is not theological reflection about Christian faith. And any form of Christian ethics that does not look for guidance to the doctrines and symbols contained in Christian narrative may be a form of morality but not really a "Christian" ethic.

In the very fabric of Christian narrative understanding is what emerges when knowing is intertwined with doing. For the Deuteronomists, Israel's faith means that the performance of those statutes that govern the community's life is intelligible only in light of the community's narrative history. Neither the moral imperatives that govern Israel's common life nor its liturgical practices are intelligible or compelling in themselves. They have their rationale in Israel's narrative history. Similarly that narrative history is never recited merely in order to amuse or to entertain. It is recited or spoken as significant speech; that is, it has a purpose—"that it may go well with you" (Deut. 6:3). Israel continues to recite that narrative in order to remember whence she comes and what she is to be about in the world.

So too in Mark's Gospel the theological question of the identity of Jesus Christ leads necessarily to the question of what it means to be a disciple of him. To claim that Jesus of Nazareth is the crucified one and that his cross is the primary event in his narrative history means that the same cross casts a long shadow in the lives of those who confess that Jesus is Lord and who claim to be disciples of him. Christian faith is finally a matter of confession, and confession—for both Augustine and Barth—is as much an act of the will as it is an act of the intellect.

The structure of Christian faith is such that what one knows in faith cannot be separated from ethical questions about how one should live faith. Perhaps in the identity narratives of other religious communities understanding is not a matter of both knowing and doing, but in Christian narrative the objective content of faith—what one knows—is only one side of the coin. Equally important is the subjective side of faith, the faith that is lived in the world. That is one reason, among others, why the subjective reality of revelation should be subjected to the kind of analysis we have undertaken in this essay. If revelation is reduced to its objective form, then faith, the Christian response to revelation, could be interpreted as the mere acceptance of some external authority—Scripture, creeds, teaching office of the church, etc. When that happens what one knows in faith is easily separated from the question of how one lives that faith, and faith degenerates into one of its many idolatrous forms, the most common of which Paul Tillich accurately described as the "intellectualistic distortion" of faith.[33] Only if the subjective reality of revelation and the nature of faith are understood to be the necessary correlates of the objectivity of revelation will the gospel not become an exercise in gnosticism. The most convincing argument that knowing and doing are inseparably related in Christian understanding is the nature of Christian faith itself, which derives its theological principles from a careful analysis of the confessional narrative which gives the Christian community its identity and its location in the world.

It is in the confessional narrative which the Christian community recites that we discover the fundamental reasons why Christian faith involves issues of social ethics and why Christian faith is world-embracing and in this sense "ecumenical" in its reach. Because of the very nature of the narrative it recites, Christian faith cannot be reduced to a private ethic. Nor can Christian faith be identified with the social and moral customs of any given culture. Although Christian faith clearly has consequences for personal, moral decisions about interpersonal relationships, marriage, sex, the abuse of the body, etc., it cannot be identified with the moral mandates of any given culture. More importantly Christian faith cannot be reduced to questions of personal ethics. Equally significant are questions about the social consequences of Christian faith. It is unnecessary to engage in arguments about whether Christian faith means that the individual Christian and the Christian community have a responsibility for what happens outside of their community in the larger social nexus. That debate, like many others, can be resolved by a careful examination of Christian narrative. Although there have been Christian communities which have interpreted biblical narrative to mean that Christians should withdraw from participation in the secular world and although there are texts in Scripture which could be used to justify such a decision, the primary thrust of Christian narrative is in the direction of what H. Richard Niebuhr described as "Christ the transformer of culture."[34] Christian discipleship is a way of living in the world in light of the meaning of the cross, and the Christian life, as Calvin observed, includes "bearing the cross." But the cross is both a religious symbol and a historical event and it has its meaning and its significance for the life of Christian discipleship only in the larger context of the narrative identity of Jesus Christ. In biblical narrative the cross represents not withdrawal from the world but costly engagement with it in the expectation of the coming kingdom of God.

The claim that in understanding Christian narrative knowing entails doing does not answer the question of what it is that is to be done. Christian narrative never answers that question prescriptively. The confessional narratives of the Christian community only provide the context in which ethical questions are asked and answered. Although the theological symbols and the ethical principles for answering that question are derived from Christian narrative, the narrative does not prescribe an answer to the moral question. In that sense Christian narrative is not a moral answer book with quick and easy responses to difficult and complex questions. Christian narrative simply provides the moral posture or disposition the Christian community assumes in relation to its larger social world, and Christian narrative provides the symbols and principles by which the community responds to moral issues.

Perhaps the most important of these principles is the distinctive interpretation of freedom that emerges from Christian narrative. Paul's comment in his letter to the church in Galatia— "For freedom Christ has set us free" (5:1)—is not simply an abstract comment about the nature of Christian freedom. It is a theological and ethical principle gleaned from the identity narrative of Jesus Christ. The peculiar nature of Christian freedom is intelligible only in light of the narrative identity of Jesus Christ, and any Christian ethic which does not reflect the significance of that interpretation of freedom in its understanding of Christian discipleship has distorted the Christian gospel. The question of whether liberation theology as it is emerging from third-world and oppressed Christian communities is a legitimate interpretation of Christian faith is a false issue. In the light of Christian narrative there can be no question that Jesus Christ identifies with the poor and the oppressed and that he calls those communities who publicly claim to be disciples of him to do the same. Understanding Christian faith means not only knowing that the cross and resurrection are the decisive moments in the narrative identity of Jesus Christ; it means knowing that the cross and resurrection compel the Christian to live the freedom of the cross in the world, to ask and answer difficult questions about the distribution of wealth, national health insurance, and the size of the defense budget in light of what the cross says about the identity of Jesus Christ and what the cross means for discipleship and Christian freedom.

Knowing and doing are interrelated in the understanding of Christian narrative, but they do not exhaust the nature of understanding, for understanding, as we have seen, is something that happens in the context of the life of the Christian community. As the final form of faith, confession involves both knowledge and the freedom to act in response to God's gracious transformation of an enslaved will, but knowing and doing are not all there is to understanding Christian narrative. In their different ways Augustine and Schleiermacher have demonstrated that Christian faith emerges from the experience of redemption as that is mediated in the life of the Christian community. Hence an interpretation of Christian understanding must take into account the sense in which both knowing and doing are related to the experience of grace or what Schleiermacher calls "feeling."[35] I would only add that it is in Christian narrative that the individual and the community are addressed by that Word which redeems them, and if we want to examine the precise relation between knowing, doing, and feeling we first must examine the nature and function of narrative in the life of the Christian community.[36]

5. Truth and Meaning

The identity narratives of the Christian community differ from those of some other religious communities in one important respect. Although they rely heavily on the use of myths, legends, sayings, and other literary forms, at their center the identity narratives of Christian faith are rooted firmly in history. Although many of the sagas in Genesis have no immediate reference to events in history, they must be interpreted in the light of Israel's historical experience. Neither the creation stories nor most of the patriarchal stories refer to historical events, but they are included in the canon of Scripture because they articulate important aspects of Israel's history. The exodus from Egypt and the occupation of the land of Palestine are events of overwhelming significance in Israel's history, but these events raise further questions for Israel about the meaning of creation and the nature of Israel's relation to Yahweh, questions that are dealt with confessionally by the sagas in Genesis. It would be a mistake of the first order, however, to describe Israel's faith and the identity narratives of the Christian community as uninterested in history. They are thoroughly historical, and the theological claims that emerge from them are convictions based on the community's historical experience.

There are several reasons why the Christian community has a stake in its claim that the narratives it recites are anchored in history, not the least of which is its understanding of the nature of redemption. From the beginning the Christian community has insisted that the incarnation of God's Word in Jesus of Nazareth means that salvation is an utterly concrete, tangible, earthy reality that takes place in the particularity of one person's narrative history. It does not take place in the realm of ideas or someplace apart from the empirical, historical world. When Christians talk about redemption, what is redeemed is not just the human soul, but the whole person and his or her narrative history. Indeed, the entire historical order, including nature, is the object of God's redemptive activity in Jesus Christ.

The historical referent in Christian faith is important because it bears on a crucial hermeneutical issue in the understanding of Christian narrative. In some quarters it is argued that the significance of Christian narrative is its meaningfulness. Christian narrative provides a set of symbols and a worldview or interpretation of reality which is internally coherent and externally consistent with human experience. Anyone in the market for a new understanding of the world and one's place in it should try the interpretation of Christian faith because it will imbue life with meaning and it comes complete with a warranty that guarantees a lifetime of satisfaction. Or at least that is the way the advertisements often read. But occasionally discerning shoppers for worldviews raise sticky questions about the category of "meaningfulness" and its application to Christian faith. They suspect that a meaningful narrative is not sufficient for their needs, and understand themselves to be in the market for a narrative that is not only meaningful but true. In order to satisfy that demand some hawkers of worldviews have developed an improved model of the original argument that Christian narrative is compelling because it provides meaning. Not only is it meaningful—so the new argument runs—but it is also "true," in the sense that it is both adequate to human experience and appropriate to the Christian tradition.[37]

The difficulties with this "revisionist model" of Christian theology are twofold. In the first place the truth of any interpretation of Christian narrative is not simply whether it is adequate to human experience and appropriate to the Christian tradition. Such an interpretation diminishes the elements of conversion and transformation which are clearly a part of the narrative of Christian faith. It may well be that Christian narrative is not adequate to human experience, but it still may be true. There is not much in human experience that justifies the claim that the cross should be the primary symbol for understanding human existence or that "whoever would save his life will lose it; and whoever loses his life for my sake and the gospel's will save it" (Mark 8:35). We have insisted that the encounter between personal identity and Christian narrative is best described in terms of the metaphor of "collision" precisely because the encounter is not necessarily adequate to human experience but jarring and world-transforming. The weakness in Gadamer's idiom of the "fusion of horizons" is that it ignores this theme of transformation. Furthermore, in the encounter between human experience and Christian narrative conflicts emerge and the question of authority cannot be evaded. It simply is not the case that every interpretation of Christian narrative is both adequate to human experience and appropriate to the Christian tradition. Those interpretations of Christian faith which are true may well be those which are appropriate to the Christian tradition and Christian narrative and inadequate to a person's experience in the world. Hence the very "appropriateness" of Christian faith may be that it is inadequate to human experience and demands a fundamental reinterpretation of personal history and personal identity. While the conflict cannot be arbitrated by proof texts from Scripture, the theological resolution of the issue must entertain at least the possibility that human experience may have to be reassessed in light of the truth claims of Christian narrative.

Secondly, interpretations of Christian faith which stress the categories of adequacy and appropriateness run the risk of collapsing truth into meaning.[38] The truth of Christian narrative and its symbols is not simply that they are appropriate to the reality to which they refer (or in which they participate), nor that they are consistent with the Christian tradition. That may be an important question to ask about the sense in which Christian narrative is meaningful, but it is not the primary question that must be asked if we want to know whether it is true. There may be other narratives, even religious narratives, in which the questions of truth and meaning can be collapsed, but such is not the case with Christian narrative, for at its center it makes claims about what has taken place in history and those truth claims are historical assertions. That does not mean that "understanding" is primarily a matter of reconstructing the mind of the author of the biblical text or any other text. Understanding takes place in the encounter between personal identity and Christian narrative, and what it is that is understood is the meaning of personal history in light of the symbols and vision of reality in Christian narrative. But because of the nature of Christian narrative, understanding in Christian hermeneutics cannot be restricted to the question of meaning. The question of truth must also be asked, and at crucial points in Christian narrative that is necessarily a question about the relation between narrative and history. For many Christians the discovery that the tomb of Jesus Christ was not and is not empty would not invalidate the narrative's claim that God raised Jesus of Nazareth from the dead. The discovery by historians that Jesus did not die on the cross but died fat and happy of old age in Palestine would render the claims of Christian narrative false.

The very nature of Christian narrative is such that the task of understanding it is primarily a matter of learning to use it in the reinterpretation of personal history and the reconstruction of personal identity. A person learns to do that when his or her narrative identity is fused to that of Christian narrative. When this "event" takes place, a narrative hermeneutic focuses on the meaning of the text and not on something external to the text—such as the intentions of the author or the *Sitz im Leben* of the text. But understanding is never satisfied simply with the question of meaning. It is driven by faith itself to ask the question of truth. Hence a Christian hermeneutic, an analysis of understanding as it takes place in Christian narrative, has no choice but to employ both the methods of theological or literary analysis and historical criticism, "that you may know the truth concerning the things of which you have been informed" (Luke 1:4).

Chapter VIII
Narrative
and Revelation

Our thesis throughout this book has been that the Christian community in our day is in the midst of a crisis of identity, that for various reasons its traditional resources and norms no longer function, and that to many people participation in the Christian community seems to be indistinguishable from participation in any of the civil or social groups that make up middle-class America. Furthermore, this crisis in Christian experience has a theological correlate in the confusion that surrounds the meaning of revelation, a doctrine which has served as the centerpiece for much of contemporary theology. In Chapter II we reviewed the development of the doctrine of revelation in recent theology and summarized some of the objections that have been raised against it. In subsequent chapters we have not attempted to offer a description of revelation that will answer all of the criticisms that have been made of the doctrine. Our project has been considerably more modest. By analyzing the nature and function of Christian narrative and the hermeneutical principles involved in understanding it, we have attempted to describe the "event" of revelation—how revelation becomes a reality in the subjective experience of individuals and communities. We have undertaken that project because of the strong suspicion that the crisis in Christian identity and the confusion surrounding the doctrine of revelation are interrelated. The one cannot be successfully resolved without attending to the other.

In the final pages of this book we will examine briefly the significance of a narrative description of revelation for some of the larger issues that were mentioned in Chapter II. And we will sketch some of the implications of narrative theology for related theological topics, such as the authority of Scripture, the meaning of the sacraments, and the relation between memory and hope.

1. Revelation and the Word of God

In Christian theology revelation does not refer simply to a numinous event nor to an event that can be described only in experiential categories. We might have reduced our description to these categories if our subject were a quasi-phenomenological approach to the history of religions, but even in that case our description would miss the most important features of what Christians mean by revelation. It may well be that the Christian experience of revelation is characterized by mystery, ecstasy, and miracle, but these formal categories are only a part of what revelation refers to in Christian faith.[1] In the Christian tradition revelation is both an objective reality and a subjective event and must be described accordingly. To put it more simply, revelation in Christian faith refers both to something that is disclosed and to an event of disclosure. What is disclosed is not primarily a piece of information, a proposition, or an idea, but the Word of God as it appears in Jesus of Nazareth. On the other hand, revelation is not merely a historical artifact that lives only in the distant past, but also an event that occurs in the contemporary experience of individuals and communities. Consequently, revelation is not a mystical event which can be experienced but not described, a "contentless" moment. It has a content, an object, something (or in this case "someone") which can be known, talked about, and proclaimed, which Christians refer to as the Word of God and which they insist is both a reality in the narrative history of Jesus of Nazareth and something that is heard in the midst of the human words of contemporary Christian communities.

In Christian faith revelation is always the revelation of God's Word. But what do Christians mean by God's Word and how does this Word become a reality in contemporary experience? A comprehensive answer to these questions would require additional volumes on christology and pneumatology. Questions about the nature of God's Word and its relation to human words are only thinly disguised questions about what Christians mean by the incarnation, their confession that "God was in Christ reconciling the world to himself." And questions about how God's Word becomes a reality in contemporary experience lead inexorably to a discussion of what Christians mean by the Spirit and how the Spirit makes Christ present in the world.

The relation between God's Word and human words, therefore, is closely related to traditional christological issues that surround the doctrine of the incarnation. One objection in recent theological discussion to traditional interpretations of Word of God theology is that the Word often seems to be a supernatural form or substance.[2] Interpreted in this fashion the doctrine of the incarnation appears to refer to a *tertium quid*, some kind of divine man who is neither fully human nor fully divine but some kind of intermediary between the two. Clearly that is not what the theologians of the early church intended when they described Jesus Christ as "one and the same Son, the same perfect in Godhead and the same perfect in manhood," but despite their best intentions classical incarnation theology which has not degenerated into Docetism or Ebionitism has bequeathed the church not a paradox but a third creature.[3]

In contemporary theology one alternative that has been proposed to some of the classical interpretations of the incarnation is the claim that God's Word in Jesus Christ is not the presence of another nature (*phusis*) but the presence and activity of God's power and love in the one person, Jesus of Nazareth. God's Word is not another word in addition to human words lurking above or behind the visible world; rather God's Word is that power which enables human words to become true words.[4] If this model of the incarnation is applied to the hermeneutics of Christian narrative, the relation between God's Word and human words takes on a different form in comparison to some of its earlier interpretations.

Christian narrative, as we have been describing it, does not have a final and fixed form. It does, however, have a center, which can be found in Scripture but cannot be identified with Scripture. Christian narrative includes the history of the diverse ways in which Scripture has been read and interpreted by Christian communities, a history that culminates in the particular interpretation of that narrative by the contemporary community. Christian narrative is not, therefore, the Word of God. But Christian narrative is the context, the sphere, in which God's Word is heard in the midst of human words. The Word of God cannot be identified with Christian narrative, nor is it some other word in an ethereal realm which must be added to Christian narrative in order for that narrative to become God's Word. Rather, God's Word refers to those moments in which Christian narrative becomes disclosive, those moments when Christian narrative ceases to be merely an object for historical curiosity, when its horizon collides with that of the reader and hearer, when the process of understanding commences, and acknowledgment, recognition, and confession become a possibility, when the human words of Christian narrative witness to Jesus Christ.

The claim that Christian narrative is the context in which God's Word appears is something that the Christian community confesses. That claim does not mean that God's Word does not and cannot appear elsewhere, in the midst of other human words and other narratives. On that question the Christian community can only confess what it does know, report where it has heard God's Word, and remain steadfastly agnostic about what it does not know. Christian faith confesses that God's Word refers to those moments in which human words point to Jesus Christ and become the occasion for transformation and confession.[5] Consequently, the only criteria Christians have for determining which human words have become an occasion for God's Word are twofold. Do those human words witness to Jesus Christ and do they lead to the transformation of personal identity and the act of confession? In principle, of course, any human word may become an occasion for God's Word.[6] Neither the church nor its theologians can prescribe where grace must or must not become a reality. Whether some human words witness to Jesus Christ in ways unknown to the Christian community is one of the many questions Christian faith cannot answer. Neither Christian faith nor the theology that reflects on that faith claim to be able to answer all questions. There are indeed limits beyond which Christian theology should not speculate and those limits are established by the confessional nature of the symbols and narratives of Christian faith.[7]

The confession that the faith narratives of the Christian community are the context in which God's Word is heard has implications as significant for those within the circle of Christian faith as it does for those without it. Although God's Word cannot be identified with the human words that make up any specific interpretation of Christian narrative nor even with the narrative as a whole, it is significant that the Christian community claims that regardless of what may be said about other words and other narratives it has heard God's Word within this narrative history.

That claim is significant because it implies a great deal about the nature of revelation, the meaning of redemption, and the God whom Christians claim encounters them in their narrative identity. In the first place, that claim suggests that not only is the category of history fundamental for understanding the structure of human identity but that the relation between God and the world is mediated by history. Legitimate criticisms have been leveled against traditional forms of Christian theology because they have ignored the importance of nature and the physical world in their explication of Christian faith. In most cases the criticisms are justified and the omission must be corrected, but any redress of the imbalance cannot alter the fact that history is indeed the primary medium in which the Christian community hears God's Word and the sphere in which it looks for God's activity and abiding presence. The created order is good and nature has its own value, not an intrinsic value, but the value it derives from its Creator. The Christian hope in redemption refers to the whole of the created order as the object of God's redemptive activity, but although redemption certainly includes nature Christian faith confesses that it is history and not nature that is the medium through which God brings about the redemption of creation.[8] By redemption Christians do not mean simply the salvation of the individual person, but the final location of the individual and the community within the life of God. What is redeemed is not just the soul, some disembodied specter in the human psyche, but the whole person, and since personal history is what gives a person his or her identity, it is personal history that is redeemed and preserved within the life of God.

Secondly, Christian faith does not claim that universal history is the sphere in which God's Word is heard—either directly or indirectly. That may be true in the gospel according to Hegel but not in the gospel of Christian faith. What Christian faith confesses is simply what it knows—that it has encountered God's grace not in history as a whole but in a particular narrative history that has its origin in those events which form Israel into one people and the church into one body. That narrative is radically inclusive and thoroughly open-ended, but it does not refer to history as a whole as the sphere for revelation, either in the past or in the future. Christian narrative has a determinateness and a particularity about it which preserve the concreteness and this-worldliness of the Christian understanding of grace and redemption. Revelation, for Christians, is always the revelation of God's Word and that Word can never be separated from the narrative history of Jesus Christ, because it is only in relation to Christian narrative that the Word has its power to engraft the identities of individuals and communities into Jesus Christ.

2. The Disclosiveness of Christian Narrative

Although Christian narrative is not itself God's Word, it is the context in which Christians listen for and believe they hear that Word. Christian narrative is not what is disclosed in revelation, but it does provide the occasion for hearing God's Word. The content of revelation—what it is that is revealed—is not Christian narrative. Christian faith confesses that what is disclosed in revelation is a personal reality it calls "God." While Christian narrative is not itself the object of revelation, it is closely tied to what Christians understand that object to be. In Christian faith revelation refers to the unveiling or disclosing of something that is hidden from view and inaccessible to human discovery, but this "something" is not a series of propositions nor an insight nor an idea. What is disclosed is a profoundly personal reality who has the status of an agent, indeed the status of the primary agent in the affairs of human history. Or as H. Richard Niebuhr made the same point some time ago, "Revelation means God, God who discloses himself to us through our history as our knower, our author, our judge and our only savior."[9] As Neibuhr described it, revelation refers to a moment or an event "in which

we find our judging selves to be judged not by ourselves or our
neighbors but by one who knows the final secrets of the heart;
revelation means the self-disclosure of the judge." [10] But what
Niebuhr did not emphasize sufficiently is the relation between
the God who is known in revelation and the narrative history
which serves as the forum for that encounter.

The God who is disclosed in revelation, the God who makes
himself accessible in his Word, cannot be identified with
Christian narrative. Yet just as the identity of every person is
constituted by his or her history so too God's personhood in relation to the world is a function of God's history. Christians speak
of God as a personal agent, a person with whom they believe they
have a relationship that reaches into the center of reality. But
God's identity is an interpretation of God's history, and the narratives of the Christian community, while not identical with
God's Word, are a report of God's history with the world. Consequently, questions about who God is cannot be answered in the
Christian community primarily by means of metaphysical speculation about the nature of God's attributes. That form of reflection is a necessary theological task, but the primary referent for
Christian discussions of the reality of God must always be the
narrative history of God's relation with the world. [11] Christian
narrative, therefore, in as much as it is a report of God's relation
with the world, provides the only resource that Christians have
for identifying the nature of God's person.

Recently it has become fashionable to speak of God's relation
to the world in terms of "God's trinitarian history," and there are
many advantages to this formula, not the least of which is that it
identifies God's being with his activity and emphasizes that God's
activity and hence his identity are available only in God's narrative
history. [12] Furthermore, the formula reminds us that the Christian
doctrine of the Trinity is not the product of speculation but
emerges from Christian reflection about the nature of God and
his relation to the world as that is disclosed in the narrative his-

tory of the Christian community. During the fourth and fifth centuries the Christian community was driven to the doctrine of the Trinity in order to make intelligible the true identity of the person with whom it has to do in its narrative history. Scripture does not itself contain a doctrine of the Trinity, nor does Christian narrative. But in so far as Christian narrative records the activity of an agent, the details of that narrative are the basis for the community's understanding of God's identity. The metaphysical questions that make up the doctrine of the Trinity are not self-generated, but emerge out of the particularity and complexity of Christian narrative. The doctrine of the Trinity is the Christian answer to the question, "Who is the person that is identified as 'God' in the church's narrative history?" The Trinity is the way in which Christians answer that question, the way they identify the nature of God. The Trinity, therefore, is a necessary description of God's identity, but it presupposes those narratives which witness to God's relation to the world. The claim that personal identity is always an interpretation of personal history applies to all persons—human beings and the triune God.

Part of what is disclosed in Christian narrative is the personal identity of the triune God. But that is only one part of the Christian doctrine of revelation. Revelation has both an objective and a subjective side; it is both content and event. Our attention has been focused more on the latter than the former, more on the nature of that event in which the relation between God and the world is disclosed and appropriated in Christian narrative. The subjective appropriation of revelation is the human activity called "faith," and faith is not so much something a person has or possesses as it is something that is lived and exercised. Confession is the final moment in the human act of faith because it completes a process which includes acknowledgment and recognition. In its form as confession, however, faith is indeed a human act. It is a human activity that involves the exercise of understanding. Interpreted in this larger context revelation refers not only to the history and personal identity of the triune God but also to the histories and identities of Christian communities and individuals, for in the act of Christian confession these are inextricably related. In revelation Christian narrative mediates or serves as the occasion for the encounter between the triune God and the community and its members. Self-knowledge, or what we have been calling personal identity, is interwoven with knowledge of God. Hence the disclosiveness of Christian narrative is not only its revelation of the identity of God but also its revelation of the true identity of the individual, insofar as that person's history has been reinterpreted in the context of the community's life and history with God.

We began this essay by pointing to the emphasis that both Augustine and Calvin place on the interrelatedness of self-knowledge and knowledge of God. The relation between knowledge of self and knowledge of God constitutes the fundamental dynamic for Christian identity and for the doctrine of revelation. Knowledge of self and knowledge of God are intrinsically related in Christian faith. The one depends on the other. Knowledge of God that does not bear on the understanding that a person has of his or her personal identity may be a matter of historical or sociological interest, but it is not truly knowledge of God, because the latter is possible only when personal history is reconstructed in the larger context of Christian narrative. On the other hand, the Christian doctrine of revelation insists that what takes place in the collision between personal history and Christian narrative is that personal identity is illumined, the ultimate meaning of one's existence is disclosed, and one is called to a new form of life. The self can be fully known only when it is understood in its relation to that reality who is its source, its life, and its final destiny.

As we have seen, the Christian doctrine of revelation and the nature of Christian identity are closely related. The present crisis in Christian identity is a theological problem and its source is the confusion that surrounds the meaning of revelation. Revelation, we have suggested, should be interpreted in its proper setting, that is, in the context of Christian narrative, for it is in this narrative that the encounter between God and the individual takes place in the life of the community. Only when revelation is understood as an event that takes place in the midst of the life of the community will it be clear why the deepest secrets of personal identity must be sought in the narrative history of the triune God. Only then will it be clear why Scripture must not be allowed to fall silent in the community's life, why the history of the community's interpretation of Scripture (what we have been calling "tradition") must not be ignored, and why the significance of theological reflection is that it enables the individual and the community to understand how Christian faith bears on questions of personal and communal identity.

3. The Authority of Scripture

A traditional concern in Protestant theology is the relation between revelation, the Word of God, and the authority of Scripture. One of the hallmarks of the Protestant tradition has been the great importance it attributes to Scripture. The Westminster Confession of 1647, for example, declares that "The whole counsel of God, concerning all things necessary for his own glory, man's salvation, faith, and life, is either expressly set down in Scripture, or by good and necessary consequence may be deduced from Scripture: unto which nothing at any time is to be added, whether by new revelations of the Spirit or traditions of men." And many contemporary interpretations ascribe authority to Scripture because it reveals God's Word.[13] Many Protestant communities traditionally have understood themselves to be a "people of the book," and questions about the authority of Scripture often have been perceived by Protestants to be of utmost importance for the interpretation of Christian faith. That is one reason why the contemporary phenomenon of the silence of Scripture in the Christian community, which we discussed in Chapter I, is a serious symptom of the crisis in Christian identity and indicates that the crisis has progressed to advanced stages.

A narrative interpretation of the doctrine of revelation and the nature of Christian identity will not resolve the arguments in the Protestant community over the interpretation of Scripture and the sense in which it is and is not "authoritative." Clearly narrative theology places great emphasis on the role of Scripture in the explication of revelation, faith, and Christian identity, because biblical narrative is the foundation for the different sediments that make up what we have been calling "Christian narrative." Christian narrative cannot be restricted to Scripture, but it is also the case that Christian narrative is always an interpretation of the contemporary world in light of the church's history of interpreting Scripture.

It should be apparent that in narrative theology, as we have been describing it, the authority of Scripture must be interpreted in terms of its function in the life of the Christian community and not in terms of some property intrinsic to it as Scripture. A case might be made that all interpretations of the authority of Scripture, even those which insist on its inerrancy and verbal inspiration, finally are arguing a functional interpretation.[14] In other words, despite what a theologian says about the inerrancy of Scripture, that position is actually derived not from Scripture itself but from the theologian's interpretation of Christian faith as a result of his or her participation in the life of a Christian community that reads Scripture in a particular fashion. In any case, within narrative theology the authority of Scripture is its function, and that function is twofold.

On the one hand, the authority of Scripture is its authority as a witness. It directs our attention to those events which are at the center of Christian narrative and therefore at the center of Christian faith. The metaphor of "witness" as a description of

Scripture's function has been carefully developed by Karl Barth.[15] Scripture is an authority in Christian faith and theology because it witnesses to those events in which the Christian community believes it sees and hears God's Word. The writers of Scripture are "witnesses" in one sense of the word because they were "contemporaries of the history in which God established his covenant with men."[16] The writers of Scripture are not authoritative because of some quality or property that distinguishes them or their words from other people and other human words. Their authority is not who they are but what they do. They witness to "Yahweh's Word itself, as it was spoken in his history with Israel, which they brought to the hearing of their people."[17] The writers of Scripture did not exercise their function as witnesses in the manner of a historian who attempts the greatest possible degree of objectivity and detachment in his or her critical assessments. Their witness is not simply that of observers of historical events; rather, they witness to events in which "Jesus' history was real, and real to *them*, pre-eminently as a history of salvation and revelation."[18]

Consequently, Scripture's function as a "witness" must be interpreted in two senses. On the one hand it is a witness, as Barth suggests, because of the writer's proximity in some cases to the events reported in the text. Obviously that is not true in every case, or even in most, but even though none of the writers of the Gospels were eyewitnesses to the events they report still they preserve oral traditions and the faith of the early church, and some of those traditions appear to preserve first-hand reports. It is precisely because some parts of Scripture do function in this fashion as a witness that Scripture must be investigated and interpreted by means of historical-critical methods. But that is not the only sense in which Scripture is a witness. It is also a witness in that it reports what was real to its authors—what Barth refers to as "a history of salvation and revelation." In this "history of salvation" what the writers of Scripture witness to is the grace of

God as they have seen it and experienced it in the proclamation that "God was in Christ reconciling the world to himself." In this second sense of "witness" what the writers of Scripture report may be true without being historically accurate. If historical proximity and historical accuracy were the only two criteria for determining which texts were gospel, then the church would have a different biblical canon than it now possesses. Just as important to the early church as the criterion of historical proximity was the question of whether a text witnessed to the truth about Jesus Christ, and that issue could not always be determined simply on the grounds of historical proximity.[19] The early church chose to exclude from the biblical canon some texts which may have been written earlier than texts which it decided to include.

In narrative theology Scripture is authoritative in these two ways. On the one hand, it witnesses to events which are the basis of the church's proclamation. The Christian community is gathered around these events, and they are the bedrock to which all other Christian communities return in order to understand what they mean by their confession that God was in Christ. Because the Christian community insists that its faith rests on the interpretation of particular historical events, the authority of Scripture in narrative theology is always subject to and vulnerable to historical-critical investigation.[20] But there is no such thing in narrative theology—or for that matter in any other form of historical narrative—as a bare fact or an uninterpreted fact. The historical events at the center of Christian narrative have their meaning only in the larger interpretive context of the narrative itself. Consequently the historical-critical investigation of Scripture can never suffice as the only method for determining the sense in which biblical narrative is true. It must be complemented by a literary analysis that examines the meaning of biblical claims in the larger context of the narrative itself. Both methods are necessary for a balanced assessment of the truth claims in biblical narrative.

Even if the metaphor of "witness" is used as a twofold interpretation of authority of Scripture, we have not yet exhausted the description of Scripture's function and therein the nature of its authority. As it is described in narrative theology, revelation and its culmination in the activity of confession suggest that the authority of Scripture is not just its witness to historical events or to the truth of the gospel but its function in the ongoing life of the Christian community.[21] Scripture's authority is not something intrinsic to it as Scripture; its authority is its role in the life of the Christian community. Once one interprets biblical authority in these functional terms it is clear that authority is something that Scripture can lose. If the community no longer turns to biblical narratives and their depiction of reality as the basis for the interpretation of personal and communal identity, then Scripture can no longer be described as "authoritative" for that community. At the same time, if Christian identity is as dependent on biblical narrative as we have argued, then it is not clear how a community which no longer listens to or uses Scripture can be said to be "Christian." Although Christian narrative in its form as confession is not simply a repetition of Scripture, still biblical narrative functions as the core material in the reconstruction of Christian identity.

Scripture's authority is not just its witness to historical events or its preservation of the truth of the gospel. It performs its function as a witness only when the Christian community allows it to do so, and it is Scripture's function in the larger life of the community that is its real authority. Scripture provides those narratives and symbols to which all Christian communities return in order to understand the substance of Christian faith. If Christian identity, as we have suggested, is a reinterpretation of personal identity by means of the narratives of the Christian community, then Christian identity cannot finally be separated from biblical narratives. And if biblical narratives are no longer allowed to function in the life of the Christian community, then Christian identity will quickly become confused with the narrative identities of other communities and traditions, both religious and secular.

4. Narrative and Sacrament

Some Protestant traditions insist that the celebration of the Lord's Supper and baptism always be accompanied by a sermon. The theological presupposition for that position is that the spiritual presence of the Word in the sacraments should not be separated from the appearance of the Word in Scripture and sermon. Certainly in narrative theology it would not be possible to celebrate the sacraments apart from the narratives of Christian faith. It is Christian narrative which provides the proper and necessary context for the interpretation and celebration of the sacraments. On this issue the arguments in Deuteronomy apply not only to the Jewish celebration of the Seder but also to the Christian celebration of the sacraments. In themselves and by themselves the sacraments are meaningless. They receive meaning only when they are located in the larger context of the confessional narratives they presuppose. The Deuteronomists insisted that the statutes, ordinances, and commandments that gave structure and order to Israel's communal life were not intelligible apart from those narratives that recounted Israel's history and faith. Not only do the narratives provide the context in which the commandments have their meaning, but even more importantly the narratives provide the reason for the continued observance of Israel's laws and rituals. The narratives are the answer to the child's question about the meaning and necessity of the statutes, ordinances, and commandments.

The Deuteronomists' arguments also hold for the Christian celebration of the Lord's Supper and baptism. It is not accidental that many Christian traditions insist that the celebration of the Lord's Supper begin with the so-called "words of institution": "For I received from the Lord what I also delivered to you, that the Lord Jesus on the night when he was betrayed took bread, and when he had given thanks, he broke it, and said, 'This is my body which is for you. Do this in remembrance of me'" (1 Cor. 11:23–24). The elements of bread and wine mediate the spiritual presence of Jesus Christ only insofar as they are celebrated in the larger context of those narratives that identify Jesus as the Christ. The injunction in the words of institution is "This is my body which is for you. Do this in remembrance of me" (1 Cor. 11:24). It is Christian narrative which mediates between the bread, the body of Christ, and Jesus Christ's spiritual presence. To "remember" him is not simply to bring Jesus of Nazareth to mind but to "actualize" those narratives in which he has his identity, to engage in that form of confession which fuses the narrative identity of the self to the narrative history of Jesus Christ. In the act of confession, in the collision of these narratives, understanding may take place and remembrance becomes a possibility. Apart from the narratives that identify Jesus as the Christ, the sacraments are vulnerable to gross misinterpretation and abuse. What Paul received from the Lord and delivered to the Corinthians was the narrative about the passion, and he appeals to this narrative in his correspondence with the Corinthians. Some of the Corinthians celebrate the Lord's Supper "in an unworthy manner," profane the sacrament, and eat and drink judgment upon themselves. The sacrament will be taken properly only when it is celebrated in the context of Christian narrative, only when the Corinthians understand the sacrament in terms of the narrative which Paul has received and delivered to them. Paul does not appeal directly to the cross, as he does in 1 Corinthians 1, but the narrative he does appeal to ("the Lord Jesus Christ on the night when he was betrayed . . ." [1 Cor. 11:23]) culminates in the cross, and it is the cross and the identity of the one crucified there that Paul asks the Corinthians to remember.

Similar issues surround the practice of baptism. To the same church at Corinth, a church suffering from internal dissension,

Paul writes, "Is Christ divided? Was Paul crucified for you? Or were you baptized in the name of Paul?" (1 Cor. 1:13). Apparently the Corinthian church was divided into factions and individuals were identifying with a particular group depending on who had baptized them ("each of you says, 'I belong to Paul,' or 'I belong to Apollos,' . . .").[22] Against this factionalism Paul appeals to the unity of all Christians in Jesus Christ (1 Cor. 3:21–23). He returns to this argument in 1 Cor. 12, the well-known passage in which Paul compares the diversity of spiritual gifts in the church with the various tasks that different parts of the body perform. "For by one Spirit we were all baptized into one body—Jews or Greeks, slaves or free—and all were made to drink of one Spirit" (1 Cor. 12:11).

Baptism, for Paul, marks the transition from the life of the flesh to the life of the Spirit. To be baptized is to be "in Christ Jesus" (Gal. 3:26); "For as many of you as were baptized into Christ have put on Christ" (Gal. 3:27). Life "in Christ" is a life of faith in which Christians "walk by the Spirit," and for Paul there is a distinct difference between the life of the flesh and the life of the Spirit lived in the body of Christ (Gal. 5:16–17). Those who are baptized into Christ become Abraham's offspring, "heirs according to promise" (Gal. 3:29). The images and metaphors Paul uses to explain the transition represented by baptism suggest not only the rejection of one form of life, but the adoption of a new way of being in the world. An important image Paul uses to explain this transition is that of the tree and the branch. In Romans 11 those who are "in Christ" replace the broken branches on the olive tree; "and you, a wild olive shoot, were grafted in their place to share the richness of the olive tree" (Rom. 11:17).[23] To be baptized into Jesus Christ, to be grafted to the tree, means that the Christian becomes part of a living, dynamic reality as the images of "body" and "tree" suggest. Hence the importance of the metaphor "body of Christ" in Paul's thought is what it implies about Paul's understanding of the

Christian community and the meaning of baptism. While Paul's use of the image of the "body" captures an essential dimension of the church, the meaning of baptism, and the nature of Christian life, it is not exhaustive. In addition to the image of the body Paul appeals to the image of "people of God" in order to explain the meaning of baptism.

To be baptized is to be grafted to the body of Christ, but for Paul that means that one becomes "Abraham's offspring, heirs according to the promise." The body into which one is baptized is the body of Christ, but what it means to be "in Christ" is to become a part of those who are "Abraham's offspring," those who are descendents of Abraham, Isaac, and Jacob not by the flesh but by means of faith in the promise. To be "in Christ" is to become through faith a part of that history that begins with Abraham and culminates in the narrative history of Jesus Christ. The transition from one form of life, which Paul describes by means of the term "flesh," to another, life in Christ, is not simply a sociological transition from one community to another. The transition goes to the very depths of human identity and marks the movement from one interpretation of personal history to another. To be "in Christ" is to find one's personal history grafted to the larger history that extends from Abraham to Jesus of Nazareth to the activity of the Spirit of Christ in the Christian community.

An interpretation of baptism in light of Christian narrative does not resolve the question of how baptism should be celebrated, whether the church should practice infant baptism or believer's baptism. Themes such as "promise" and "convenant" traditionally have played prominent roles in the arguments that emphasize the sovereignty of God's grace and that advocate the baptism of children as a sign and seal that the children of believers are also heirs of the convenant. Yet while narrative theology also emphasizes the themes of promise and convenant, equally important is the collision of the personal history of the individual with the faith narratives of the Christian community. Only then is "Christian understanding" a possibility and only then may faith come to fruition in the act of confession. Even if baptism is understood as a visible sign and seal of the invisible reality of God's grace, in narrative theology baptism means that an individual's personal identity finally is to be found in the identity of that agent who is the subject of Christian narrative, the triune God. In narrative theology baptism cannot be separated from faith, and faith is not fully a reality until it issues in confession. Believer's baptism, therefore, is an appropriate form for the acknowledgment, recognition, and confession that a person is in Jesus Christ and consequently a child of the promise.[24]

Finally, a major issue in most discussions of the sacraments is the question of "presence." In what sense is Jesus Christ "present" in the sacraments? In the narrative theology we have been sketching in this essay the question of sacramental presence is related to the question of the relation between God's Word and Christian narrative and to the issue of the authority of Scripture. Just as Jesus Christ as God's Word cannot be identified either with Scripture or with Christian narrative so too the Word cannot be identified with the physical elements of the sacraments. Revelation occurs when Christian narrative collides with personal identity and the latter is reconstructed by means of the former. That event is not the intrusion of a Word from a supernatural realm into the natural order, but the moment when human words become true and authentic, when that Word which is the depth and the ground of everything human enables human words to discover their true referent in Christian narrative. The presence of God's Word is the presence of a transforming and world-altering power. God's Word is present in Christian narrative when that narrative becomes disclosive of the truth about personal and communal identity, and the same Word is present in the community's celebration of the sacraments when the elements of bread, wine, and water become the occasion for the transformation of personal identity by means of Christian narrative. While God's Word cannot be identified with human words or with the bread, wine, and water of the sacraments, the Word is present when the Spirit enables personal and communal identity to be fused to the narrative history of God's grace. Apart from the recital of Christian narrative the sacraments are vulnerable to distortion and misinterpretation, which is simply to say that the sacraments have their proper setting in the church's narratives of thanksgiving and confession.

5. Memory and Hope

The structure of Christian narrative reflects the distinctively Christian understanding of temporality. Because Christian narrative is an interpretation of the community's narrative history, Christians look to the past in order to understand the present and anticipate the future. The God who Christians believe is revealed in their narrative history is the same God to whom they offer their confessions and prayers in the present and to whom they look for the ultimate meaning of a narrative identity that is open-ended and unfinished, for the identity of the Christian community is wedded to that narrative which recounts God's activity and therein God's identity. The identity of Christian individuals and communities is finally rooted in and dependent on the yet unfinished narrative in which God has his identity in relation to the world. Christian hope, therefore, is based not on a repetition of the past, but on the expectation of a future in which God's promises in the past will be consummated in new and unexpected ways. Christians look to the future not simply as a repetition of the past, but as the final, yet undisclosed meaning of the past and present.

Christian hope is not simply a summary of Christian history cast in the future tense. The future in Christian narrative is unknown and open. But at the same time, Christian hope is not radically discontinuous from that which Christians remember and celebrate in their narrative history. Christian hope is not simply the repetition of Christian memory, but neither is Christian hope discontinuous with and unrelated to what Christians remember about God's activity in the past. In other words, Christians do indeed look to the future for the consummation of that narrative in which they have their unfolding history and identity, and the content of that future cannot be known simply by looking to the past. The future, however, is not something that Christians approach in anxiety and dread. The God to whom they are related in their narrative history is the same God to whom the future belongs.

Furthermore, Christians are compelled to look to the future for the consummation of their narrative identity in the yet unfinished narrative of God's history with the world. But it is Christian memory of the past that prompts Christian hope in the future. The future cannot be determined from what has taken place in the past and in that sense it is "new," but the future which Christians anticipate is the future of the God to whom they are related in their narrative history, and although that future may be new and unknown, Christians trust in the faithfulness of God who is celebrated and confessed in Christian memory. It is precisely Christian memory, however, that will not allow faith to look solely to the past; it is Christian memory that turns the attention of Christian faith to the future and to the consummation of that which has been promised in the past.

Christian identity, we have suggested, is constructed around the narrative event of the cross. The narrative identity of Christian individuals and communities is reinterpreted by means of the narrative identity of Jesus Christ, a narrative that culminates in the passion and the cross. Christian confession is not just the recognition that redemption is found in Jesus Christ but the understanding that confession entails discipleship and that Christian discipleship is defined by the cross. But if the cross were the final event in the narrative identity of Jesus Christ, then

Christian discipleship would be simply a life of heroic despair and Christians would look to the future in grim determination rather than in confident expectation. In Mark's Gospel, as in all Christian narrative, the meaning of the cross in Jesus' narrative history is intelligible only in relation to that other event in the narrative that Christians refer to as "resurrection." It is the resurrection that has enabled Christians, both those in the first century and those in the twentieth, to identify Jesus of Nazareth as the crucified Messiah, and it is the event of the resurrection that links Christian memory to Christian hope. What Christians remember about Jesus Christ is that in the resurrection God confirms that the crucified Jesus is the Christ, that he who proclaimed the kingdom is he in whom the kingdom has come and is coming. The memory of the resurrection of the crucified Christ compels the Christian community to look to the future in hope and anticipation of the consummation of Christian narrative.

If the relation between memory and hope in Christian narrative is dissolved, then neither the past nor the future are understood properly, and Christian identity becomes confused and uncertain. Either Christian identity hides in history and seeks to interpret the present by repeating the past, or Christian identity looks to the future as an escape from the past and loses itself in whatever is novel. In neither case is the tension between past and future, between memory and hope, which is at the center of Christian narrative, preserved. The symptoms of the crisis in Christian identity, which we discussed in Chapter I, appear in either case. Scripture falls silent in the life of the church when it is presented either as a narrative that does not need interpretation in the present or when it is dismissed as irrelevant for the task of understanding the future. The same thing happens to theological tradition and the practice of theology, with the predictable result that Christian identity becomes the repetition of a single historical form or it bears little or no resemblance to any of its historical forms and is shaped entirely by whatever forces are at work in the present and hover on the horizon of the future.

If Christian identity is closely tied to the task of interpreting and understanding Christian narrative, then every contemporary interpretation of Christian narrative—that is, every new form of Christian identity—must preserve the tension in Christian narrative between the past and the future, between memory and hope. Within that tension Scripture, tradition, and the sacraments have their proper function, and in that context, although its form may change in any given interpretation, the dynamics of Christian identity are not distorted. In the tension between memory and hope, Scripture, tradition, and the sacraments provide the Christian community the resources for understanding the present and anticipating the future. Christian identity is neither simply a repetition of the past nor a construction unrelated to the past, but the result of faith's struggle to extend Christian narrative into a new and unforeseen future. Christian identity in every age hopes in the coming future of God's kingdom, and it hopes not anxiously but in confident expectation because it remembers the narrative history of the God who is faithful even through death.

Notes

Chapter I

1 See Chapter VI for an extended discussion of Augustine's *Confessions*.
2 I have borrowed this description of the correlative relation between knowledge of God and knowledge of self from Edward A. Dowey, Jr., *The Knowledge of God in Calvin's Theology* (New York: Columbia University Press, 1952), pp. 18–24.
3 John Calvin, *Institutes of the Christian Religion*, 2 Vols., ed. John T. McNeill, "The Library of Christian Classics," Vols. XX and XXI (Philadelphia: The Westminster Press, 1960), I:35.
4 For a detailed discussion of the development of hermeneutics in the eighteenth and nineteenth centuries see Hans W. Frei, *The Eclipse of Biblical Narrative* (New Haven: Yale University Press, 1974).
5 James D. Smart, *The Strange Silence of the Bible in the Church* (Philadelphia: The Westminster Press, 1970).
6 Part I: The Book of Confessions of *The Constitution of The United Presbyterian Church in the United States of America* (New York: The Office of the General Assembly of The United Presbyterian Church in the United States of America, 1970), 5.001.
7 See the first chapter of Smart's *The Strange Silence of the Bible in the Church*.
8 See Wolfhart Pannenberg, "The Crisis of the Scripture Principle" in *Basic Questions in Theology*, Vol. 1 (Philadelphia: Fortress Press, 1970), pp. 1–14.
9 Karl Barth, "The Strange New World Within the Bible" in *The Word of God and the Word of Man* (Gloucester, Mass.: Peter Smith, 1978), pp. 28–50.
10 Rudolf Bultmann, "New Testament and Mythology" in *Kerygma and Myth*, ed. Hans Werner Bartsch (New York: Harper & Row, Harper Torchbooks/The Cloister Library, 1961), p. 5.

11 Walter Wink, *The Bible in Human Transformation* (Philadelphia: Fortress Press, 1975), p. 1.

12 These are issues which have important implications for our central question about the role of Scripture in the formation of Christian identity. We will return to them in Chapter V.

13 For a perceptive and illuminating discussion of the diverse senses in which Scripture has been understood to exercise authority in the Protestant church, see David H. Kelsey, *The Uses of Scripture in Recent Theology* (Philadelphia: Fortress Press, 1975).

14 Gerhard Ebeling describes the relation between Scripture and tradition perceptively: "Since the truth of *sola scriptura* depends on the reliable transmission of the Gospel, the Scripture-principle necessarily involves a doctrine of tradition." See his essay, " 'Sola Scriptura' and Tradition" in *The Word of God and Tradition*, trans. S. H. Hooke (Philadelphia: Fortress Press, 1968), p. 144.

15 See Ebeling's essay, "Church History Is the History of the Exposition of Scripture," ibid., pp. 11–31. Also instructive is John H. Leith's discussion of "traditioning" in his *An Introduction to the Reformed Tradition* (Atlanta: John Knox Press, 1977), pp. 17–31.

16 In his book *Ecclesial Man*, Edward Farley argues the importance of what he calls "the principle of positivity." The principle asserts that *"each general stratum undergoes transformation when it is incorporated into the strata more determinate than itself"* (p. 60). General structures of Christian faith, therefore, are modified and transformed in any given faith community. See Farley's fifth chapter, "Ecclesia and Language," *Ecclesial Man* (Philadelphia: Fortress Press, 1975), pp. 106–126.

17 Gordon D. Kaufman discusses the importance of history and memory for the individual in a way that can easily be extended to the life of the community. See his *God the Problem* (Cambridge, Mass.: Harvard University Press, 1972), pp. 187–188.

Chapter II

1 For a discussion of the development of revelation in modern theology, see Jürgen Moltmann, *Theology of Hope* (London: SCM Press, 1967), pp. 37–94.

2 Emil Brunner lists six basic features of the biblical concept of revelation. See his *Revelation and Reason* (Philadelphia: Westminster Press, 1946), pp. 20–32.

3 "To know God is to be known of him, and therefore also to know

the self as it is reflected in God." H. Richard Niebuhr, *The Meaning of Revelation* (New York: Copyright, 1941, by Macmillan Publishing Co., Inc., renewed 1969 by Florence Niebuhr, Cynthia M. Niebuhr, and Richard R. Niebuhr; Macmillan Paperbacks Edition, 1960), pp. 64–65.

4 Karl Barth, *Church Dogmatics*, trans. G. T. Thomson, Harold Knight, G. W. Bromiley, T. F. Torrance, *et al.* 4 vols. in 13 parts (Edinburgh: T. & T. Clark, 1936–1969), I/1:133. Permission to quote granted by the publisher.

5 "By 'proclamation of the Word of God' we are to understand withal, primarily and decisively, preaching and the sacraments" (ibid., p. 89). For Barth's interpretation of the relation between preaching and sacrament and his differences with Roman Catholicism on this issue, see ibid., pp. 71–77.

6 Ibid., p. 104.

7 Ibid., p. 61.

8 "Proclamation is human language in and through which God Himself speaks, like a king through the mouth of his herald, which moreover is meant to be heard and apprehended as language in and through which God Himself speaks, and so heard and apprehended in faith as the divine decision upon life and death, as the divine judgment and the divine acquittal, the eternal law and the eternal gospel both together" (ibid., p. 57).

9 Ibid., p. 106.

10 Ibid., p. 105. See also Barth's footnote on p. 57.

11 Barth discusses the metaphor of "witness" in *Evangelical Theology: An Introduction*, trans. Grover Foley (New York: Holt, Rinehart and Winston, 1963), pp. 26–36.

12 Barth, *Church Dogmatics*, I/1: 126.

13 Ibid., p. 123.

14 Ibid.

15 Ibid., p. 133.

16 Ibid., p. 134.

17 Barth distinguishes between one form of the Word of God, that of Incarnation, where the Word is present "originally and immediately [ursprünglich and unmittelbar]" and the other two forms, Scripture and proclamation, where human words become God's Word "derivatively and mediately [abgeleitet und mittelbar]" (ibid., p. 131); *Kirchliche Dogmatik*, I/1: 120.

18 Barth discusses the objectivity of revelation at length in *Church Dogmatics*, I/2: 1–44.

19 "Humiliation" and "exaltation" are the terms Barth uses to construct his christology. See *Church Dogmatics*, IV/1: 157–357 and IV/2: 3–377.

20 According to Barth, there are three senses in which the human words of proclamation and Scripture are "elevated" and become God's Word: (1) they are lifted up and made visible and knowable; (2) they are made relative and signify the limits of what human words can accomplish; and (3) they are secured in the sense that they are confirmed, preserved, and fulfilled. *Church Dogmatics*, I/1: 132–133.

21 For Barth, "Subjective revelation can consist only in the fact that objective revelation, the one truth which cannot be added to or bypassed, comes to man and is recognised and acknowledged by man. And that is the work of the Holy Spirit." *Church Dogmatics*, I/2: 239. Barth discusses the subjective reality and possibility of revelation in the same volume, pp. 203–279.

22 Martin Luther, "Avoiding the Doctrines of Men," *Luther's Works*, Vol. 35, ed. E. Theodore Bachmann (Philadelphia: Fortress Press, 1960), p. 132.

23 Barth, *Church Dogmatics*, I/2: 237.

24 Brunner, *Revelation and Reason*, p. 198.

25 Gerhard Ebeling, "Word of God and Hermeneutics," *Word and Faith* (Philadelphia: Fortress Press, 1963), p. 325.

26 In his essay "Reflections on the Doctrine of the Law," Ebeling discusses Barth's "formalism." See *Word and Faith*, pp. 247–281 (especially, pp. 267–268), and "Word of God and Hermeneutics," ibid., pp. 325–328.

27 Ebeling, "Word of God and Hermeneutics," p. 325.

28 Several important articles have been written on the meaning of the claim "God acts in history." See Langdon B. Gilkey, "Cosmology, Ontology, and the Travail of Biblical Language," *The Journal of Religion*, Vol. XLI, No. 3 (July 1961), pp. 194–205; Schubert M. Ogden, "What Sense Does It Make to Say 'God Acts in History'?" *The Reality of God* (New York: Harper & Row, 1963), pp. 164–187; Gordon D. Kaufman, "On the Meaning of 'Act of God,'" *God the Problem*, pp. 119–147.

29 Wolfhart Pannenberg, "Introduction" to *Revelation as History*, ed. Wolfhart Pannenberg (London: Macmillan, Macmillan Paperbacks,

1969). p. 4. The volume also contains essays by other members of the "Pannenberg circle": Rolf Rendtorff, Trutz Rendtorff, and Ulrich Wilkens.

30 Ibid.

31 Ibid., p. 13.

32 See Pannenberg's essay, "Dogmatic Theses on the Doctrine of Revelation" ibid., pp. 123–158.

33 For a more recent statement of Pannenberg's "theology of history" see his book, *Human Nature, Election, and History* (Philadelphia: Westminster, 1977). For his views on Hegel see his essay, "The Significance of Christianity in the Philosophy of Hegel" in his collection of essays, *The Idea of God and Human Freedom* (Philadelphia: Westminster, 1973), pp. 144–177.

34 James Barr, "Revelation Through History in the Old Testament and in Modern Theology," *Interpretation*, Vol. XVII, No. 2 (April 1963), p. 193, by permission. See also Barr's third chapter, "The Concepts of History and Revelation," in his book, *Old and New in Interpretation* (New York: Harper & Row, 1966), pp. 65–102.

35 Barr, "Revelation Through History," p. 195.

36 Barr, *Old and New in Interpretation*, p. 77.

37 For Barr's most recent statements about the relation of "history" to "story," see his article "Story and History in Biblical Theology" in *The Journal of Religion* Vol. 56, No. 1 (Jan. 1976), pp. 1–17.

38 Barr, "Revelation Through History," pp. 198–199.

39 Paul Althaus, "Die Inflation des Begriffs der Offenbarung in der gegenwärtigen Theologie" in *Zeitschrift für systematische Theologie*, Vol. 18 (1941), pp. 134–149.

40 F. Gerald Downing, *Has Christianity a Revelation?* (Philadelphia: Westminister, 1964).

41 Ibid., p. 10.

42 Ibid., p. 21. Or, as he argues elsewhere in the book, "*'Revelation,' in any of its modern theological uses, as a major term (or even the sole adequate term) with which to convey the purpose of the life, death, resurrection of Jesus, does not occur in the New Testament*" (ibid., p. 123).

43 Ibid., p. 284. Downing also argues, curiously and unconvincingly, that either God did intend to reveal himself in Christ and failed, since we are still left in uncertainty, or that he did not intend to reveal himself but only to make the "'revealing of God' a possibility in some sort of future." But, he insists, if the latter is the case, "A

'revelation' of what cannot now be seen is not a 'revelation'" (ibid., p. 238).

44 Niebuhr, *The Meaning of Revelation*, p. 10.

45 "We are in history as the fish is in water and what we mean by the revelation of God can be indicated only as we point through the medium in which we live" (ibid., p. 36).

46 Ibid., p. 16.

47 Ibid., p. 40.

48 Ibid., p. 44.

49 Ibid., p. 51.

50 Ibid., p. 52.

51 Ibid., p. 65.

52 Ibid., p. 68.

53 Ibid., p. 81.

54 Ibid., p. 86.

55 Ibid., p. 85.

56 Ibid., p. 53.

57 Ibid., p. 80.

58 Although Austin Farrer did not have Niebuhr's appreciation of the importance of either external or internal history, he did understand the important role that images play in this process. "The great images interpreted the events of Christ's ministry, death and resurrection, and the events interpreted the images; the interplay of the two is revelation. Certainly the events without the images would be no revelation at all, and the images without the events would remain shadows on the clouds." *The Glass of Vision* (London: Dacre Press, 1948), p. 43.

59 Niebuhr, *The Meaning of Revelation*, p. 80. "We reason in our hearts in order that we may know the whither as well as the whence and where of our personal lives" (ibid., p. 95).

60 Ibid., p. 71.

61 Ibid., p. 73.

62 Ibid., p. 111.

63 Ibid.

64 Ibid., p. 112.

65 Ibid., p. 81.

66 Calvin, *Institutes* I:541.

67 Niebuhr, *The Meaning of Revelation*, p. 35.

Chapter III

1 I wrote an article reviewing some of the theological literature that has made use of the category of "story" and "narrative," "A Bibliographical Critique" in *Theology Today*, Vol. XXXII, No. 2 (July 1975), pp. 133–143.

2 Sam Keen, *To a Dancing God* (New York: Harper & Row, 1970); Harvey Cox, *The Seduction of the Spirit* (New York: Simon and Schuster, A Touchstone Book, 1973); Michael Novak, *Ascent of the Mountain, Flight of the Dove* (New York: Harper & Row, 1971); Robert P. Roth, *Story and Reality* (Grand Rapids: Eerdmans, 1973); John Shea, *Stories of God* (Chicago: Thomas More Press, 1978); James B. Wiggins, ed., *Religion as Story* (New York: Harper & Row, 1975).

3 Gabriel Facre, *The Christian Story* (Grand Rapids: Eerdmans, 1978).

4 John Navone, SJ, *Towards a Theology of Story* (Slough, England: St. Paul Publications, 1977).

5 David Baily Harned, *Images for Self-Recognition* (New York: Seabury Press, 1977).

6 For a brief summary of the positions of a few of the figures in the German discussion see Bernd Wacker, *Narrative Theologie?* (Munich: Kösel, 1977).

7 Dietrich Ritschl and Hugh O. Jones, *"Story" als Rohmaterial der Theologie* (Munich: Kaiser, 1976).

8 Harald Weinrich, "Narrative Theology," and Johann Baptist Metz, "A Short Apology of Narrative" in *The Crisis of Religious Language*, eds. Johann Baptist Metz and Jean-Pierre Jossua (New York: Herder and Herder, 1973), pp. 46–56 and 84–96. Josef Meyer zu Schlochtern, *Glaube-Sprache-Erfahrung* (Frankfurt: Peter Lang, 1978).

9 Hans W. Frei, *The Identity of Jesus Christ* (Philadelphia: Fortress Press, 1975); Edward Schillebeeckx, *Jesus: An Experiment in Christology* (New York: Seabury Press, A Crossroad Book, 1979); Eberhard Jüngel, *Gott als Geheimnis der Welt* (Tübingen: J.C.B. Mohr [Paul Siebeck], 1977).

10 Stephen Crites, "The Narrative Quality of Experience," *Journal of the American Academy of Religion*, Vol. 39, No. 3 (September 1971), pp. 291–311, by permission.

11 Ibid., p. 291.

12 Ibid., p. 301. In a subsequent article, "Angels We Have Heard," Crites appears to qualify his argument by insisting, "I do not mean

to imply that this convergence of art and experience occurs in narrative form alone." See *Religion as Story*, ed. James B. Wiggins (New York: Harper & Row, 1975), p. 57.

13 Crites, "The Narrative Quality of Experience," p. 296.

14 Ibid., p. 295.

15 Ibid., p. 305.

16 James Wm. McClendon, Jr., *Biography as Theology* (Nashville: Abingdon Press, 1974), p. 36.

17 Ibid., p. 37. "Convictions," according to McClendon, are "those tenacious beliefs which when held give definiteness to the character of a person or of a community, so that if they were surrendered the person or community would be significantly changed" (ibid., p. 34). See also James Wm. McClendon, Jr., and James M. Smith, *Understanding Religious Convictions* (Notre Dame: University of Notre Dame Press, 1975), p. 7.

18 John S. Dunne, *A Search for God in Time and Memory* (London: Copyright © 1967, 1969 by John S. Dunne, C.S.C., Macmillan Paperbacks Edition, 1970), p. 170, by permission.

19 Ibid., p. xi.

20 Ibid.

21 McClendon, *Biography as Theology*, p. 89. By "image" he means "metaphors whose content has been enriched by a previous, prototypical employment so that their application causes the object to which they are applied to be seen in multiply-reflected [sic] light; they are traditional or canonical metaphors, and as such they bear the content of faith itself" (ibid., p. 96–97).

22 Stanley Hauerwas, with Richard Bondi and David B. Burrell, *Truthfulness and Tragedy*, copyright 1977 (University of Notre Dame Press, Notre Dame, Indiana, 46556), p. 8. See also Hauerwas' other books, *Character and the Christian Life: A Study in Theological Ethics* (San Antonio: Trinity University Press, 1975) and *Vision and Virtue: Essays in Christian Ethical Reflection* (Notre Dame: Fides, 1974).

23 Hauerwas, *Truthfulness and Tragedy*, p. 76.

24 Ibid., p. 75.

25 See Gerhard von Rad, *Old Testament Theology*, 2 Vols. (New York: Harper & Row, 1962, 1965); Oscar Cullmann, *Christ and Time* (Philadelphia: Westminster, 1964); G. Ernest Wright, *God Who Acts* (London: SCM, 1952).

26 Amos N. Wilder, *The Language of the Gospel: Early Christian Rhetoric* (New York: Harper & Row, 1964), p. 64.

27 Ibid., p. 67.
28 William A. Beardslee, *Literary Criticism of the New Testament* (Phila-
    delphia: Fortress Press, 1970), p. 14.
29 Eric Auerbach, MIMESIS: THE REPRESENTATION OF RE-
    ALITY IN WESTERN LITERATURE, transl. by Willard R. Trask
    (copyright 1953 by Princeton University Press; Princeton Paper-
    back, 1968), p. 45. Reprinted by permission of Princeton Univer-
    sity Press.
30 Ibid., p. 23.
31 Ibid., pp. 14–15.
32 Ibid., p. 15.
33 Frei, *The Eclipse of Biblical Narrative*, pp. 28–30.
34 Frei, *The Identity of Jesus Christ*. An early version of this manuscript
    appeared under the title "Theological Reflections on the Accounts
    of Jesus' Death and Resurrection" in *The Christian Scholar*, Vol. 50
    (1967), pp. 263–306.
35 Norman Perrin, *What Is Redaction Criticism?* (Philadelphia: Fortress
    Press, 1969). See also Perrin's *The New Testament: An Introduction*
    (New York: Harcourt Brace Jovanovich, Inc., 1974), pp. 164–165.
36 James A. Sanders, *Torah and Canon* (Philadelphia: Fortress Press,
    1972), p. 4. See also Sander's article, "Torah and Christ" in *Interpre-
    tation*, Vol. XXIX, No. 4 (October 1975), pp. 372–390.
37 Brevard S. Childs, *Introduction to the Old Testament as Scripture* (Phila-
    delphia: Fortress Press, 1979), p. 71. See also Childs' article, "The
    Old Testament as Scripture of the Church" in *Concordia Theological
    Monthly*, Vol. 43. No. 11 (December 1972), pp. 709–722.
38 Brevard S. Childs, *Introduction*, p. 72.
39 The book was published under the name Sallie McFague TeSelle,
    Speaking in Parables (Philadelphia: Fortress Press, 1975). For other
    works on parable in the New Testament see Dan Otto Via, Jr., *The
    Parables: Their Literary and Existential Dimension* (Philadelphia: For-
    tress Press, 1967); John Dominic Crossan, *The Dark Interval* (Niles,
    Illinois: Argus, 1975); and Robert W. Funk, *Language, Hermeneutic,
    and Word of God* (New York: Harper & Row, 1966).
40 TeSelle, *Speaking in Parables*, p. 13.
41 For example, see Ted L. Estess, "The Inerarrable Contraption: Re-
    flexions on the Metaphor of Story," *Journal of the American Academy of
    Religion*, Vol. XLII, No. 3 (September 1974), pp. 415–434.
42 TeSelle, *Speaking in Parables*, p. 3.

272   THE PROMISE OF NARRATIVE THEOLOGY

43 Dietrich Ritschl and Hugh O. Jones, *"Story" als Rohmaterial der Theologie*, pp. 7–41.
44 I have tried to suggest how the category of narrative might be applied to some problems in christology in an article, "Chalcedon Revisited" in *Theology Today*, Vol. XXXV, No. 1 (April 1978), pp. 52–64.
45 In *The Nature of Narrative* (London: Oxford University Press, 1966), Robert Scholes and Robert Kellogg describe plot as "the dynamic, sequential element in narrative literature" which makes minimal reference to character (p. 207).
46 Crites, "The Narrative Quality of Experience," pp. 301–302.
47 Dietrich Ritschl and Hugh O. Jones, *"Story" als Rohmaterial der Theologie*, p. 14 (my translation).
48 On the nature of autobiography see Roy Pascal, *Design and Truth in Autobiography* (London: Routledge & Kegan Paul, 1960), James Olney, *Metaphors of Self: The Meaning of Autobiography* (Princeton: Princeton University Press, 1972), and James Olney, ed., *Autobiography: Essays Theoretical and Critical* (Princeton: Princeton University Press, 1980).

Chapter IV

1 For example, see the Second Part of Friedrich Schleiermacher's *The Christian Faith* (Edinburgh: T.&T. Clark, 1928).
2 Sydney Shoemaker, *Self-Knowledge and Self-Identity* (Ithaca, New York: Cornell University Press, 1963), p. 2.
3 The major philosophical arguments can be found in two anthologies: John Perry, ed., *Personal Identity* (Berkeley: University of California Press, 1975) and Amélie Oksenberg Rorty, ed., *The Identities of Persons* (Berkeley: University of California Press, 1976).
4 I am indebted to Diogenes Allen for this distinction.
5 John Locke, *An Essay Concerning Human Understanding*, 2 Vols. (New York: Dover Publications, 1959), I:448–449.
6 Ibid., I:449.
7 Ibid., I:458.
8 For example, see the essays by H. P. Grice and Anthony Quinton in John Perry, ed., *Personal Identity*.
9 Shoemaker, *Self-Knowledge*, pp. 195, 243.
10 Sydney Shoemaker, "Personal Identity and Memory" in John Perry, ed., *Personal Identity*, p. 129, and Shoemaker, *Self-Knowledge*, p. 246.

11 Shoemaker, *Self-Knowledge*, p. 250.

12 Josiah Royce, *The Problem of Christianity*, 2 Vols. (Chicago: Henry Regnery Company, A Gateway Edition, 1968), II:40.

13 Wolfhart Pannenberg, *What Is Man?* (Philadelphia: Fortress Press, 1970), p. 139.

14 Ibid.

15 The "life cycle" and "identity formation" are major themes in most of Erikson's work. For example, see *Childhood and Society*, Second edition (New York: W. W. Norton, 1963), *Identity: Youth and Crisis* (New York: W. W. Norton, 1968), and *Insight and Responsibility* (New York: W. W. Norton, 1964).

16 Erikson, *Identity*, p. 163.

17 Erik H. Erikson, *Life History and the Historical Moment* (New York: W. W. Norton, 1975), pp. 113–114.

18 The claim that a person or self is always a reality in transit, something in the process of becoming, is a basic theme in the work of Søren Kierkegaard. More recently Ray Hart has described personal identity in similar terms: "The concentration of re-enacted past and intended future in the self's present act is not the long-distance pastime of a remote and static nature; it is the act of a being whose life is just such activity." *Unfinished Man and the Imagination* (New York: Herder and Herder, 1968), p. 154.

19 See Gadamer's discussion of "Prejudices as Conditions of Understanding," pp. 245–274. From TRUTH AND METHOD by Hans-Georg Gadamer, English Translation Copyright © 1975 by Sheed & Ward Ltd., Reprinted by permission of The Continuum Publishing Corporation.

20 Ibid., p. 259. We will return to this theme in Chapter VII.

21 Ibid., p. 258.

22 "We define the concept of 'situation' by saying that it represents a standpoint that limits the possibility of vision. Hence an essential part of the concept of situation is the concept of 'horizon.' The horizon is the range of vision that includes everything that can be seen from a particular vantage point" (ibid., p. 269).

23 "The anticipation of meaning that governs our understanding of a text is not an act of subjectivity, but proceeds from the communality that binds us to the tradition" (ibid., p. 261).

24 "After a self has arisen, it in a certain sense provides for itself its social experiences, and so we can conceive of an absolutely solitary self. But it is impossible to conceive of a self outside of social ex-

perience." George Herbert Mead, *On Social Psychology*, ed. Anselm Strauss (Chicago: University of Chicago Press, Phoenix Books, 1956), p. 204.

25 For example, in his essay, "The Foundations of Belief," Gordon Kaufman argues that persons are constituted by their social relations. "Selves are not simply self-forming; nor do they gain their structure simply as an autonomous evolution from the biological organism that is their base. They are social and historical realities largely constituted by their relations to other selves and thus by the communities and histories in which they participate" (*God the Problem*, p. 229).

26 Peter Berger has described this process of interpretation in terms of what historians call "periodization." See his *Invitation to Sociology: A Humanistic Perspective* (Garden City, New York: Doubleday, Anchor Books Edition, 1963), p. 54. Also of importance in Berger's book is his third chapter, "Excursus: Alternation and Biography (Or: How to Acquire a Prefabricated Past)."

27 Hauerwas, *Truthfulness and Tragedy*, p. 76.

28 Ibid.

29 W. B. Gallie, *Philosophy and the Historical Understanding*, Second ed. (New York: Schocken Books, 1964), pp. 22–71.

30 Crites, "The Narrative Quality of Experience," p. 291. Crites also argues that, "Only narrative form can contain the tensions, the surprises, the disappointments and reversals and achievements of actual, temporal experience" (ibid., p. 306).

31 Ibid., pp. 301–302.

32 Scholes and Kellogg, *The Nature of Narrative*, p. 211.

33 Ibid.

34 See W. H. Walsh's essay, "'Plain' and 'Significant' Narratives in History," *The Journal of Philosophy*, LV (Jan.-Dec. 1958), pp. 479–484.

35 Arthur C. Danto insists that the distinction between chronicle and history is false because history is of a single piece. See the chapter, "History and Chronicle" in *Analytical Philosophy of History* (Cambridge: The University Press, 1965), pp. 112–142.

36 Howard L. Harrod makes a similar point in his article "Interpreting and Projecting: Two Elements of the Self as Moral Agent" in *Journal of the American Academy of Religion*, XLI (March 1973), pp. 18–29. I am not, however, using the term in the same way that Harrod does. He divides self-identity into two processes: "retrospective in-

terpreting," in which the self "builds up a consistent picture of its own past," and "projecting," in which "the self seeks to employ its identity in action." I am using the one term "interpretation" to describe both of these processes.

37 What Josiah Royce called "the self" we are referring to as "person." "The self," Royce wrote, "is no mere datum, but is in its essence a life which is interpreted, and which interprets itself, and which, apart from some sort of ideal interpretation, is a mere flight of ideas, or a meaningless flow of feelings, or a vision that sees nothing, or else a barren abstract conception" (*The Problem of Christianity*, II:61).

38 Paul Ricoeur, *Freud and Philosophy* (New Haven: Yale University Press, 1970), p. 369.

39 "The experience of conversion to a meaning system that is capable of ordering the scattered data of one's biography is liberating and profoundly satisfactory" (Peter Berger, *Invitation to Sociology*, p. 63).

40 Gadamer, *Truth and Method*, p. 269.

41 Malcolm Little, *The Autobiography of Malcolm X*, with the assistance of Alex Haley (New York: Grove Press, Copyright © 1964 by Alex Haley and Malcolm X, Copyright © 1965 by Alex Haley and Betty Shabazz, Introduction © 1965 by M. S. Handler, Paperback Edition, 1966), p. 35. Permission to reprint granted by Random House who now controls publication rights.

42 Ibid., p. 150.

43 Ibid., p. 159.

44 Ibid., p. 170.

45 Ibid., p. 150.

46 Ibid., p. 164.

47 Ibid., pp. 194–195.

48 Novak, *Ascent of the Mountain, Flight of the Dove*, esp. pp. 43–87.

49 Novak describes religion as "a conversion to the sense of the sacred." And by conversion he means "a focusing of one's way of life: I mean taking up one standpoint, after having occupied another" (ibid., p. 28).

50 Ibid., p. 53.

51 Ibid., p. 15.

52 In *A Search for God in Time and Memory*, Dunne attempts to develop a "method" for "passing over" into the life stories of other people, "the process of passing over by sympathetic understanding to others and coming back to a new understanding of ourselves" (p. x).

53 Herbert Fingarette, *Self-Deception* (London: Routledge & Kegan Paul, 1969), pp. 49–50.

54 Stanley Hauerwas and David B. Burrell, "Self-Deception and Autobiography: Reflections on Speer's *Inside the Third Reich*" in Hauerwas, *Truthfulness and Tragedy*, p. 87.

55 Dietrich Bonhoeffer, *Creation and Fall; Temptation* (New York: Macmillan, 1959), p. 81.

56 "If then there is to be a self there must also be an other in space and time. The Self cannot exist in isolation" (John MacMurray, *The Self as Agent* [London: Faber and Faber, 1957], p. 142).

Chapter V

1 Royce, *The Problem of Christianity*, II:36–37.

2 See Chapter 6, "The Church: A Community of Memory and Understanding: in James M. Gustafson's *Treasure in Earthen Vessels* (New York: Harper & Row, 1961), pp. 71–85.

3 John E. Smith, *The Analogy of Experience* (New York: Harper & Row, 1973), p. 129. Smith's comment is reminiscent of H. Richard Niebuhr and James Gustafson, and all three acknowledge a debt to Royce's discussion of time and community in *The Problem of Christianity*.

4 Scholes and Kellog, *The Nature of Narrative*, p. 207.

5 Gerhard von Rad describes Israel's deliverance from Egypt as it is interpreted in the credo in Deuteronomy 26:5ff. as "the dramatic mid-point around which the historical events detailed are grouped." Furthermore, von Rad insists that despite later embellishments ("when the tellers of the story come to describe it, they introduce a plethora of words, some allegedly spoken by Jahweh and some by Israel") this historical event is the basis of Israel's faith; "This datum ancient Israel never spiritualised" (*Old Testament Theology*, I:176).

6 See John Van Seters' study of the Abraham tradition in his book *Abraham in History and Tradition* (New Haven: Yale University Press, 1975).

7 Barth, *Church Dogmatics*, III/1: 81ff.

8 Ibid., p. 76.

9 Ibid., p. 84.

10 Ibid., p. 81.

11 Ibid., p. 82.

12 Frei, *The Eclipse of Biblical Narrative*, p. 4.

13 Ibid., p. 24.

14 For example, see Peter Stuhlmacher's book, *Schriftauslegung auf dem Wege zur biblischen Theologie* (Gottingen: Vandenhoeck & Ruprecht, 1975), part of which has been translated into English under the title, *Historical Criticism and Theological Interpretation of Scripture*, trans. Roy A. Harrisville (Philadelphia: Fortress Press, 1977).

15 For example, see Brevard S. Childs' essay, "The Old Testament as Scripture of the Church" pp. 709–722.

16 One ambiguity that remains unresolved in canonical criticism, particularly in Childs' formulation of it, is the precise relation between a historical-critical analysis of the text and what Childs calls "theological reflection." See Brevard S. Childs, *The Book of Exodus* (Philadelphia: Westminster, 1974).

17 For example, see Gerhard Ebeling's essay, "The Significance of the Critical Historical Method for Church and Theology in Protestantism," *Word and Faith*, esp. pp. 55–56.

18 See Chapter III, pp. 83–84.

19 An early discovery of the importance of the "framework" of the Gospels is C. H. Dodd's article, "The Framework of the Gospel Narrative," *The Expository Times*, Vol. XLIII, No. 9 (June 1932), pp. 396–400.

20 Sanders, *Torah and Canon*, p. 4.

21 "When the Christian in any time or place confesses his faith, his confession turns into a narrative. When the Christian observes Christmas or Easter, in either case it is with reference to a story of things that happened" (Wilder, *The Language of the Gospel*, pp. 64, 67).

22 von Rad, *Old Testament Theology*, I:123. For von Rad's description of "The Oldest Pictures of the Saving History," see ibid., I:121–128.

23 Ibid., I:122.

24 I am using an alternative translation which is listed in the notes to Deuteronomy 6:4a in *The Oxford Annotated Bible*.

25 Or as S. Dean McBride, Jr., puts the matter: "The Deuteronomists addressed a fragmented community whose links with the transcendent realities, that alone were able to sustain it, had become strained or broken. No longer were the heirs of Jacob a single nation unified through exclusive allegiance to Yahweh, bound together in his service, and living in the shadow of his protection. No longer were they a contemporary manifestation of the Israel which had escaped bondage to the hostile dominions of the world. Nor were they the people—alive and yet to be born—who had stood at Sinai to

enter into solemn pact with their divine deliverer" ("The Yoke of the Kingdom: An Exposition of Deuteronomy 6:4–5" in *Interpretation*, Vol. XXVII, No. 3 [July 1973], p. 305).

26 Brevard S. Childs, *Memory and Tradition in Israel*, "Studies in Biblical Theology, No. 37" (Naperville, Illinois: Allenson, 1962), p. 82.

27 Ibid., p. 55.

28 Ibid., p. 85.

29 Ibid., pp. 78–79.

30 Frei, *The Identity of Jesus Christ*, pp. 126–138.

31 Norman Perrin, "Towards an Interpretation of the Gospel of Mark" in *Christology and a Modern Pilgrimage: A Discussion with Norman Perrin*, ed. Hans Dieter Betz (Missoula, Montana: Society of Biblical Literature, 1971), p. 55; and Theodore J. Weeden, *Mark—Traditions in Conflict* (Philadelphia: Fortress Press, 1971).

32 Nils Alstrup Dahl, "The Purpose of Mark's Gospel" in *Jesus in the Memory of the Early Church* (Minneapolis: Augsburg, 1976), p. 56.

33 Ibid., p. 64.

34 Ibid.

35 Perrin, "Towards an Interpretation of the Gospel of Mark," p. 54.

36 Ibid., p. 55.

37 For discussions of the structure of Mark's Gospel see Vincent Taylor, *The Gospel According to Mark* (London: Macmillan, 1966), Second Edition, pp. 105–113; Willi Marxsen, *Mark the Evangelist* (Nashville: Abingdon, 1969), pp. 54–116; Norman Perrin, *The New Testament: An Introduction*, pp. 143–167.

38 The other passage is the "little apocalypse" in Chapter 13, or what Dahl, following F. Busch, refers to as "'Jesus' farewell discourse according to Mark'" (Dahl, "The Purpose of Mark's Gospel," p. 62).

39 See also Mark 3:11.

40 Although he misinterprets the meaning of the passage, Paul Tillich rightly observes that Peter's confession at Caesarea Philippi "marks the turning point in the narrative." Reprinted from *Systematic Theology* by Paul Tillich by permission of The University of Chicago Press. Volume I Copyright 1951, Volume II © 1957, Volume III © 1963 by The University of Chicago.

41 Dahl, "The Purpose of Mark's Gospel," p. 64.

42 Perrin, "Towards an Interpretation of the Gospel of Mark," p. 55.

Chapter VI

1 Alfred Schutz, "The Stranger," *Collected Papers*, 3 Vols. (The Hague: Nijhoff, 1964), II: 91–105, by permission.

2 Ibid., p. 96.

3 Ibid., p. 97.

4 Ibid., p. 100.

5 Alfred Schutz, "The Homecomer," *Collected Papers*, II: 106–107.

6 Ibid., p. 107.

7 Ibid., pp. 115–116.

8 Saint Augustine, *Confessions*, trans. R. S. Pine-Coffin (Middlesex, England: Penguin Books, 1961), X. 1, p. 207, Copyright © R. S. Pine-Coffin, 1961, Reprinted by permission of Penguin Books Ltd. In references to the *Confessions* I will note chapter and section in addition to the pagination in the Pine-Coffin edition.

9 Ibid., V.2; p. 92.

10 Ibid., II.4; p. 47.

11 Ibid., V.6; p. 98.

12 Ibid.

13 Ibid., V.7; p. 98.

14 Ibid., V.7; p. 99.

15 Ibid., IV.1; p. 71

16 For example, see I.5; p. 24 and IX.4; p. 188.

17 Robert Goff, "The Language of Self-Transformation in Plato and Augustine," *Man and World*, Vol. IV (November 1971), p. 423, by permission.

18 Ibid.

19 Saint Augustine, *Confessions*, IV.15; p. 85.

20 Ibid., IV.16; pp. 89, 88.

21 Ibid., IV.10; p. 104.

22 Ibid., VII.20; p. 154.

23 Ibid., XII.15; p. 290.

24 Ibid., IV.1; p. 71.

25 Ibid., VI.6; p. 118.

26 Ibid., X.8; p. 215.

27 Ibid., VII.12; p. 148.

28 Ibid., VII.17; p. 151.

29 Ibid., VIII.12; p. 178.

30 "Thus, in Book VIII of the *Confessions*, the problem of the will leaps into focus" (Peter Brown, *Augustine of Hippo* [London: Faber and Faber, 1967], p. 173).

31 J. L. Austin, "Performative Utterances," *Philosophical Papers*, ed. J. O. Urmson and G. J. Warnock (Oxford: Oxford University Press, 1961), pp. 220–239.

32 Barth, "The Holy Spirit and Christian Faith," *Church Dogmatics*, IV/1: 740–779.

33 Ibid., p. 744.

34 Ibid.

35 Ibid.

36 Ibid., p. 749.

37 Ibid., p. 751.

38 Ibid., p. 755.

39 Ibid., p. 760.

40 See Chapter II, pp. 44–51. Barth also discusses the concept of acknowledgment in the first volume of his *Church Dogmatics*, in the section on "The Word of God as the Criterion of Dogmatics." See *Church Dogmatics*, I/1: 233–238.

41 Barth, *Church Dogmatics*, IV/1: 761.

42 Ibid., p. 762.

43 Ibid., p. 761.

44 Ibid., p. 763.

45 Ibid., p. 766.

46 Ibid., p. 769.

47 Ibid., p. 774.

48 Ibid., p. 776.

49 Ibid.

50 Ibid., pp. 776–777.

51 Ibid., p. 778.

52 Ibid.

53 In Paul Tillich's categories faith that is nothing more than acknowledgment is an instance of heteronomy, a person's acceptance of an external authority, and faith that is reduced to recognition is a form of autonomy. Only when faith becomes confession is it theonomous faith, a faith in touch with its depth.

Chapter VII

1 Saint Augustine, *Confessions*, VI.6; p. 118.

2 In the following discussion of understanding as a learned facility I am obviously indebted to the work of Ludwig Wittgenstein. See Wittgenstein's *Philosophical Investigations* (Oxford: Basil Blackwell, 1967), especially ## 1–202 (# designates sections numbered in

the text rather than page numbers). In footnotes I shall indicate both.

3 Ibid., #19, p. 8.
4 Ibid., #23, p. 11.
5 Patrick Sherry, "Is Religion a 'Form of Life'?" *American Philosophical Quarterly*, IX, No. 2 (April 1972), pp. 159–167.
6. For example, see Wittgenstein's remarks in *Philosophical Investigations*, ##1–22, especially #11, p. 6.
7 Gadamer, *Truth and Method*, p. 321.
8 Ibid., p. 271.
9 Ibid., p. 346.
10 Ibid.
11 David B. Burrell, *Exercises in Religious Understanding* (Notre Dame: University of Notre Dame Press, 1974), p. 26.
12 Calvin, *Institutes*, I: 726 (III, 11, 1), and Tillich, *Systematic Theology*, III: 223.
13 Tillich, *Systematic Theology*, III: 223.
14 Calvin, *Institutes*, I: 727 (III, 11, 2).
15 Or as Calvin puts it, "as Christ cannot be torn into parts, so these two which we perceive in him together and conjointly are inseparable—namely, righteousness and sanctification" (ibid., I: 732 [III, 11, 6]).
16 See Tillich's well-known sermon, "You Are Accepted," *The Shaking of the Foundations* (New York: Scribner's, 1948) pp. 153–163; also see Tillich's *Systematic Theology*, III: 223–228.
17 See Paul Ricoeur's discussion of guilt in *The Symbolism of Evil* (New York: Harper & Row, 1967), pp. 100–150, especially p. 101.
18 Ibid., pp. 47–99.
19 Martin Luther, "Two Kinds of Righteousness," *Luther's Works*, Vol. 31, "Career of the Reformer, I," ed. Harold J. Grimm (Philadelphia: Fortress Press, 1957), p. 297.
20 Ibid., p. 298.
21 Ibid., p. 299.
22 Ibid., p. 300.
23 Ibid., p. 299.
24 Calvin, *Institutes*, I: 595 (III, 3, 3).
25 Ibid., I: 684 (III, 6, 1).
26 Ibid., I: 707 (III, 8, 7).
27 Tillich, *Systematic Theology*, III: 228 ff.
28 Ibid., pp. 231–237.

29 Berkhof translates the categories of condemnation-justification-sanctification as despair-relaxation-effort. Hendrikus Berkhof, *Christian Faith: An Introduction to the Study of the Faith* (Grand Rapids: Eerdmans, 1979), p. 467.

30 Barth, *Church Dogmatics*, IV/2: 503.

31 Ibid., p. 507.

32 Ibid., p. 508.

33 Paul Tillich, *Dynamics of Faith* (New York: Harper & Row, Harper Torchbooks, The Cloister Library, 1957), pp. 30–35.

34 H. Richard Niebuhr, *Christ and Culture* (New York: Harper & Row, Harper Torchbooks, The Cloister Library, 1951), pp. 190–229.

35 Schleiermacher, *The Christian Faith*, pp. 5–12 (§3).

36 Schleiermacher would surely agree; see his discussion of the relation between the experience of redemption in the Christian community and the biblical picture of Jesus Christ (ibid., pp. 361–365 [§88]).

37 This caricature is not a fair interpretation of David Tracy's description of the sources and criteria for theology. See his discussion of criteria and his analysis of "meaning," "meaningfulness," and "truth" in *Blessed Rage for Order* (New York: Seabury, A Crossroad Book, 1975), pp. 64–87, 172–203.

38 For example, Paul Tillich argued that there is a double sense in which a symbol is true. "A symbol *has* truth: it is adequate to the revelation it expresses. A symbol *is* true: it is the expression of a true revelation," (*Systematic Theology*, I: 240).

Chapter VIII

1 Paul Tillich describes mystery, ecstasy, and miracle as the "marks" of revelation (*Systematic Theology*, I: 106–118).

2 See the criticisms of revelation in Chapter II, pp. 51–59.

3 The use of the category of "paradox" to describe the incarnation is a common theme in Christian theology. See Søren Kierkegaard, *Philosophical Fragments* (Princeton, New Jersey: Princeton University Press, 1936) and D. M. Baillie, *God Was in Christ* (London: Faber and Faber, 1956).

4 For example, see Gerhard Ebeling's argument that "in every word event there is present a depth dimension which is indicated by the word 'God'—not, so to speak, as a prolongation of the causal series into the adjacent realm of the hyper-macrocosmic and the hyper-microcosmic, but as a hidden and tacit word event to which every word owes its existence," (*God and Word* [Philadelphia: Fortress

Press, 1967], p. 29). See also Peter C. Hodgson's discussion of "homologous word" in *Jesus—Word and Presence* (Philadelphia: Fortress Press, 1971), pp. 136–155.

5 For a discussion of the occasional nature of God's Word see James Wharton, "The Occasion of the Word of God," *Austin Seminary Bulletin*. Faculty Edition 84 (September 1968).

6 See Barth's comments on this point in *Church Dogmatics*, I/1: 42.

7 See Paul Ricoeur's discussion of the relation between myth and gnosis in *The Symbolism of Evil*, pp. 164–171. A case in point is his perceptive interpretation of original sin in his essay "'Original Sin': A Study in Meaning," in the collection of essays *The Conflict of Interpretations*, ed. Don Ihde (Evanston: Northwestern University Press, 1974), pp. 269–286.

8 Or as Paul writes, "because the creation itself will be set free from its bondage to decay and obtain the glorious liberty of the children of God" (Rom. 8:21).

9 Niebuhr, *The Meaning of Revelation*, p. 111.

10 Ibid., pp. 111–112.

11 That is one reason why the interpretation of the reality of God in process theology is inadequate and unsatisfactory. The metaphysical scheme has no necessary relation to Scripture or to "Christian narrative" (in the broader sense in which we have been describing it). Process theologians use Scripture when it is convenient or when it can be used to lend weight to an argument, but the witness of Scripture is of little or no significance in comparison to the authority of Whitehead's metaphysical scheme.

12 Jürgen Moltmann has developed the concept of God's trinitarian history in his book *The Church in the Power of the Spirit* (New York: Harper & Row, 1977). Also of importance is the word of Eberhard Jüngel, *The Doctrine of the Trinity* (Grand Rapids: Eerdmans, 1976) and *Gott als Geheimnis der Welt*.

13 It should be noted, however, that while The Westminster Confession affirms the authority of Scripture it also argues that the "inward illumination of the Spirit of God" is necessary "for the saving understanding of such things as are revealed in the Word." Because The Westminster Confession understands the authority of Scripture in terms of a doctrine of inspiration it differs significantly from some contemporary interpretations of Scripture's role, such as The Confession of 1967, which appeal to a doctrine of revelation.

14 See Kelsey, *The Uses of Scripture in Recent Theology*, pp. 139–155.

15 See Karl Barth, *Evangelical Theology*, especially pp. 26–36, and his *Church Dogmatics*, I/1: 111–124.

16 Barth, *Evangelical Theology*, p. 26.

17 Ibid., p. 27.

18 Ibid., p. 29.

19 Hans von Campenhausen, *The Formation of the Christian Bible* (Philadelphia: Fortress Press, 1972), especially pp. 252–268.

20 Consequently, we must disagree with Tillich's claim that "historical research can neither give nor take away the foundation of the Christian faith" (*Systematic Theology*, II:113).

21 To be fair to Barth it should be noted that in *Evangelical Theology* his chapter on "The Witnesses" is followed by a chapter on "The Community," which begins with the observation, "When theology confronts the Word of God and its witnesses, its place is very concretely in the *community*, not somewhere in empty space" (*Evangelical Theology*, p. 37).

22 Hans Conzelmann, *I Corinthians* (Philadelphia: Fortress Press, 1975), pp. 31–34.

23 Calvin makes extensive use of the language of "engrafting" in Books III and IV of the *Institutes*.

24 For recent proposals on baptism see Karl Barth, *Church Dogmatics*, IV/4 and Jürgen Moltmann, *The Church in the Power of the Spirit*, pp. 226–242.

Subject Index

Author Index